Demythologizing Educational Reforms

There are many myths surrounding today's educational reform movemement. These include the beliefs that student achievement is responsible for our economy's success, that there are great numbers of deficient teachers, that testing represents knowledge, and that the market values of privitization and competition lead to success. In this volume, the editors have welcomed articles that discuss how educational discourse has been appropriated to reflect the values of politicans, financial elites, the media, and educational foundations. These writers tackle the mythic nature of issues such as neoliberalism, competition, testing, suburban and urban schooling, charter schools, teacher education, and parental involvement. The contributors expose the "logic behind the talk" and offer authentic possiblities for reform that are grounded in the actual social, economic, political and educational realities of contemporary society.

Arthur T. Costigan is Associate Professor of Education at Queens College, City University of New York, USA.

Leslee Grey is Assistant Professor of Educational Foundations, Secondary Education and Youth at Queens College, City University of New York, USA.

Routledge Research in Education Policy and Politics

The Routledge Research in Education Policy and Politics series aims to enhance our understanding of key challenges and facilitate on-going academic debate within the influential and growing field of Education Policy and Politics.

Books in the series include:

1 **Teacher Education through Active Engagement**
   Raising the Professional Voice
   Edited by Lori Beckett

2 **Health Education**
   Critical Perspectives
   Edited by Katie Fitzpatrick and
   Richard Tinning

3 **US Education in a World of Migration**
   Implications for Policy and Practice
   Edited by Jill Koyama and Mathangi Subramanian

4 **Student Voices on Inequalities in European Higher Education**
   Challenges for Theory, Policy and Practice
   Edited by Fergal Finnegan, Barbara Merrill and Camilla Thunborg

5 **Social Context Reform**
   A Pedagogy of Equity and Opportunity
   Edited by P. L. Thomas, Brad Porfilio, Julie Gorlewski, and Paul R. Carr

6 **Narrowing the Achievement Gap for Native American Students**
   Paying the Educational Debt
   Edited by Peggy McCardle and Virginia Berninger

7 **Demythologizing Educational Reforms**
   Responses to the Political and Corporate Takeover of Education
   Edited by Arthur T. Costigan and Leslee Grey

Demythologizing Educational Reforms
Responses to the Political and Corporate Takeover of Education

Edited by Arthur T. Costigan and Leslee Grey

NEW YORK AND LONDON

First published 2015
by Routledge
711 Third Avenue, New York, NY 10017, USA

and by Routledge
2 Park Square, Milton Park, Abingdon, Oxfordshire OX14 4RN

First issued in paperback 2016

*Routledge is an imprint of the Taylor & Francis Group,
an informa business*

© 2015 Taylor & Francis

The right of Arthur T. Costigan and Leslee Grey to be identified as the authors of the editorial material, and of the authors for their individual chapters, has been asserted in accordance with sections 77 and 78 of the Copyright, Designs and Patents Act 1988.

All rights reserved. No part of this book may be reprinted or reproduced or utilised in any form or by any electronic, mechanical, or other means, now known or hereafter invented, including photocopying and recording, or in any information storage or retrieval system, without permission in writing from the publishers.

Trademark Notice: Product or corporate names may be trademarks or registered trademarks, and are used only for identification and explanation without intent to infringe.

Library of Congress Cataloging-in-Publication Data
A catalog record has been requested for this book.

Typeset in Sabon
by IBT Global.

ISBN 13: 978-1-138-28672-6 (pbk)
ISBN 13: 978-0-415-73555-1 (hbk)

Contents

Foreword   vii

1   Demythologizing Educational Reforms: 30 Years Since *A Nation at Risk*   1
ARTHUR T. COSTIGAN

2   The Neoliberal Myth: Narrative Resistance to Democratic Education   20
BRYAN METCALFE

3   Class Struggle and Education: Neoliberalism, (Neo)-Conservatism, and the Capitalist Assault on Public Education—A Marxist Analysis   34
DAVE HILL

4   Debunking the Myth of Standardized Education to Promote Equity and Rigor   68
DEBRA A. ROOT

5   An Inquiry into the Myth of Neutrality: Curriculum and Pedagogy in an Age of Terrorism   87
JESSICA A. HEYBACH

6   Deceptive Data: How the Corporate Reform Movement Uses Standardized Tests to Achieve the Neoliberal Agenda   104
DAVID HURSH

7	Behind the Common Core Standards Movement: OECD's PISA and Global Education Policy RICHARD D. LAKES	117
8	Charter Schools: Appearance Versus Essence SHAWGI TELL	133
9	The Myth of Preparation and the Futility of Teacher Education Programs ERIC C. SHEFFIELD	153
10	From K to EdD: Understanding the Cycle of Compliance and Teacher Education's Complicity in Neoliberal School Reform DAVID GABBARD	170
	Afterword: Implications and Discussion LESLEE GREY	183
	Contributors	195
	Index	199

Foreword

Demythologizing Educational Reforms: Responses to the Political and Corporate Takeover of Education is a book that critically analyzes the current discourses of contemporary educational reforms in the US and other countries today. While the deleterious effects of the neoliberal, corporatized reform movement are increasingly being documented (Ravitch, 2013), there is still the need to analyze and to understand why these reforms are taking place in hope that such analysis can lead to political action. To paraphrase the comedian George Carlin: Once *they* have you thinking using *their* terms, you've already lost. This book is an attempt to see the thinking behind the neoliberal reform agenda and "get it out of our heads," and out of our schools.

The current neoliberal corporatized educational reform movement has become the chief reality in which anyone involved in public education now lives. This is true for families who must scramble for their children's "seats" in schools run by for-profit and nonprofit corporate bodies; for students who experience relentless high-stakes testing and scripted curricula; for teachers who are losing autonomy, professionalism, and job rights; and for teacher educators whose educational programs are being replaced by "alternative certification" programs that contain only a few weeks of training. If those of us in this educational community are honest, it is this paradigm that we are made to respond to, attempt to subvert, acquiesce to, and ultimately participate in (Taubman, 2009). In short, the educational reform movement has taken over our lives. This is the ecology, habitat, or landscape in which we all now live (Costigan, 2014). This book asks the questions: How did things get this way? Why do they continue this way? And, will we be able to *reform these reforms*?

This volume explores the educational reform movements' many seemingly commonsense myths that serve the reformers' own cultural, economic, and political values and ideologies, such as neoconservatism, neoliberalism, and corporatism, and that do not address the actual social, political, economic, and educational realities of teaching and learning in the US and other English-speaking countries today. Such reforms are not commonsensical, and they are not inevitable. These reforms are based on a carefully crafted mythology that serves particular economic, political, and social interests. And, as this volume explores, these myths do not address the inherent social and economic inequities of life in the US today. Rather, they mask them over. We hope that this volume offers an analysis of educational reforms that is more congruent with reality, and one that offers real possibilities for educational and social change. This volume asks:

- What are the myths and belief systems, or worldviews, of educational reform? What is behind, and what drives, the seemingly commonsense discourses of educational reforms? From where did these beliefs originate? Whose interests do they serve? What values are promulgated through these reforms? What sustains this type of thinking? What is its future?
- What is the relationship of these myths, or these seemingly commonsensical understandings, to the actual social, cultural, and economic realities of the US today? How are these myths, or thought processes, beneficial or harmful to improving education?
- What improvements can be made to conversations about education reform to make them congruent with the political, economic, and social realities of life in the US today? Is there any answer to the current climate of educational reform?

We hope that you find in this book an examination of the key elements of the current landscape of educational reform that balances research into the current realities and implementations of educational reforms, analysis and synthesis of theoretical and conceptual frameworks of thinking about educational reforms, and specific suggestions that point towards more authentic educational policies and practices.

Arthur T. Costigan
Leslee Grey
Coeditors

REFERENCES

Costigan, A. T. (2014, Winter). Ecological perspectives of learning to teach: Introduction to a special issue of *Teacher Education Quarterly*. *Teacher Education Quarterly*, 41(1), 3–8.

Ravitch, D. (2013). *Reign of error: The hoax of the privatization movement and the danger to America's public schools*. New York, NY: Knopf.

Taubman, P. M. (2009). *Teaching by numbers: Deconstructing the discourse of standards and accountability in education*. New York, NY: Routledge/Taylor & Francis.

1 Demythologizing Educational Reforms
30 Years Since *A Nation at Risk*
Arthur T. Costigan

> We find that whole communities suddenly fix their minds upon one object, and go mad in its pursuit that millions of people become simultaneously impressed with one delusion, and run after it, till their attention is caught by some new folly more captivating than the first. We see one nation suddenly seized from its highest to its lowest members, with a fierce desire.
> —Charles Mackay, *Memoirs of Extraordinary Popular Delusions and the Madness of Crowds* (1852, location 1)

THE MYTHOLOGY OF EDUCATIONAL REFORMS

After a decade of educational reforms since the Elementary and Secondary Education Act, commonly called No Child Left Behind (NCLB) (US Congress, 2001), and 30 years since the alarms of *A Nation at Risk* (National Commission on Excellence in Education [NCEE], 1983), such statements as the following can be still be found almost daily in the media, in politicians' speeches, in the press releases of educational reform groups, at in-school teacher workshops, and around kitchen tables:

- American public schools are failing.
- Student graduation rates and test scores are historically low.
- Failing schools jeopardize the economic future of the US.
- There are many bad teachers, and they need to be weeded out.
- Young people are unprepared to be workers in the global economy.
- Students in the US are behind other countries, such as Finland, Japan, or China, in math and science.

Because of such commonsensical beliefs, schools are closed, teachers are fired, students are relentlessly tested, the media sell articles about the failure of the nation's schools, and families submit to nerve-wracking and often futile application processes for privatized charter schools. In New York City, students have lost their historic right to attend their neighborhood public schools (Gootman, 2009). However, educational writers and researchers, as well as the general public, are increasingly seeing that there is something radically wrong with the corporatization and privatization of public schooling, and the attendant unfairness of the testing and accountability movement (Ravitch, 2013).

This chapter, as well as this entire volume, is an attempt to go behind the increasingly well-documented effects of corporate style educational reforms and to look at some causes why these reforms continue to exist. This chapter first considers the mythological nature of the educational reform movement that has overtaken the country for the past 30 or so years. Second, this chapter opens a conversation about the reasons why the mythology of educational reform is so important to elites and why they find it necessary to impose this mythology on students, teachers, and families. Ultimately, this chapter examines the myths and myth-making processes that have seduced the educational community and the general public into accepting or tolerating, now for over one generation, an education reform movement that has reaped no discernable benefits, has caused much pain, and has caused what Dewey a century ago called "waste in education" (Dewey, 1907/2011).

In contrast to these myths, in the US today more students are graduating, more students are passing tougher tests, and our students know more than previous generations. Furthermore, there have been successful schools in the US for decades (Muskal, 2013; Ravitch, 2013; Snyder, 1993).

A Word About Myths

Contrary to the popular definition, myths are neither simply nor necessarily lies, untruths, or delusions. Myths, in and of themselves, are not necessarily false or even harmful. In fact, myths are important meaning-making devices because they are a way of explaining the complex nature of the world. Myths are like stories; they may seem to be fictitious, but they hold within themselves a powerful way of making meaning. Myths are commonly accepted statements, stories, or beliefs that coalesce and unify a perceived reality. Myths are similar to "mental constructs," which can be held personally or collectively. They are the tentative belief systems humans hold about reality. In order for them to work at all, however, they must be continually tested for accuracy against reality (Kelly, 1962). Statements such as, "People are poor because they are basically lazy" or "All students can achieve college or workplace readiness in school," are myths in that they are mental constructs, meaning-making devices. Whether these statements are reprehensible (as in the first statement) or simplistic (as in the second statement) is not primarily the point. The immediate point is that they *are* mythological statements. They are a means of ordering, defining, and simplifying a complicated world.

Myths are highly useful in that they reduce or eliminate the need for the constant effort of complex and time-consuming critical analysis. But of course they can be helpful, as when a teacher says, "All my students can achieve!"; and they can be harmful, as when a popular journal article implies that it is a good thing that 55% of new teachers did not get tenure because there are simply too many defective teachers right now (see Baker, 2012). And myths can have a powerful negativity, as with the political myths of Willie Horton, the Cadillac-driving welfare mother, and Obama's birth certificate.

Since the publication of *A Nation at Risk* (NCEE, 1983), almost 30 years ago, a very strong mythology of educational reform has arisen. The myths that this report codified and popularized have become the commonsensical discourse of educational reform. However, these myths are not neutral. They serve a particular cultural, economic, and political agenda that benefits specific groups of people who have taken over the discourse of educational reform. And, as we shall see later in this chapter, these myths serve a profound psychological need of the creators of these myths of reform. But first a word about what myths are and what they do.

What Myths Do

Take the story of the Garden of Eden. Many people believe that this story is not literally true, that it is a myth. Yet we know that for those of us who live in a Western culture, this myth has been spectacularly meaningful. We may not like the myth, and we may even be violently opposed to what the myth seems to be saying—as in the notion of Original Sin—but the fact remains that it has a powerful hold on our personal and collective imagination. In fact, there was, and continues to be, a "Garden of Eden time" when humans were basically naked and innocent, where there probably were no wars, where people cooperated rather than competed with each other, where food was readily available—literally for the picking—where there was far less disease than at more "civilized" times in human history, and when humans typically were healthy, well nourished, basically happy, and lived relatively long lives (Ryan & Jetha, 2010). We call these hunter-gatherer societies. In human history, this was followed by a time when people moved to cities, ate less healthy and less varied diets, had to work very hard at unpleasant and tedious jobs to live, became physically smaller and prone to host of previously unknown diseases, and lived briefer lives (Ryan & Jetha, 2010). We call this civilization. So the "garden" myth continues to be useful. We might not want to go back to hunter gathering and give up our cheeseburgers, our central heating, or our Lexus, but we can't argue that there don't exist hunter and gatherer societies that have few incidences of diabetes or substance abuse, and where poverty is literally an unthinkable concept. Yet these peoples are also without credit cards, the internet, Cabernet Sauvignon, and antibiotics. However, we do know at the very core of our being that the benefits of modern society are at the expense of our basic human innocence. It is the "garden" price we have had to pay for the benefits of civilization.

Likewise, the American Dream is also a myth, but it is also very true. We know that it is useful because we are very well aware when our current economic system doesn't live up to the myth. When we worry and complain about the growing divide between the top 1% and the other 99%, we are not denying the myth of the American Dream, we are affirming its power.

However, calling a myth true or false or not is not the best way of thinking of myths. Perhaps the best way of thinking of a myth is that it is *useful* or not. The story of the Garden of Eden, the American Dream, and even urban folk tales and religious parables help us create meaning about a complex and confusing world. A myth is like a story in that it is a lie. But at the heart of the lie is a truth. Thus various groups of people find helpful various meaning-making myths such as dystopian stories, zombie videos, MM novels,[1] young adult (YA) novels about sexy teenage vampires, and the ongoing *Star Trek* saga.[2] These can be useful things to help us make sense of a complex and often confusing world (Pinker, 2002). Conversely, myths can be not only useless but dangerous when they do not conform to reality, as in such myth making found in ungrounded conspiracy theories, cultish religious beliefs, and quick money-making schemes (Mackay, 1852; Sagan, 1996). And they are the more dangerous the more they become divorced from the facts grounded in the way the world really is.

How Educational Reform Became Educational Myth

A Nation at Risk was published in 1983 by a highly ideological and hand-picked group with the self-important name of the National Commission on Excellence in Education (NCEE). It was published during the conservative revival nearly 30 years ago in the Reagan era, and it put into words the beliefs of neoconservatives about education. This alarmist text was quite simple: Schools are failing miserably, teachers are woefully deficient, students are unchallenged and underperforming, and the curriculum is so watered down as to be meaningless. And because of these factors, so the myth goes, the very economic survival of our nation is literally *at risk*. The beginning of the report is rhetorically magnificent: "If an unfriendly foreign power had attempted to impose on America the mediocre educational performance that exists today, we might well have viewed it as an act of war" (NCEE, 1983, p. 5).

It needs to be pointed out that there were, from the outset, two objections to the report. The first objection is that *A Nation* doesn't deal in evidence or facts but in summaries of cherry-picked studies that support its conclusions. Furthermore, these summaries don't bear up under investigation (Berliner & Biddle, 1995; Bracey, 2004). But this hardly matters for the mythological purposes of the report.

The second objection is that the report revitalizes the trend of equating our individual and societal happiness almost exclusively with economic success, a myth that subsequent educational reforms have built on eagerly (Gabbard, 2007; Harvey, 2005). This is a vision to which many may not subscribe. It is a great stretch to move from saying that "economic health is important for people" to saying "the primary purpose of existence for a human is to be a *homo economicus*."[3]

However, neither of these two objections are why the report was influential as the *cri de coeur* of educational reform. What the report did is to put into words, to codify and clarify, several educational myths. These myths are useful to economic and political conservatives, and appear so tacit and commonsense that even liberals and the general public can be made to agree with them, as when avowed liberals such as Ted Kennedy voted in 2001 for NCLB and when Obama assumed the educational reformist mantle of the G. W. Bush years.

Myth #1: Schools Create the Economy

The central myth of this educational reform movement is actually not the deficiency of our school system, but the belief that the school system is ultimately responsible for the success and failure of American society. When Arne Duncan, the secretary of education, can tell an audience, "I remain interested in hearing from you about how Americans can educate our way to a better economy," he's immersed in this myth (Duncan, 2010). Thomas Friedman is in the middle of this myth when he tells the *New York Times* readership that "there's something to" the fact that "our struggling public schools [are] actually a critical, but unspoken, reason for the Great Recession," and, "While the subprime mortgage mess involved a huge ethical breakdown on Wall Street, it coincided with an education breakdown on Main Street" (Freidman, 2009; see also Friedman, 2005).

In fact, first, our schools weren't "failing" before the Great Recession any more than they were failing in 1800, 1900, or 2000 (Ravitch, 2000, 2013). And forget the fact that, second, even if someone could prove schools were failing now more than ever (and they aren't), then it does not follow that the correlation of phenomenon (school failure) indicates causation (Main Street failure) (Karier, 1986; Kliebard, 2004; Ravitch, 2000). No less a thinker than Friedman, who has won three Pulitzer Prizes and is the author of six highly regarded and popular books on economics, actually is susceptible to the myth that not only are our schools failing, but these failing schools are actually a *cause* of the nation's economic failure. Ultimately, he believes the myth that schools create a society's economy. This myth does not seem to be found in any other country with successful schools (Ravitch, 2013).

In contrast to this myth, the reality is that the US has exactly as many school systems it deserves. I have to say "school systems" (plural) because the US is the only postindustrial country in the world where schools are financed locally, primarily through local property taxes, a fact that amazes people from other developed countries when they learn the incredible fact that in the US, wealthy areas of the country finance well-funded, well-maintained, and adequately resourced schools, and that poor areas can fund only dilapidated, overcrowded, antiquated, and underresourced schools. The result of this economic situation, however, is that the US really does have many excellent school systems. We have the best schools, the best students, and the best teachers, equal to any school system in the world. They are just found in highly selective areas.

Imagine if we had a population of citizens who basically shared the same homogeneous culture, spoke the same language, were all native born, had excellent health care and nutrition from birth, were relatively economically well off, were relatively safe from violence, and had excellent housing and job security for life. Imagine if we had universally well-educated, well-paid, and (yes) strongly unionized teachers teaching students from supportive and involved families. We then would have an excellent school system. We'd also be Finland (Sahlberg, 2011).

But we aren't Finland, of course. However, we have pockets of Finland. Take my current home, the Bronx, New York. The Bronx has one of the five poorest congressional districts in the US and about 30% of population is below the poverty line. But besides having poor areas such Hunts Point, Morrisania, and the South Bronx, it has wealthy areas such as Riverdale, Fieldston (probably you've heard of the über-privileged Fieldston School), and Country Club (yes, that's the actual name of a neighborhood). It has many so-called underperforming schools, many of which are being closed, and it has DeWitt Clinton High School, with the most recoded incidences of violence in an educational system that is the largest in the country and twice as large as the next largest (Los Angeles). However, where I live, in Parkchester, there is a strongly middle-class, highly diverse neighborhood. Here the public schools are pretty good, and we have one of the top five schools in the New York City, the Bronx Charter School for Excellence. The smart, hardworking, middle-class African Americans, Caribbean immigrants, Dominicans and Puerto Ricans, Bengalis, and a large Muslim population know how to support and demand from the city good schools.

The Bronx also has the Bronx High School of Science, a school whose students have earned more doctorates than those from any other high school in the US. It has had 132 finalists in the Intel Science Talent Search (formerly Westinghouse scholarships) and has the largest number of any school in the country. Seven graduates have won Nobel Prizes, more than any other high school in the world.[4] Obviously, this is a school that, in *A Nation*'s words, is able to allow students to "stretch their minds to full capacity" (NCEE, 1983, p. 17).

Nevertheless, it is a useless myth to say that anything Bronx Science is doing is anything to create the social and economic realities of the Bronx, or that this school is creating a population of highly competitive workers to enhance the economy of either the Bronx or New York City or the US. Rather, the myth is the other way around. Bronx Science attracts students from culturally advantaged or culturally striving families and communities in New York City. Not only does Bronx Science not create any economic conditions in the Bronx, it has nothing to do with the Bronx at all.

The school could be in Westchester or Bora-Bora or Finland for all that it matters.

Barring Dewey's ideal of school and society as a collaborative enterprise expressed in the early part of the last century (Dewey, 1907/2011), there is as of yet no evidence, from *A Nation* to the *New York Times* (Friedman, 2009) to Arne Duncan (2010), that schools create society.

Myth #2: Many Teachers Are Deficient

Almost universally, the media, whether these are liberal or conservative, simply assume that great numbers of teachers are deficient, ineffective, or lazy, and that such teachers are protected by unions. The defectiveness of teachers is measured, as always with reformers, by test scores, which over time, as adjusted for other factors, really don't rise much or fall much without manipulation by the test creators themselves. However, as Ravitch (2013) points out, scores are rising, and this is from the only consistent and valid test given over time that we have, the National Assessment of Educational Progress (NAEP). There is no reason to believe that today students are doing less well on tests than they did in some mythological previous era of wonderful schools and superb students. Nevertheless, test scores, whether rising or falling, or whether they are manipulated or not, don't matter. Reformers simply believe the myth that there are massive numbers of deficient teachers and deficient students, just as *A Nation* stated 30 years ago.

Additionally, from a logical perspective, why should there be more defective teachers than there are defective doctors, lawyer, cops, morticians, or cooks? Furthermore, there is good evidence that teachers become teachers because they want to (Costigan, 2005a; Costigan & Crocco, 2004). They know their students will often be unprepared, resistant to learning, and have low test scores, and will come with all sorts of social and economic issues that hinder learning. But teachers come anyway. Teaching is a vocation, not a job (Weiss, 2006). Teachers don't need the carrot of competitive financial incentives, and they don't need the stick of threats of termination because of fluctuating test scores (Ravitch, 2013).

But if you hold the myth that teachers are deficient, they can be considered "at will" employees without job security. Not only that, you want them to turn over their population after two years, as the Teach For America (TFA) model advocates. This myth devalues the development of expertise in teaching over time that comes from years of experience and, rather, puts faith in for-profit corporations that provide scripted "teacher proof" curricular materials and online learning. Paying for these materials and computer programs is very expensive, but less so than paying experienced teachers higher salaries and benefits.

The more a teacher teaches, the better she gets (Huberman, 1993; Levin, 2003), and this goes against the myth that a novice with a strong academic background needs to commit to only two years of teaching based on a short, intensive "boot camp" induction (Costigan, 2005b; Ravitch, 2013). Those who are personally invested enough, or crazy enough, to want to teach, particularly in poor urban schools, probably are doing it for the right reason and will be pretty good at it. As for the stick of firing, always due to variable test scores, that does nothing but increase anxiety and disenfranchisement, and increase the exodus from the profession (Ingersoll, 2003, 2012).

Myth #3: Students Are Unchallenged

Educational reformers have to be careful because it is so-called minority students who are failing, even despite their best test-based reform efforts. Children and adolescents who are wealthy, White, native-born, and native English speaking are doing just fine by schools. Black and Hispanic and immigrant kids from upwardly mobile families are doing fine also. The system is working for them. In fact, wealthy kids in private schools and working-class kids in parochial schools don't even have to take the standardized and high-stakes tests reformers put in place for poor kids in public schools. Still, no reformer wants to be called a racist, despite the fact that it is the poor, the immigrant, the non-native English speaking, or persons of color who schools are "failing." Rather than call failing students "deficient," the reformers maintain that they are "unchallenged," that teachers are doing something wrong, and that these minority populations are ill-served by schools.

The sociologist James Coleman's landmark study in the 1960s, sponsored by the US government, revealed that the best students are not the brightest but rather those willing to be bored and work at relatively meaningless tasks with little intrinsic or immediate reward (Coleman, 1966). The best students are those whose families, friends, and local communities value schooling, and who can see the financial and social rewards at the end of a (usually) tedious and joyless round of schooling. Schooling, for successful students, is a long slog of darkness for the economic light at the end of the tunnel.

It is interesting that there is not one sentence in any text of educational reform that speaks of the joy of learning, or the wonders of being aesthetically engaged with English, math, or science. The inherent joy of learning found in life—of reading a good book, playing a musical instrument, discovering something about plants or bacteria, or solving a math puzzle—is of no interest to educational reformers.

When would we find massive amounts of student who *were* challenged and engaged in school? During the Revolutionary War? Back during Teddy Roosevelt's presidency? During World War II? In the 1950s or 1960s? In fact, today's youths generally are better nourished, are healthier, and have higher IQs at any point in human history (Flynn, 2012a, 2012b). If they are unchallenged by school, it is not because they are stupid, or otherwise deficient, it is because they choose not to be engaged by formal schooling, or that they are so economically, psychologically, or socially stressed that they *can't* be engaged by formal schooling. And then there is the inconvenient fact that for many students, disengagement from schooling is not an insane or irrational act; it is a perfectly logical act of rational self-interest. Dropouts, even if they are ultimately self-destructive, are acting rationally based on the evidence they have at hand (Csikszentmihalyi, Rathunde, & Whalen, 1993).

But educational reformers are completely disinterested in what students think, feel, or believe. If they did talk to young people, they would find that the myth of student disengagement first promulgated by *A Nation* is not the case. As the sociologist Csikszentmihalyi—one of the few researchers who is actually concerned with what young people think, feel, and believe—finds, young people are interested in all sorts of things, from music, to games, to computers, to sports, to writing, to reading (Csikszentmihalyi, 1996). Junior high school students, for instance, are reading many books all the time. It's just that they are not engaged with school reading, or with much else of the curriculum of school.

The reformers never talk to young people (or teachers or parents for that matter) because these people are seen as deficient and defective. They need to be "worked on" by reformers who come from, and think like, people from the corporate marketplace. These educational reformers engage in a kind of destructive tautology: If many young people are disengaged from schooling, then the solution is to make schooling *become more of what it already is*, to make the appurtenances of schooling harder, faster, and more intense, what Hargreaves (2000) calls the *intensification* of schooling. Statistics are hard to come by, but there are some 25% to 45% of students in the US who never graduate at all. Doing traditional schooling harder and faster and at higher stakes does nothing but create a deeper fear and loathing of school. It remains a mystery how this intensification is supposed to assist "young people [in] their chance to learn and live according to their aspirations and abilities" (NCEE, 1983, p. 16).

Myth #4: Testing Reflects Knowledge

One of the most insidious myths of educational reform is that standardized tests reflect some kind of knowledge. What is interesting is that *A Nation* really doesn't speak about testing, but testing is a natural outcome of the myth of unchallenged students and deficient teachers.

The central reason for the ascendency of relentless and high-stakes testing is actually quite simple. Again, we look to where the money is. Tests, while very expensive, are considerably cheaper and seemingly easier than providing small classes, authentic learning materials, experienced teachers with pensions and benefits, and simply the time for teachers to reflect and collaborate to create an engaging curriculum for their specific students (Hargreaves,

2000). So, the US school systems spend $1.5 billion a year on testing, then these costs are justified as an efficient and relatively cheaper way to assess student progress (Chingos, 2012; Ujifusa, 2012). An important aspect of testing is that for-profit test-publishing corporations provide not only tests but also test preparation materials. Then, if many students fail their tests, these corporations for a price can provide test remediation materials. It's a win-win marketing situation, similar to the case of Bain Capital, which made a handsome profit even if the companies it took over failed.

Furthermore, most people in the US believe that tests are a commonsensical and inevitable part of schooling (Johnson & Immerwahr, 1994). Education, after all, is pretty much the same across the US, and this common experience, including testing as a norm, has been shared by almost every citizen in the country (Cuban, 1984). People *know* what schooling does. People at a party would never tell a surgeon how to remove a gall bladder or a lawyer how to win a malpractice suit, but they are ever ready to tell teachers what is needed in schooling, whether it be "more grammar" or "returning to memorizing the times tables." People just *know* what schools do. And, having been tested in schools all their lives, and having been taught that the fear and loathing of testing is just a commonsense part of schooling to be endured, most people just accept the inevitability of testing, like they do regular visits to the dentist or, for those of us over age 50, a colonoscopy every few years. However, there is no universal law that dictates that we must have tests. In fact, it is possible to conceive of schooling without testing at all through authentic assessment practices, including student presentations of expertise in learning and portfolios showing the growth of student work.

The problem is that while tests test *something*, it is not at all clear what they test. The SAT for instance, no longer stands for the "Scholastic Assessment Test" nor the "Scholastic Aptitude Test." The name did shift to the "Standard Application Test," but now the acronym "SAT" is not an acronym for anything (Gardner, 2014). By its own admission this test "doesn't test logic or abstract reasoning" but rather "readiness for college, or the skills you're learning in school."[5] However, the SAT's importance is that it is a myth, a rite of passage, something on which students hang their hopes and their futures. Actually, the SAT is a *pseudo-referential*. That is, like the unicorn, it is *supposed* to symbolize something, but it's never quite clear what that something actually is. However, it has been clear since 1974 that the one thing the test is able to test more accurately than any other variable is family income (Karier, 1986, pp. 333–334).

The fact remains that all tests are flawed instruments. They predict a person's knowledge of English or math as much as polls accurately predict a presidential race. An IQ test or the SAT certainly indicate *something*. If you get an 85 on an IQ test or a 600 on your SATs, you're probably not going to do a doctorate in nuclear physics—but, hey, you never know. However, it is another thing to say that the Stanford-Binet IQ test measures something called "g" (some intelligence factor), and that the SAT measures something called "readiness for college" (whatever this is). In any event, while many things can be measured, what is really important in life cannot be measured at all. You cannot measure the meaning of *Hamlet* or string theory or *The Magic Flute* on a test. What is measurable may not be meaningful, and the meaningful things may not be measurable at all (Bruner, 1990). And, of course, what is certainly tested in every test is family income.

The problem with tests and test- and standards-based curricula is that they have very little to do with what writers, readers, scientists, artists, mathematicians, or other people actually do. I can only really speak with any authority in my subject area, which is English; however, I am sure the situation is the same in other relentlessly tested subject disciplines, such as math, science, and history. In English Language Arts, the reality is that tests have almost nothing to do with what readers and writers actually do in the real world. For instance, English Language Arts (ELA) tests given to high school students in Texas, Florida, California, New York, and Massachusetts, to name a few, all look remarkably the same. In fact, they *are* the same, despite some very minor differences (Costigan, 2008). Yet a test-based essay never looks like an essay in the *New York Times* or on the *Huffington Post*. Someone reading poetry never needs to stop and consider such archaic terms for "literary devices" such as *alliteration*, *assonance*, or *caesura*, which routinely appear on ELA tests. Whatever it is English tests test, it is not the subject discipline of English.

The more devious aspect of tests is that, even if they were able to really assess what makes good history, science, math, or English, then they can test only information. Information does not equal knowledge (Bruner, 1990). Information, or facts, is necessary but not sufficient for knowledge. This is because any subject discipline has—and *is*—a language, a way of thinking, a way of looking at the world. If the facts of the theory of relativity, the reason for JFK's assassination, or T. S. Eliot's understanding of *Hamlet* (Eliot, 1922/1980) become outmoded or incorrect, more is the power of the disciplines of science, history, or English who have furnished new understandings of these phenomena. Subject disciplines are not just the facts that have been found out, either historically or recently; they are *conversations*, a way of doing things, a way of making sense of the world. And this, of course, has nothing to do with testing.

Myth #5: Competition Is Good

Educational reforms are grounded in the notion of competition, but it is a highly selective notion of competition. The notion of corporation-style competition as a *good* is opposed to educational cooperation as a *good* (Dewey, 1907/2011). Of course the type of competition imposed on schools, teachers, and students by corporate-style reformers is far different from how the heads of the corporations, or corporate-style reform groups, compete among themselves.

The Race to the Top (RTTT) initiative is even more blatant in seeing educational resources literally as a "race," a competition for athletes in which there are clear winners and losers. The fact that some athletes are competing in the latest running shoes, whereas others have to run in flip-flops and others barefoot, is beside the point to educational reformers. More perversely, somehow the race is supposed both to be *on* a level playing ground and at the same time *to create* a level playing ground, a glaring logical and empirical inconsistency. In fact, those with the running shoes come in first, and those in bare feet are predetermined to lose. The vast majority of us, the middle, are destined to do our running in flip-flops.

So, it is fairly easy to see how the general public and even academics can be induced to swallow these educational myths, along with many others. Myths are easy to digest. Myths are comforting. Myths are simple, unified, fast-food processed nuggets of meaning. However, these processed nuggets of meaning did not just appear from nowhere; they were *created*. And they were created by real people with a real agenda. The question remains about their creation: Why were they created, by whom were they created, and for what purpose?

REFORM MYTHOLOGY AS EXISTENTIAL JUSTIFICATION

From a socio-psychoanalytic perspective, Erich Fromm states, "We know that a person, even if he is subjectively sincere, may frequently be driven unconsciously by a motive that is different from the one he believes himself to be driven by" (Fromm, 1947/1965, p. 85). Educational writers and researchers do not have to subscribe to theories of the unconscious to note that we ourselves, and the people we encounter, often do not know the motivations that drive us, even when we think we are working for good. To paraphrase the 17th-century philosopher Pascal, "The heart has reasons which reason does not know" (Pascal, 1995). Nevertheless, "a great number of apparently insoluble problems disappear at once if we decide to give up the notions that the motives by which people *believe* themselves to be motivated are necessarily the ones which actually drive them to act, feel, and think as they do" (Fromm, 1947/1965, p. 156; emphasis in original). The same approach may assist us to understand the reasons behind reformers' language of simply helping children achieve success in life as *homines economicam*.

What then are the causes behind the demonizing of teachers and the disparagement of local public schools? What are the reasons for closing schools in poor neighborhoods, eliminating teachers' rights to job security and due process, the elimination of union-level benefits, or firing as many of them as possible; in short, what is the effect of the "Walmartization of schooling"? (Costigan & Crocco, 2004; Ravitch, 2013). What are the intentions behind the "fierce desire" (Mackay, 1852) for the privatization of schooling; the corporatization of education; the creation of systems to enhance relentless competition among teachers, schools, and students for meager funding;

relentless testing; the creation of an audit culture; the panopticon-like surveillance of workers; and viewing education as a resource for personal and corporate profit?

In these varied elements of educational reform, is there an existential need that is met? What is "in it" for the reformers themselves, from millionaire mayors of major cities now in charge of school systems, to charitable foundations such as the Bill and Melinda Gates foundation, to President Obama who surprised the educational community with his continuation of the neoliberal reform agenda legally that was formalized in the Reagan years with *A Nation* and imposed in the George Bush era with NCLB? Why do these myths endure so well?

The answer lies in the nature of myth itself. Myths make a person feel good when they confirm that person's, or a group of people's, conception of reality, of their very means and ways of existing. However, myths not only coalesce, order, and simplify facts to give them meaning, but it is in this act of making meaning that people are allowed to feel good about themselves, to "self-affirm," if you will. The myths of reform enhances the existence of personal and class justification, creating satisfaction.

As explained at the outset of this chapter, myths are best thought of as neither true nor untrue but as useful and beneficial, or as not useful and harmful. Myths are seen as useful and beneficial when they conform to and explain reality, as in, "The deck is stacked against poor rural high school graduates getting into Harvard" (Hoxby & Avery, 2012; Leonhardt, 2013). Myths are not useful and are even harmful when they are divorced from reality, as in, "Those poor rural high school graduates are not smart enough to get into in Harvard." Yet myths work also in the opposite direction. If a person convinces her or himself that a myth feels good and is personally rewarding, then that myth also enables that person to assemble facts of agreeing with the myth that is so important to her or his mode of existing, as in, "It is regrettable that there exist rural poor high school graduates who can't succeed in Harvard—as people like me can." After all, as Fussell (1983) notes, it hardly matters if you get in to Harvard unless there are also masses of people who can't.

Myths don't only make sense of and coalesce reality; they are able to *create* reality. As the economist John Kenneth Galbraith said, "To a very large extent, of course, we associate truth with convenience—with what most closely accords with self-interest and individual well-being or promises best to avoid awkward effort or unwelcome dislocation of life.... Therefore we adhere, as though to a raft, to those ideas which represent our understanding" (Galbraith, 1958/1998). What is true in economics is true in education.

What then, are the myths of self-understanding of educational reformers? Making some myths here about the reformers may help clarify thinking about them. These myths can then be tested for conformity to reality as researchers continue examine the motivations for the reformers' zeal:

- They know at the core of their being that their wealth is a mixture of native talent that is coupled to the accidents of privilege and fortune. Deep down, they know that their good fortune is built on ordinary talent and initiative combined with lots of luck and personal ambition. They know, in essence, that they are average people.
- They know deep down that poor people are poor not primarily because they are weak or defective, but because they don't have access to successful wealthy communities of people, to select private schools, to joining country clubs, to living in comfort in desirable areas, to being able to rub shoulders with other successful people who can help them access more power, money, and privilege. This access to the corridors of privilege could be called "the law of proximal opportunity." Those who have access to power and privilege are those most likely to get it.

Steve Jobs may have been a genius who invented the first personal computer in his garage, but the fact is *he had a garage*. And his parents were college professors, and they were wealthy enough to live in San Francisco. Michelle Rhee may make much of the fact that her parents were South Korean immigrants, but her father was a physician and her mother owned a clothing store. Michael Bloomberg may have "made" his billions through hard work and much luck, but he started his life as his real estate father moved his family up in status through three increasingly upscale suburbs of Boston. These reformers are not the poor people whom they wish to act upon. In New York City, for instance, there are 15 charter school principals and "leaders" who make more than the school chancellor, and the top two leaders make more than double the chancellor's salary (Monahan, 2013).

When people become successful—as opposed to those who were lucky enough simply to be born wealthy—they usually forefront their own genius and initiative, while at the same time they downplay the very real social factors that enhanced their success. For example, there are probably about as many good-looking poor people as there are good-looking wealthy people, just as there are certainly just as many smart poor people as there are smart wealthy people (Fussell, 1983). The accidents of money and the proximity to success, however, are very unequal and in essence unfair. Educational reformers, all of whom are relatively well educated, privileged, and wealthy—or were clever enough, and driven enough, and lucky enough to become so—must affirm and bolster the sense of their self-sufficiency and self-worth, while at the same time must downplay, or even deny, that there is anything fundamentally wrong with contemporary society, which enabled them to acquire and maintain wealth, status, and power. The ultimate myth that enhances their self-worth, and that even justifies their status, is the myth that "you just need a leg up in life," that your background, social status, finances, and proximity to power and privilege do not matter at all.

But of course proximity to power not only matters, it is central to success. By ignoring the effects of poverty and other social inequities, and by maintaining that it's just hard work on the part of a student to "achieve" status as the *homo economicus*, reformers draw away attention from their own proximity to avenues of wealth, power, and privilege, and focus solely on the isolated factors of their presumed intelligence, abilities, and merit. If these economic and social strivers were to admit that society is basically unfair, and that this unfairness has worked to their benefit, their whole secure world, along with their feelings of personal accomplishment and self-worth, their sense of self-actualization, their "justification," is deflated. This is the principle of educational reform systems such as TFA, as if those who join this group were mythologizing to themselves:

> We will descend, for two years from our great universities, down to your level, to teach you. We will give you the knowledge and skills that we have due to our privilege and our fine education. We will show you the way to do the same. Then more of you will be enlightened by our efforts. Then, after having enlightened you, we will ascend back into the higher realms of corporate management."[6]

The myths of educational reform, therefore, provide privileged reformers with a playing field to impose the kinds of ruthless competition they would never like to experience themselves. By pointing the finger of educational reform primarily at the urban or rural poor, the non-native English speaking, the immigrant, and persons of color, they can feel more secure that they made it by the same rules they are imposing on teachers and young people.

More importantly, reformers nowhere advocate any love of learning or appreciation of the disciplines of the arts and sciences. These are irrelevant to the *homo economicus*, solely concerned with the "enlightened self-interest" of making money and achieving high social status. Steve Jobs was a notoriously bad student. Bill Gates spent his time forming Microsoft in a poker room at Harvard and then dropped out. Almost all educational reformers have had privileged backgrounds and attended private schools and top-rated colleges, and an overwhelming number have MBAs or similar business-oriented degrees from top universities. Neither Bill and Melinda Gates, Michael Bloomberg, Michelle Rhee, nor those sitting on the boards of educational foundations have demonstrated anything more than a tangential love for their own educational histories. Education serves primarily the means for bringing to the most competitive social standing, money, and the trappings of power. This worldview is, of course, in stunning contrast to what motivates most teachers.

But that's beside the point. They made their money by talent, pluck, opportunism, and privilege. By imposing rigorous rules and relentless competition on others, they affirm the myth that they came to their own wealth by playing the game fairly and competing relentlessly. Through the myths of educational reform, they can impose their own myths of the self-made opportunist on those who have been less fortunate. In this act of self-affirmation, self-actualization, and self-justification, reformers never have to address the inherent economic and social inequalities in the US. They never have to confront the fact that these inequalities continue to create bad schools, and they are enabled to pin our nation's problems on the mythology of bad schools, bad teachers, and bad students, and not on the facts of the economic and social inequities that aided their own ascendancy.

In the neoliberal paradigm of educational reform, teachers, students, families, and even schools themselves are reduced to the gladiators of the Roman Empire who were forced to fight in the arena of "excellence." Rubrics, testing, standards, and "value added" accountability are only modern equivalents of the trident, net, and sword. Like those forced to fight in the arena, educators are obliged to compete for the amusement and condescension of the elites. When those in the arena fail, then, like the injured gladiators of old, they are blamed for their own lack of skill. Those who do survive in the arena of standards know that, like the gladiators in the ancient world, they have only delayed the one eventual outcome.

NOTES

1. "Male–male," a relatively new genre of gay romance fiction.
2. See Sheffield's example of the Borg in his chapter in this volume.
3. See Metcalfe's chapter in this book for one explication of *homo economicus*.
4. See en.wikipedia.org/wiki/The_Bronx_High_School_of_Science.
5. http://sat.collegeboard.org/why-sat/topic/sat/what-the-sat-tests.
6. See teachforamerica.org/our-mission.

REFERENCES

Baker, A. (2012, August 18). Many New York City teachers denied tenure in policy shift. *The New York Times*, p. A1. Retrieved April 30, 2013 from http://www.nytimes.com/2012/08/18/nyregion/nearly-half-of-new-york-city-teachers-are-denied-tenure-in-2012.html?pagewanted=2

Berliner, D., & Biddle, B. (1995). *The manufactured crisis: Myths, fraud and the attack on America's public schools*. New York, NY: Basic Books.

Bracey, G. (2004). *Setting the record straight: Responses to misconceptions about public education in the U.S.* (2nd ed.). Portsmouth, NH: Heinemann.

Bruner, J. (1990). *Acts of meaning*. Cambridge, MA: Harvard University Press.

Chingos, M. M. (2012, November 29). *Strength in numbers: State spending on K–12 assessment systems*. Retrieved March 1, 2014 from Brookings Institution website: http://www.brookings.edu/research/reports/2012/11/29-cost-of-ed-assessment-chingos

Coleman, J. S. (1966). *Equality of educational opportunity*. The Coleman Study. Washington, DC: US Department of Education.

Costigan, A. (2005a, Spring). Choosing to stay, choosing to leave: New York City Teaching Fellows after two years. *Teacher Education Quarterly, 32*(2), 125–142.
Costigan, A. (2005b). A "traditional" alternative route to certification: Narrative research and implications for teacher education and teacher retention. In J. R. Dangel & E. M. Guyton (Eds.), *Research on alternative and non-traditional education: Association of Teacher Education Yearbook* (Vol. 13, pp. 27–38). Lanham, MD: Scarecrow Education/Rowman & Littlefield.
Costigan, A. (2008, Spring). Canaries in the coal mine: Urban rookies learning to teach language arts in "high priority" schools. *Teacher Education Quarterly, 35*(2), 85–103.
Costigan, A. T., & Crocco, M. S. (2004). *Learning to teach in an age of accountability*. Mahwah, NJ: Erlbaum.
Csikszentmihalyi, M. (1996). *Creativity: Flow and the psychology of discovery and invention*. New York, NY: HarperCollins.
Csikszentmihalyi, M., Rathunde, K., & Whalen, S. (1993). *Talented teenagers: The roots of success and failure*. New York, NY: Cambridge University Press.
Cuban, L. (1984). *How teachers taught: Constancy and change in American classrooms, 1890–1980*. New York, NY: Longman.
Dewey, J. (2011). *The school and society & the child and the curriculum* (Kindle ed.). US: Seven Treasures Publications. (Original work published 1907)
Duncan, A. (2010, September 2). There's courage in our country's classrooms. *The Huffington Post*. Retrieved from news.yahoo.com/s/huffpost/20100903/cm_huffpost/704341
Eliot, T. S. (1980). Hamlet and his problems. In T. S. Eliot, *The sacred wood: Essays on poetry and criticism* (pp. 63–67). New York, NY: Macmillan. (Original work published 1922)
Flynn, J. R. (2012a). *Are we getting smarter?: Rising IQ in the 21st century*. Cambridge, England: Cambridge University Press.
Flynn, J. R. (2012b, September 22). Are we really getting smarter? *The Wall Street Journal*, p. C3.
Friedman, T. L. (2005). *The world is flat: A brief history of the twenty-first century*. New York, NY: Straus & Giroux.
Friedman, T. L. (2009, October 20). The new untouchables. *The New York Times*, p. A31. Retrieved November 3, 2019 from http://www.nytimes.com/2009/10/21/opinion/21friedman.html?scp=1&sq=the+new+untouchables&st=nyt
Fromm, E. (1965). *Escape from freedom*. New York, NY: Avon Books. (Original work published 1947)
Fussell, P. (1983). *Class: A guide through the American status system*. New York, NY: Touchstone.
Gabbard, D. A. (2007). *Knowledge and power in the global economy: The effects of school reform in a neoliberal/neoconservative age* (2nd ed.). New York, NY: Erlbaum/Taylor & Francis.
Galbraith, J. K. (1998). *The affluent society* (4th ed.). New York: NY: Houghton Mifflin. (Original work published 1958)
Gardner, W. (2014, March 10). Still unsatisfactory. *The New York Daily News*. Retrieved March 11 2014 from http://www.nydailynews.com/opinion/unsatisfactory-article-1.1714714
Gootman, E. (2009, March 24). Children are rejected by schools near their home. *The New York Times*, p. A21. Retrieved March 25, 2009 from http://www.nytimes.com/2009/03/24/education/24schools.html?_r=0
Hargreaves, A. (2000). *Changing teachers, changing times: Teachers' work and culture in the postmodern age*. Professional Development and Practice Series. New York, NY: Teachers College Press.

Harvey, D. (2005). *A brief history of neoliberalism*. Oxford, England: Oxford University Press.
Hoxby, C. M., & Avery, C. (2012). *The missing "one-offs": The hidden supply of high-achieving, low income students*. Working Paper No. 18586. Cambridge, MA: National Bureau of Economic Research. Retrieved February 1, 2014 from http://www.nber.org/papers/w18586
Huberman, M. (1993). *The lives of teachers* (J. Neufeld, Trans.). New York, NY: Teachers College Press. (Original work published 1989)
Ingersoll, R. M. (2003). *Who controls teachers' work?: Power and accountability in America's schools*. Cambridge, MA: Harvard University Press.
Ingersoll, R. M. (2012). Beginning teacher induction: What the data tells us. *Phi Delta Kappan, 93*(8), 47–61.
Johnson, J., & Immerwahr, J. (1994). *First things first: What Americans expect from the public schools*. New York, NY: Public Agenda.
Karier, C. J. (1986). *The individual, society, and education: A history of American educational ideas* (2nd ed.). Urbana-Champaign: University of Illinois Press. (Original work published 1967)
Kelly, G. A. (1962). *A theory of personality*. New York, NY: Norton, 1963.
Kliebard, H. (2004). *The struggle for the American curriculum*. New York, NY: Routledge/Falmer.
Leonhardt, D. (2013, March 17). Better colleges failing to lure talented poor. *The New York Times*, p. A1. Retrieved April 20m 2013 from http://www.nytimes.com/2013/03/17/education/scholarly-poor-often-overlook-better-colleges.html?pagewanted=all&_r=2&
Levin, B. B. (2003). *Case studies of teacher development: An in-depth look at how thinking about pedagogy develops over time*. Mahwah, NJ: Erlbaum.
Mackay, C. (1852). *Memoirs of extraordinary popular delusions and the madness of crowds* (Kindle ed.). Public domain book. Retrieved January 2, 2013 from http://www.amazon.com/dp/B004TP6B1O/ref=rdr_kindle_ext_tmb
Monahan, R. (2013, October 27). Top of class: 16 charter bigs out-earn chancellor. *New York Daily News*, p. 13. Retrieved October 28, 2013 from http://www.nydailynews.com/new-york/education/top-16-nyc-charter-school-execs-out-earn-chancellor-dennis-walcott-article-1.1497717
Muskal, M. (2013, January 22). U.S. high school graduation rate hits highest level in decades. *The Los Angeles Times*. Retrieved September 23, 2014 from http://articles.latimes.com/2013/jan/22/nation/la-na-nn-high-school-graduation-rate-increasing-20130122
National Commission on Excellence in Education. (1983). *A nation at risk: The full account*. Portland, OR: USA Research.
Pascal, B. (1995). *Pensées and other writings* (H. Levi, Trans.). Oxford, England: Oxford University Press.
Pinker, S. (2002). *The blank slate: The modern denial of human nature*. New York, NY: Penguin.
Ravitch, D. (2000). *Left back: A century of failed school reforms*. New York, NY: Simon & Schuster.
Ravitch, D. (2013). *Reign of error: The hoax of the privatization movement and the danger to America's public schools*. New York, NY: Knopf.
Ryan, C., & Jetha, C. (2010). *Sex at dawn: The prehistoric origins of modern sexuality*. New York, NY: HarperCollins.
Sagan, C. (1996). *The demon-haunted world: Science as a candle in the dark*. New York, NY: Ballantine/Random House.
Sahlberg, P. (2011). *Finnish lessons: What can the world learn from educational change in Finland?* New York, NY: Teachers College Press.

Snyder, T. D. (Ed.). (1993). *120 years of American education: A statistical portrait*. National Center for Educational Statistics. Washington, DC: US Department of Education, Office of Educational Research and Improvement. Retrieved October 23, 20113 from http://nces.ed.gov/pubsearch/pubsinfo.asp?pubid=93442

Ujifusa, A. (2012, November 29). Standardized testing costs states $1.7 billion a year, study says. *Education Week, 32*(13). Retrieved November 30, 2012 from http://www.edweek.org/ew/articles/2012/11/29/13testcosts.h32.html?tkn=VLMFJUQpeyvKkTzwuCHPd%2FuQG%2BPWLRrD1lNp&cmp=clp-edweek

US Congress. (2001). *Elementary and Secondary Education Act: No Child Left Behind Act of 2001*. Washington, DC: Author.

Weiss, L. (2006). *Urban teaching: The essentials*. New York, NY: Teachers College Press.

2 The Neoliberal Myth
Narrative Resistance to Democratic Education

Bryan Metcalfe

Over the course of the last 30 years, neoliberalism has come to be understood by many as antithetical to democracy (Bourdieu, 1998; Giroux, 2004; Harvey, 2005). It is for this reason that educators who are committed to democratic change in and through education have long been concerned with how neoliberalism has embedded itself in North American schools and eroded democratic practices, values, and beliefs in classrooms. And while many critical democratic educators have discussed the various characteristics of neoliberalism as an "ethic" and ideological force in society and schools (Freire, 1998; Giroux, 2004), little analysis has occurred on how a neoliberal economic theory has become a pervasive and powerful sociopolitical myth.

Central to this chapter is examining how neoliberal economic theory has become an important sociopolitical myth that is circulating and accepted by educational policy makers, administrators, teachers, and students alike. Crucial to this reexamination of neoliberalism is coming to a more substantive conception of sociopolitical myths. More specifically, drawing on the philosophical works of philosophers Hans Blumenberg (1979/1985) and Chiara Bottici (2007), this chapter resituates neoliberalism in a Blumenbergian conception of sociopolitical myth. In doing so, this rethinking of sociopolitical myths provides important insight into the ideological force of the neoliberal myth; it reveals how the neoliberal myth provides a gripping narrative that has come to dominate much of educational discourse. More than this, it reveals how the neoliberal myth, as a powerful normative narrative, fundamentally undermines and erodes any meaningful democratic aspirations in schools.

This chapter will open, for the sake of conceptual clarity, with an examination of a Blumenbergian conception of sociopolitical myth. It will then examine how neoliberal economic theory, which is traditionally conceived as a morally neutral theoretical model, spurred the neoliberal myth that currently circulates in North American education systems. Far from the development of neoliberalism into a sociopolitical myth being benign, it has ultimately led to educators and students accepting and even promoting a normative myth that is morally and ethically vacuous. Finally, as this chapter will reveal in the final section, this vacuity is particularly antithetical to educators' democratic aspirations in terms of both setting the aims of education as well as understanding the notions of quality and excellence in education.

WHAT ARE SOCIOPOLITICAL MYTHS?

Central to neoliberalism's ideological influence in education is that it has become a "sociopolitical myth" that informs both current education systems and current reforms. For the most part, educators understand "myth" in its popular pejorative sense: as a commonly held illusion that should be demystified by reason to uncover the truth or reality about a subject matter. However, more can be said on how neoliberalism grips the current education system by coming to a deeper and more substantive understanding of sociopolitical myths. German philosopher Hans Blumenberg's (1979/1985) conception of myth established in his treatise *Work on Myth*, later adapted and applied to the realm of politics by philosopher Chiara Bottici (2007) in her work *A Philosophy of Political Myth*, is particularly insightful in shedding light into myth.

Several important characteristics define sociopolitical myths in the Blumenbergian sense. First, myths are understood as "stories that are distinguished by a high degree of constancy in their narrative core" (Blumenberg, 1979/1985, p. 34). In this sense, the meaning of myth is consistent with what people traditionally think of as great ancient narratives such as the myth of Odysseus or Sisyphus. However, this general understanding of myth can also be extended to include more contemporary political myths (Bottici, 2007). An example of a modern political myth that Chiara Bottici uses in her work is the myth of the "clash of civilizations" (Bottici, 2007; Bottici & Challand, 2006). She argues that this myth is a political narrative that tells the story of the West's inextricable cultural battle with Islam. According to Bottici, this narrative was raised to particular prominence after the 9/11 attacks, which led to an increased popularity of various academic works such as Samuel Huntington's *The Clash of Civilizations and the Remaking of the World Order* (1996).

More than simply a story, however, myths provide a sense of unity and what Blumenberg denotes as "significance" to reality. As myths are formed and embraced within communities, certain people, acts, and events gain importance and significance as people locate them within the mythic narrative itself. In this way, the myth provides symbolic unity to people's orientation in the world and infuses their reality, which is perceived as indifferent to humanity's existence, with a heightened sense of meaning and significance (Blumenberg, 1979/1985, p. 67). For example, according to Bottici, the myth of the clash of civilizations has emerged as a particularly powerful narrative that provides communities and individuals a symbolic means of understanding the world as well infusing various aspects of people's social order within a heightened sense of significance. One can see that this myth has become so banal that it continues to infuse many debates, people, and events with significance both in North America and abroad from the use of drones in air strikes on foreign soil and the continued imprisonment of "unlawful combatants" to other domestic debates such as the legitimacy of women wearing burkas.

The ability of a narrative to provide significance to communities is essential to understanding the power and resiliency of sociopolitical myths even in the contemporary society. While it is tempting to think that contemporary communities do not rely on sociopolitical myths because science and rationally constructed organizations have made such narratives obsolete, Blumenberg challenges this notion by arguing that insofar as humans need to orient themselves in a complex and indifferent world, they will necessarily rely on myths to provide unity and significance to it. Furthermore, he argues that given the significant epistemological limitations of reason and science providing a symbolic guide for acting in the world, in many cases it is reasonable for humans to turn to rhetoric, of which myth is a part, as part of their everyday praxis (Blumenberg, 1996). For Blumenberg, then, people in contemporary culture necessarily use both reason and myth to aid in their symbolic interaction with the world around them.

Another essential feature of sociopolitical myths in the Blumenbergian sense is that myths are always particularized within communities to meet their specific social and political needs (Bottici, 2007). What this means is that while politicians and academics might understand the overarching narrative in the general sense, myths are always contextualized, or what Blumenberg calls "worked on," by particular communities to meet their specific sociopolitical needs. To use Bottici's example of the clash of civilizations again, one can understand the general narrative core of this myth as the cultural battle between the West and Islam, but the myth is contextualized and particularized differently in communities within New York City from those in Toronto, Canada. This conceptual element of myth is an important one in discussing the function of sociopolitical myths in education insofar as one will find that a sociopolitical myth, such as the neoliberal myth, while sharing a general narrative core will marginally vary based on how particular communities receive and work on it.

NEOLIBERALISM: FROM THEORY TO SOCIOPOLITICAL MYTH

One important implication of embracing a more substantive Blumenbergian conception of sociopolitical myths is that it provides important insight into the effects of neoliberalism *qua* myth. Neoliberal theory, for the most part, is insulated from criticism insofar as it is understood by its defenders as an economic theory that merely informs free-market policy rather than an ideology that shapes normative discourse, values, beliefs, and action. However, a more substantive version of sociopolitical myth opens the possibility that this controversial economic theory has become a political narrative that provides unity, significance, and mode of symbolic orientation within various communities beyond government think tanks, academia, and corporations.

Neoliberalism as an economic theory provides social scientific predictions regarding capitalist growth; in turn, these scientifically grounded predictions provide the theoretical basis for various policies of economic institutions. This conception of neoliberalism is notably discussed by economists Arthur Denzau and Douglass North (1994) in their work "Shared Mental Models: Ideologies and Institutions." According to Denzau and North, neoliberalism as an economic theory is understood as a mental model that conceives of humans as rational, self-interested utility maximizers in order to interpret how humans potentially interact in a free-market environment. Further, Denzau and North (1994) argue that a neoliberal economic theory is directly related to variety of applied neoliberal projects in real political contexts insofar as it is part of a shared mental model, which is best understood as a shared systemic sets of ideas and related principles used by people to interpret the world (Denzau & North, 1994, p. 2).

Crucial to traditional neoliberal economic theory is using a "constrained vision" of humans as rational, self-interested utility maximizers (Roy, Denzau, & Willett, 2007). The concept of a constrained vision originates in Thomas Sowell's (1980) view of theoretically conceiving the human state as having a specific limited content (Roy, Denzau, & Willett, 2007, pp. 5–7). In this sense, a constrained utopian vision requires a certain type of human to make it possible, namely understanding humans as *homo economicuses*: solely self-interested individuals that always try to maximize their consumption of goods and services in an economic order. By using a constrained vision of humans as self-interested utility maximizers, economists are presumably able to create a mental model that attempts to accurately predict and describe free-market-orientated ideas within theoretical contexts that later can be applied to real political contexts through the shared mental model.

One important element of neoliberal theory, which this chapter discusses further in the context of education, is that as a social scientific theory it is understood to be morally neutral in terms of its descriptions and predictions of economic change. In this way, neoliberal economic theory, like physics or chemistry, tries to provide accurate hypotheses and predictions about how individuals act in a free-market economy, but such hypotheses and predictions are thought to be neutral and distinct from humanity's moral and political values. Specifically, neoliberal economic theorists are concerned with accurately describing how *homo economicus*'s beliefs and desires subsequently lead to utility maximization within a free-market environment rather than what constitutes a just society or how people should treat one another.

However, despite neoliberalism positivist theoretical roots, it is evident that over the course of the last 30 years neoliberalism has become much more than an economic model to make predictions with or a set of theoretical principles that help guide public policies through a shared mental model. In fact, neoliberalism has emerged as a powerful sociopolitical myth that provides an important mode of symbolic orientation and normative guide for many individuals and groups in North America. While neoliberalism began as a theoretical construct, as neoliberal economic theory became implemented as public policies, the normative values, beliefs, and ideas, as well as the narrative of economic progress began to be worked on as a myth by economists, politicians, bureaucrats, and the general public alike. As neoliberalism became part of people's sociopolitical discourse, the myth emerged as an important and distinct narrative that provides an important mode of symbolic orientation and sense of narrative significance to people's sociopolitical order.

At the most general level, the neoliberal myth is a narrative of individual and collective progress. Central to the narrative is the archetype of *homo economicus*—the ideal of human behavior that can lead to individual and collective betterment. To this end, every person is a potential *homo economicus* who is able to direct his or her self-interest towards economic ends by rationally maximizing his or her choices both as a consumer and as entrepreneurial producer. In this way, as neoliberal theory became part of the larger shared mental model of society, it became much more than another set of principles and ideas that led to economic growth. Instead, people embraced the view that they should act in accordance with this political and economic archetype. Hence, individuals and groups that receive and work on the neoliberal myth are able to frame their existence within a narrative of individual and collective realization through economic prosperity and progress within their sociopolitical order.

The neoliberal myth offers a unique possibility for those who receive and work on the narrative of *homo economicus* as the archetypal human. If one embraces this myth within a proper capitalist setting, it is possible for every individual to progress through material wealth via consumption and production. An individual's self-interested and utility-maximizing economic behavior is thus normatively tied to living a fulfilled economic life that progresses indefinitely to his or her death. The neoliberal myth's ability to provide significance to the individual in this world should not be dismissed or taken lightly. Amid an indifferent reality and complex sociopolitical order, the neoliberal myth offers in its narrative core the possibility of self-fulfillment and progress by acting out of one's own economic self-interest. For instance, if Bill Gates perhaps embraces the neoliberal myth, his constant striving to expand the profitability and productive power of Microsoft is not simply an effect of his ingenuity, it is an important measure of his own growth as an individual. Similarly, in embracing the neoliberal myth, Gates's consumption of goods and services, from his investment portfolio to his $147 million mansion, are also indicative of said progress. In both instances, the neoliberal myth infuses the self-interested production and consumption of goods and services with a sense significance within the larger narrative of individual progress. Hence, an individual's entrepreneurial production and consumer consumption not only provide him or her with a means of fulfilling immediate desires but also provide important feedback on his or her growth and progress. Further, this feeling of growth and sense of progress, in turn, is the psychological confirmation that the neoliberal myth, and its ideal of *homo economicus*, is an effective normative framework for making prescriptions for people in their current sociopolitical order.

While the individual is at the fundamental core of the neoliberal myth, his or her progress through self-interested production and consumption is necessarily tied to the prosperity of humanity in general. More precisely, central to the neoliberal myth is the narrative that humanity's collective prosperity and progress is possible *only* through people's collective assimilation of *homo economicus* as the ideal. In other words, individual progress as *homo economicus* not only promises individual material fulfillment, but also carries with it the added ideal and promise of worldwide prosperity through more and more groups embracing the narrative core of the myth. Bill Gates, as a hypothetical example, by acting as a perfect neoliberal individual, increases Microsoft's profitability, invests in various companies, and purchases luxury goods; consequently, his consumptions, production, and investments lead to the US's and even the world's collective betterment as this capital is distributed through various economic avenues.

It is important to emphasize the distinction between neoliberalism as a very popular myth and its theoretical counterpart. As a theory, the idea of vast, global economic growth fueled by billions of *homo economicuses* is a positivist description that can exist only hypothetically. As a political myth, however, neoliberal ideas, values, and beliefs gain real normative force as groups collectively embrace it as a narrative to live by. In embracing the neoliberal myth, politicians, policy makers, and large sections of the public accepted the language, symbols, analogies, references, and vision of neoliberal economic theory. Consequently, both deregulation of the market and *homo economicus*'s beliefs, values, and actions *should* be pursued. The problem with this view, of course, is that the neoliberal myth, founded on a morally neutral foundation, sounds suspiciously like answers to fundamental moral and ethical questions:

1. What should people make of themselves? Answer: A materially affluent group of individuals.
2. How should people live? Answer: As self-interested, utility-maximizing consumers and producers.

3. What should people do? Answer: Rationally maximize their individual utility.
4. What kind of person should people become? Answer: *Homo economicus*.

Thrust into the realm of social policy and political discourse, including in education, the neoliberal myth no longer clings to its scientifically justified moral neutrality; *homo economicus* becomes an ideal of human behavior and the free market becomes the ideal amoral environment that people are encouraged to strive to create in a world fraught with human suffering, exploitation, oppression, and violence.

THE NEOLIBERAL MYTH AND EDUCATION

It is evident that one particularly problematic area in which the neoliberal myth has profoundly influenced schools is the narrative discourse concerning the aims of education. By aims, one is referring to Dewey's view of the articulated ends that education systems as a whole aspire to achieve through directed schooling (Dewey, 1922/1974, pp. 70–80). It is the articulated aims of education that subsequently guide how institutions, curricula, pedagogy, and modes of assessment and evaluation are designed in order to achieve these aims. Furthermore, in articulating the aims of education, one is also identifying the desired effects of directed learning *both* within the educational institutions themselves as well as within various communities.

What is the neoliberal myth's aim for any education system? Simply, the neoliberal myth aims to integrate the schooling system, like any other institution, in its narrative of optimal individual and collective economic growth. As a result, all institutions and government policies are forged to achieve this goal. Of course, the primary means of achieving this aim is the active development and promotion of individuals into the *homo economicus* ideal as well as the deregulation of private business. For neoliberals, schooling is much more than a location of individual learning. Rather, education is a crucial institution that actively directs "human capital" towards achieving its single aim of immense and constant economic growth (Friedman & Friedman, 1981).

While I can identify numerous anecdotal examples that reveal the dominance of the neoliberal myth from my own experience as a teacher, the most startling one occurred during the period of my teacher training in 2005. I was placed in a Grade 7/8 split class in London, Ontario. It was during this placement that my students were forced to partake in a school program entitled Building Futures Network (Canadian Foundation for Economic Education, n.d.). The program, created by the Canadian Foundation for Economic Education, was presented by a former bank manager. During the one-day program, the students were systematically led through a series of interrelated booklets. The students began by checking off all the material things that they needed and desired in the future, ranging from a house to a car, etc. Having chosen their material needs and wants, the students, in turn, had to calculate the total cost per year of these items based on a price list provided at the start of the booklet. Once the students calculated this total, they then had to choose the profession that earned an average income that sustained this lifestyle. Finally, the students had to find the corresponding educational program that would lead to their chosen profession. The program was unquestionably trying to promote education. However, it was also trying to promote and reinforce the neoliberal myth's narrative view of education in which learning is explicitly connected to educational accreditation, economic production, and economic consumption. In other words, these 12- and 13-year-old students were encouraged to receive and work on the myth's narrative that they should be young *homo economicuses*, whose self-interested desires to acquire numerous material goods would spur their competitive drive to be productive students and economic agents. Of course, implicit in this exercise is that indefinite self-interested consumption is the locus of human progress and individual and collective fulfillment. Unsurprisingly, given the educational community's widespread embracing of the neoliberal myth and the view that the education system aim is to develop young *homo economicuses* for the competitive global economy, the program was unanimously embraced by the administration, my associate teacher, and the students involved; it was embraced by everyone except for a young woman who was laughed at for announcing that she did not want anything when she grew up.

As this example illustrates, within the neoliberal myth, education system becomes one of the primary institutional venues for what Mark Olssen (1996) calls the "manipulation of man" towards becoming *homo economicus* (p. 340). More specifically, to ensure the success of the neoliberal myth, the education system must ensure that all of the students embrace and receive the *homo economicus* narrative of individual and collective progress and, consequently, must train them to be self-interested, utility-maximizing, and productive entrepreneurs. According to the current neoliberal model of education, optimal economic growth can occur only both by actively developing the individual's capacity to produce as well as by promoting free-market values and dispositions of egoism, individualism, competition, and consumerism within schools.

The radical engulfing of education by the neoliberal myth has fundamentally altered the current discourse on the aims of education to a discussion concerning economic growth. And while educational discourse has always contained within it an important and crucial view of education as a means of training students for the economy (Freire, 1998), the current incarnation of the neoliberal myth in schools has overwhelmingly privileged this view at the cost of others. As McQuaig argues in her work *All You Can Eat* (2001), never in the history of any civilization have *homo economicus* values of self-interested greed and consumerism been so readily accepted and promoted to large portions of society than they have in North American society over the course of the last 30 years.

A significant and key effect of conceiving the neoliberal myth as separate from moral and political issues in education is that policy makers, administrators, and educators fail to see a real fundamental tension and conflict between the myth and democratic values, dispositions, and pedagogy. For example, one of the important elements of democratic education is taking differences between people seriously, and thus working with students to critically engage substantive moral and political issues, such as the unjustified inequities between community members based on religion, race, gender, class, etc. (Freire, 1998; Portelli & Solomon, 2001). However, within educational communities that embrace the neoliberal myth, the engagement of critical issues is eroded. In many cases, the critical engagement of substantive democratic issues is downplayed as inconsequential insofar as it does not contribute to the development of the students into *homo economicuses*. Worse yet, engaging substantive democratic issues in many schools is silenced because it promotes values and practices, such as the questioning of authority and openly discussing forms of systemic harm, that do not fit neatly with the neoliberal narrative of education being primarily an instrument of economic growth.

Equally problematic is that at the very moral core of engaging these substantive issues is understanding and recognizing other people as fundamentally equal in the democratic sense, and thus worthy of deep-found respect. Democratic education requires that administrators, teachers, and students take seriously (Portelli & Solomon, 2001) fundamental inequities that may undermine people's liberty, autonomy, and, in turn, ability to act as a democratic citizens. In the neoliberal myth, however, the individual's amoral framework is directed towards self rather than the consideration of the other; it considers people as economic consumers and producers but is blind and indifferent to the vast inequities that continue to undermine the autonomy and harm others. In the myth, the well-being of others is taken care of by the ever-expanding free market. For students, this means simply working hard and competing with others for grades and scarce positions in the economy, and securing the maximum amount of purchasing power with no regard to systemic inequalities and the plight of others. This, of course, is not to claim that people should not have self-interested motivations to wanting to do well in school. Rather, it is to argue that the education system, if it is going to actively contribute to the moral development of students, including the cultivation of a democratic way of life, must not promote the reception and work on a normative myth that offers no language or prescriptions on how to treat others beyond them being fellow instruments of economic development.

In addition, the neoliberal myth has also played a significant role in defining the notion of "quality" in education. While both neoliberal reformers and their critics defend having a quality education, where neoliberals and their critics differ significantly is regarding what it means for an education system to have a high or low degree of excellence and subsequently how to determine the degree to which this excellence is achieved. One significant way in which neoliberals frame the issue of quality and education is in terms of the creation of a product that is fit for its purpose (Herrnstein & Murray, 1994; Winch, 1996). To this end, to be properly fit for a neoliberal purpose means that students should acquire the highest socioeconomic position that is possible for them through the development of their talents and skills of production. Further, students are to always maximize utility in the consumption of goods and services. In this sense, the excellence of an education system is directly determined by its ability to create individuals who can maximize the economic growth of a society (Herrnstein & Murray, 1994).

More than simply redefining the notion of excellence in education, governments, policy makers, and educational think tanks that embrace the neoliberal myth also incorporate business discourse amid their myth of individual and collective progress. In doing so, neoliberalism works to redefine how the public and educators determine and understand excellence in education. Drawing on business models that emphasize quality assurance and quality controls in production, neoliberals argue that the only way to ensure that students are gaining a high-quality education is to measure their progress or lack thereof against a common and objective standard (Winch, 1996). In this sense, the neoliberal narrative of individual and collective progress is ingrained with the belief that there should be sets of "scientific" and "objective" evaluative standards in education. It is precisely these measurable standards that attempt to solidify a sense of quality and progress in schools by constantly tracking and providing feedback to students, teachers, parents, and bureaucrats alike.

In this way, quality assurance in neoliberal-influenced schools is no different than in the creation of any other complex product. Just as one constantly measures and compares a car against a standard during various points of manufacturing, neoliberals argue that schools should also constantly measure and compare students. One does not have to look too hard to see the corresponding educational policy that neoliberalism has spurred within schools. In both the US and Canada, there continues to be an unprecedented movement towards the standardization of curricula, modes of evaluating, and testing to ensure that students are properly and consistently measured. Of course, implicit in this analysis is that high-quality schools cannot be created without a mode of evaluation or assessment that objectively measures students' progress; nor can they be achieved without a single common and universal standard to measure against. Similarly, the intimate link between student progress in the neoliberal myth and standardization also implies that one cannot understand educational development, growth, and excellence without providing measurable data and feedback. As a consequence, in a school system that is engulfed with the neoliberal myth, teachers, students, administrators, and parents believe that the standards and corresponding data are the normative confirmation of their individual and collective progress.

It should be noted that evaluation and the idea of measuring students against and through standardized curricula and tests predates the advent of neoliberalism (Lemann, 1999). That said, what makes the neoliberal narrative discourse regarding standards unique is its emphasis on framing the issue in the context of quality and education. In accordance with the neoliberal myth, *all* meaningful learning and progress should be measurable against a standard in schools. Of course, this radical shift in the notion of quality in education has led to significant problems in framing educational projects in terms of the political and moral development of students. Democratic and moral values and dispositions, such as critical thinking, altruism, open-mindedness, and a deep, profound reciprocal respect for each other, are immeasurable. There is no standardized test that can measure a student's ability to be an active democratic citizen who reflects and actively seeks to transform the world into a more just, caring, and loving social order. Similarly, there is no standardized test that can measure how open-minded and critical students are.

Within the neoliberal myth, all of the political and moral values and dispositions that are necessary to nurture within oneself in order to develop an ability to resist and overcome injustices in the world are meaningless. Or to put it another way, the democratic and moral dispositions and values nurtured in students have no bearing on the quality of schooling for those embracing the neoliberal myth. The neoliberal conception of quality assurance has become so predominant in North American education systems that it has come to frame many goals within in schools. More specifically, various goals for student achievement in the future and improvements in curricula and pedagogy in the future are necessarily framed within the discourse of quality assurance and measurement. For example, currently in many school boards across the US and Canada, schools and departments are required to create SMART goals to ensure the constant progress and development of students, teachers, and schools. SMART is an acronym for framing goals: Simple, Measurable, Achievable, Relevant/Realistic, and Timely. Adopted directly from entrepreneurship classes throughout North America, SMART goals ensure that any goal administrators and teachers set for their schools are bound by a normative vision of simplicity, measurability, positivism, and economic efficiency. Any goal that cannot be framed in such a way in effect does not contribute to the quality of schools; any goal that cannot be measured and justified based on quantifiable data does not contribute to the quality of schools; any goal that educators and students collectively have to constantly struggle towards does not contribute to the quality of schools, nor does any goal that must be constantly striven towards throughout one's individual and collective existence. Based on this neoliberal mode of framing goals, schools do not and should not set goals for the ethical nurturing of teachers and students, or the creation of a just and democratic school and world order. All such goals are vague, unachievable, and immeasurable and thus are irrelevant in the dark neoliberal fatalism of educational progress.

CONCLUSION: WHAT IS TO BE DONE?

As this chapter showed, concern over how neoliberalism is influencing North American schools and eroding democracy is well placed. Given the force and how widespread this myth has become in North American schools, the only meaningful solution is resistance and abandonment of the myth altogether. This, of course, does not mean that schools abandon the importance of developing skills for employment or for training students. On the contrary, these skills and training are essential to communities as well as the well-being of students' growth both inside and outside educational institutions. Rather, the neoliberal myth and corresponding policies that propagate the view that education is purely an instrument of the market economy and that students should be developed into self-interested, utility-maximizing producers and consumers must be resisted and abandoned.

If educators are to take democracy seriously and find democratic beliefs and values both morally and politically necessary for the individual and collective betterment, then any neoliberal informed policy must be challenged. At the most fundamental level, this means that democratic educators must articulate and fight for the view that the education system has to be about more than another location of economic development; it is also a place where democratic practices, values, and beliefs, such as critical thinking and engaging substantive moral and political issues, are developed. To this end, the aim of creating a democratic order and democratic way of life must not simply be an irrelevant add-on in schools; rather, it must inform the core of educators' pedagogical practices as well as the desired outcomes of schools. Similarly, educators can no longer be complicit in encouraging students to develop into young *homo economicuses*. Schools must provide educational opportunities for students to engage in community issues that cannot be solved by self-interested utility maximization (Portelli & Vibert, 2002). They also must be spaces in which the recognition of the democratic other is developed and the inherent challenges of inequity are not ignored but taken seriously.

Finally, educators must unequivocally reject the idea that there is a single and measurable standard for determining the quality of the work and skills produced and developed by the students. In contrast, a democratic conception of quality and excellence in education embraces the view that there is a significant amount of learning and development that is essential to a student's moral and political development that is complex, difficult to develop, and, in many cases, immeasurable. Moreover, a democratic conception also fundamentally rejects the notion that by measuring students against a single, politically informed, value-laden set of standards, the education system is treating students equitably (Portelli & Vibert, 1997). In the best-case scenario, schools should provide teachers with space and time to create, articulate, and engage these learning skills and differentiated standards of development. Failing this, teachers must begin to try to do so amid the current neoliberal environment. While far from ideal, at least some students would be provided with alternative avenues to find excellence and growth in their educational experience. In the end, if democracy is to be preserved in and through education, it must be done so by understanding, challenging, and eroding the neoliberal myth.

REFERENCES

Blumenberg, H. (1985). *Work on myth* (R. Wallace, Trans.). Cambridge, MA: MIT Press. (Original work published 1979)

Blumenberg, H. (1996). An anthropological approach to the contemporary significance of rhetoric. In K. Baynes, J. Bohman, & T. McCarthy (Eds.), *After philosophy: End or transformation?* (pp. 423–459). Cambridge, MA: MIT Press.

Bottici, C., & Challand, B. (2006). Rethinking political myth: The clash of civilizations as a self-fulfilling prophecy. *The European Journal of Social Theory, 9*(3), 315–336.

Bottici, C. (2007). *A philosophy of political myth.* New York, NY: Cambridge University Press.

Bourdieu, P. (1998). The essence of neoliberalism. *Le Monde Diplomatique*, December 1998. Retrieved July 5, 2007, from http:mondediplo.com/1998/12/08bourdieu/

Canadian Foundation for Economic Education. (n.d.). Retrieved June 10, 2007, from http://buildingfuturesnetwork.com/main_en.php

Denzau, A. T., & North, D. C. (1994). Shared mental models: Ideologies and institutions. *Kyklos, 47*(1), 3–31.

Dewey, J. (1974). The nature of aims. In R. Archambault (Ed.), *John Dewey on education* (pp. 70–80). Chicago, IL: University of Chicago Press. (Original work published 1922)

Freire, P. (1998). *Pedagogy of freedom: Ethics, democracy, and civic courage* (P. Clarke, Trans.). Lanham, MD: Rowman & Littlefield.

Friedman, M., & Friedman, R. (1981). *Free to choose.* New York, NY: Avon Books.

Giroux, H. A. (2004). *The terror of neoliberalism: Authoritarianism and the eclipse of democracy.* London, England: Paradigm.

Harvey, D. (2005). *A brief history of neoliberalism.* New York, NY: Oxford University Press.

Herrnstein, R. J., & Murray, C. (1994). *The bell curve: Intelligence and class structure in American life.* New York, NY: The Free Press.

Huntington, S. (1996). *The clash of civilizations and the remaking of the world order.* New York, NY: Simon & Schuster.

Lemann, N. (1999). *The big test: The secret history of the American meritocracy.* New York, NY: Farrar, Straus and Giroux.

McQuaig, L. (2001). *All you can eat: Greed, lust and the new capitalism.* Toronto, ON: Penguin Group.

Olssen, M. (1996). In defense of the welfare state and publicly provided education: A New Zealand perspective. *Journal of Education Policy, 11*(3), 337–362.

Portelli, J. P., & Solomon, P. (2001). Introduction. In J. P. Portelli & P. Solomon (Eds.), *The erosion of democracy in education: From critique to possibilities* (pp. 11–24). Calgary, AB: Detselig Enterprises.

Portelli, J. P., & Vibert, A. (1997). Dare we criticize common educational standards? *McGill Journal of Education, 32*(1), 69–79.

Portelli, J. P., & Vibert, A. (2002). A curriculum of life. *Education Canada, 42*(2), 36–39.

Roy, R. K., Denzau, A. T., & Willett, T. D. (2007). Introduction: Neoliberalism as a shared mental model. In R. K. Roy, T. D. Willett, & A. T. Denzau (Eds.), *Neoliberalism: National and regional experiments with global ideas* (pp. 3–13) New York, NY: Routledge.

Sowell, T. (1980). *Knowledge and decisions*. New York, NY: Basic Books.

Winch, C. (1996). Quality and education [Special issue]. *Journal of Philosophy of Education, 302*(2).

3 Class Struggle and Education
Neoliberalism, (Neo)-Conservatism, and the Capitalist Assault on Public Education—A Marxist Analysis

Dave Hill

WHAT IS A MARXIST ANALYSIS?

There are many Marxisms, both at a political level and at a theoretical level, in historical terms and in contemporary terms, in different locations. All draw on the work of Karl Marx and Friedrich Engels, in particular their *Communist Manifesto*. It is startlingly powerful and relevant today in its analysis of capitalism. Capitalism, as analyzed and criticized by Marxists, is the systematic exploitation of the labor power of the working class(es), with the capitalists appropriating the surplus value created by the labor of the working class(es). Capitalist economy and society is one in which there is an ongoing system of class conflict, of class war, with each of the two (major) classes of society—capitalists (called the *bourgeoisie* by Marx and Engels) and workers (called the *proletariat* by Marx and Engels)—engaged in struggle over increasing the proportion of surplus value (the value left when raw materials, rents, and wages/salaries have been paid) that should go into capitalists' pockets as profits, or into workers' pockets as wages, and, in addition, for the benefit of workers, into what can be termed the social wage. The social wage comprises publicly funded education, publicly funded health services, and publicly funded welfare benefits such as old-age pensions, disability, unemployment, maternity, and other welfare benefits, such as subsidized travel and subsidized private housing.

In broad terms, there are two classes in capitalism—the capitalist class, the 1%, the bosses, the rulers of the universe as exemplified in films such as *Wall Street*, *The Wolf of Wall Street*, *Metropolis*, and *Blade Runner*, who own or control the means of production and leading financial institutions. These control the economy and the media and the major political parties. In the US for example, both major parties, Republicans and Democrats, are overwhelmingly funded by Big Business (Fraser & Gertsle, 2005; Sefla, 2012). The other class is the working class, the 99%, unskilled workers, skilled workers, supervisory managerial and professional workers. What each of these "strata" or groups within the (broadly defined) working class have in common is that they all must sell their labor power to capitalists, or to organizations and apparatuses in the capitalist state, in order to subsist.

It is the state apparatuses that keep this workforce trained and fit to work—schools, universities, and health services.

Marxists agree with radical Democrats, liberals, and even some conservatives that in the post–Second World War period of the 1940s, 1950s, and 1960s, there was pretty much a system of class balance. That is to say, the organizations of the working class(es), such as trade unions, were in a strong enough position vis-à-vis the capitalist class—the employers and the governments they control—to win pay rises, employee and trade union rights, and some welfare benefits.

Commentators from across the political spectrum are also in agreement that in a vigorous class war from above (Harvey, 2005; D. Hill, 2013c; Malott, Hill, & Banfield, 2013; Picketty, 2014) since the economic crisis of the mid-1970s (the oil crisis), the capitalist class has been remarkably successful in wresting back from the working class a greater and greater share of public wealth, of the share of national income and wealth, across much of the capitalist world.

Neoliberal economics, the Chicago school of monetarists, and neoliberal governments, preeminently those of Margaret Thatcher in the UK and of Ronald Reagan in the US, proved to be simply the first neoliberal governments, smashing trade unions, cutting welfare benefits, and privatizing public services. Under neoliberal governments, the rich have gotten immensely richer, the poor poorer, and what in the US are called "hardworking middle-class families" have suffered absolute immiseration, absolute sinking into poverty. They have been hard hit, with worsened and worsening pay, working conditions, and trade union rights and protections, and a degraded public sector provision/withdrawal and limitation of benefits.

Some conservatives, laughing all the way to the top of the heap, argue that inequality is not only natural but also desirable, since it fuels envy, competition, hard work, and, they argue, increased wealth that will trickle down to the rest of society. This is the Ayn Rand ideology, which can be termed by Marxists as economic fascism, and is similar to that of Friedrich Hayek, Margaret Thatcher's guru, in the belief in the very small state as liberating humanness and humanity. However, it is widely apparent in this Hayekian dystopia that wealth has not trickled down; it has funneled up. This is because of the prorich and antiworker policies of right-of-center and right-wing antiequality governments such as the Republicans and the (slightly less right-wing) Democrats in the US. It is similar across the globe—such as the Conservatives and Liberal Democrats in the UK, the AKP in Turkey, New Democracy in Greece—right-wing and center-right governments everywhere. And, in a development that is new since the 1970s, political parties and governments that were traditionally labor, social democratic, or left-of-center governments that in the 1940s, 1950s, and 1960s had seen it as their duty to redistribute some wealth and power from the top to the bottom of society have *also* subscribed to neoliberal restructuring of economies, resulting in increasing inequalities within most of the economies of the world. Socialist governments, such as those of Cuba and Venezuela, which have not gone so far along the neoliberal road, have not seen these increasing inequalities—they see their role as to make societies more equal, with both having established free health care and free education as public rights rather than as commodities to be bought and sold on the stock exchange or Wall Street, though both have capitulated to some neoliberal pressures.

Conservative critics of the increasingly apartheid-like, socially segregated societies, including some of the mega-wealthy such as Joseph Stiglitz and Warren Buffet, look to the dangers of social instability and revolt, and to the fact that if the workers (whether middle class or working class) are paid less and less, then there is less and less money in circulation to buy the goods that capitalists sell—so there is, in economic terms, a crisis of overaccumulation, with billionaires and trillionaires sitting on vast amounts of reserves with nowhere productive to invest in, apart from inflating various "bubbles" such as stock markets, housing, and commodity markets.

In contrast to neoliberal and neoconservative ideology (described below), liberal democratic and social democratic analysis is that capitalism works fine, or can work fine; it just needs some reforms, some improvements. For example: more regulation of banks post-2008.

Social democrats, such as the Labour Party in Britain, Australia, and social democratic parties in Scandinavia, do not want to replace capitalism; they want to manage it better. They cite the much more equal economies and societies of northwest Europe, such as Sweden and Finland, for example, and of Western Europe in general, prior to the 1970s and argue that societies become more equal, and happy, with more regulation—over, for example, health and medicine standards, food standards, health and safety standards, and environmental and ecological protection. (The book *The Spirit Level*, by Wilkinson and Pickett [2009], offers powerful evidence to support this, with the most equal societies such as the Scandinavian countries, and Taiwan and Japan, with their concern for communities rather than focusing on individuals, having far less homicide, rape, psychosis, violence, and social ills than the most unequal large, rich societies such as the US and the UK.)

Where Marxists disagree with other critics of these widened social and economic inequalities is the Marxist analysis that capitalism has periodic crises—of overaccumulation for example, a crisis of profitability for capital, a declining rate of profit—and that in times of crisis (such as the recession of the 1930s, the so-called oil crisis of the 1970s, and the bankers' crisis since 2008), the capitalist class will always try to tear back from the hands of the workers the benefits and living standards they had won in more profitable times.

That is to say, in times of economic crisis, of recession, even labor and social democratic governments dance to the tune of national and transnational capitalists and start cutting the real value of wages/salaries and social benefits. That is, it is the poor who pay for the crisis.

For Marxists, capitalism is not just immoral and a case of oppression. It is that capitalism is based on economic exploitation. Critics of Marxism suggest that, according to scientific socialism, Marxists believe in economic determinism, that it is inevitable that capitalism will be overtaken, surpassed, replaced by socialism and then by communism. However, most Marxists and socialists (the terms are slightly different and used differently in different situations) point to the need for agency for action, for the need for Marxist militants and activists to work to develop class consciousness, or, to use Freire's term, conscientization, and to develop strong political organizations to fight for major social and economic, revolutionary, change. For Marxists today, socialism and Marxism are not inevitable. For Rosa Luxemburg, the future is socialism or barbarism (Luxemburg, 1918/1971; Luxemburg, 2013). And that socialism has to be fought for.

Capitalism is undoubtedly, for Marxists, immoral. Workers die far earlier than bankers, have unhealthier lives, and have inferior education and health and retirement services than the rich. Furthermore, capitalism deliberately encourages division within the working class, with media whipping up hatred and division between Black and White, men and women, gay and straight, immigrant and nonimmigrant, public sector employees and private sector employees. Indeed, Marxists see Fascism and Nazism in 1920s, 1930s, and 1940s Europe, and some examples of extreme nationalism and xenophobia since then, as with the Nazi Golden Dawn party being elected to the Greek parliament in 2012, and European Parliament in 2014 as a throw of the dice by capitalists desperate to stop the red menace, to stop communism.

But, to repeat, where Marxist analysis of economic, social, human rights, and education policy differs from other critiques, even of radical-left democrats like Henry Giroux, is that Marxists prioritize class analysis, and go beyond critique, go beyond deconstruction, into reconstruction, proposals for a fundamental change in society and economy, a socialist economy. And they move beyond proposal into activism.

I return to what is specifically Marxist in terms of education policy towards the end of this chapter.

I want now to spend a couple of paragraphs on Marxism in practice. Prior to and since the McCarthyite witch hunts of suspected communists and communist sympathizers in the 1950s in the US, Marxism has not had good press. It was deliberately associated with the Stalinist dictatorship in gulag prison camps, yet, just as with capitalist states, there are democratic examples and there are authoritarian, dictatorial, even totalitarian examples. Democratic Marxist governments range from Venezuela, which, despite the protestations of the very right-wing *Fox News*, repeatedly has free and democratic elections and repeatedly returns Marxist governments (first under Chavez, now under Maduro), to the one-party communist state of Cuba (with the highest standards of education and health care in

Central and South America). It is worth adding here that Marx said that the emancipation of the working class could only be the act *of* the working class. That basic tenet, for most Marxists today, indicates that totalitarian regimes cannot be called Marxist in the true sense. This is a Trotskyist analysis, as expounded in the writing of Tony Cliff with his thesis that the Soviet Union was not a workers' state but a state capitalist society.

Wherever a people has elected a Marxist government, a government seeking to replace or very considerably control and nationalize capitalism, then the US sent in the Marines. The US has bombed more than 30 separate countries since 1945—in the process killing or supporting the killing at various times since 1945 of not just a cumulative total of millions of Indonesians, Guatemalans, Nicaraguans, Chileans, Argentineans, Brazilians, Greeks, and Yugoslavs, but also many thousands of US working-class young men and women.

In terms of ways of having collective, or public, control and management of a Communist economy, there are again a variety of models. These include the workers' control of the former Yugoslavia, where assemblies of the workers in an industrial or commercial enterprise would decide on the pay levels of various types of jobs, would interview and appoint managers, would decide how to allocate profits between reinvestment, salaries, benefits, and community facilities. Other versions of collective ownership are versions of workers' control, from the Mondragon cooperative of the Basque country in Spain, where workers completely own and manage an enterprise, to the monolithic national-level state control in the Soviet states, to the varieties of local collectives such as those practiced by the Zapatistas in Mexico in their autonomous zone.

Current developments in Marxist political and theoretical analysis have learned from the minuses of former communist states and economies as well as from the pluses (longer, healthier, more solidaristic, less selfish, less unequal lives). Thus, in many countries, the old-style top-down, tightly controlled, vertically organized parties, with a powerful central leadership, and often small memberships, are learning to amalgamate and work with the more horizontal and nonhierarchical developments of the Occupy movement, of the Movement of the Squares, of the global reactions and resistances to the widening inequalities and increasingly authoritarian there-is-no-alternative policies of big-business-supported governments and their riot police, tasers, tear gas, and bullets.

What then, in more detail, are neoliberalism and neoconservatism?

NEOLIBERALISM AND (NEO)-CONSERVATISM

Neoliberalism

Neoliberalism is marked, inter alia, by the marketization, commodification, degradation, managerialization, and privatization or preprivatization

Class Struggle and Education 39

of public services (Chrysochou, 2014; Giroux, 2004; Harvey, 2005; D. Hill, 2013a, 2013b; D. Hill & Kumar, 2009; D. Hill & Rosskam, 2009; Saad-Filho, 2011). As Saad-Filho puts it:

> In essence, neoliberalism is based on the systematic use of state power, under the ideological guise of "non-intervention", to impose a hegemonic project of recomposition of the rule of capital at five levels: domestic resource allocation, international economic integration, the reproduction of the state, ideology, and the reproduction of the working class. (Saad-Filho, 2011)

Elsewhere (D. Hill [2003], for example) I have detailed the major characteristics of neoliberalism as follows, as applied below, to education:

1. Privatization/preprivatization of public services such as schooling and universities
2. Cuts in public spending/salaries/pensions/benefits
3. Marketization, competition between schools and between universities
4. Vocational education for human capital (except for the ruling class, who, in their elite private schools, are encouraged into a wider and less basics-driven education)
5. Management of the workforce: new public managerialism in schools and colleges, with hugely increasing differentials in pay and power between managers and workforce
6. Encouragement of competition between workers, through performance-related pay and the busting of trade union-agreed national pay scales
7. Casualization/precariatization of public and private sector workers, with a decline in tenured and in full-time, secure jobs for teachers and university faculty
8. Attacks on trade unions, on workers' rights, on centralized pay bargaining
9. Management speak, e.g., students as customers, delivering the curriculum, discourse of the market replacing that of social responsibility
10. Denigration/ideological attacks of public sector workforce

Neoconservatism

Neoliberalism does not come unaccompanied. It usually has a twin, neoconservatism, albeit a twin with which it has an often fractured relationship. Gamble (1988) talked of *The Free Society and the Strong State*. Neoconservatism here refers firstly to order and control, and secondly to traditional morality.

"The systematic use of state power" referred to by Saad-Filho at the beginning of this chapter is the use by governments of the repressive state apparatuses such as law, the police, the judiciary, the security services, the armed forces, and the surveillance intimidatory forms of management control within institutions and places of work. In addition to their overtly intimidatory, law enforcement, repressive function, the repressive state apparatuses have ideological functions and impacts (Althusser, 1971). These repressive state apparatuses currently reinforce the individualistic, competitive, "commonsense" procapitalist ideology (Gramsci, 1971) and serve to naturalize capital, rendering capitalist economic relations and capitalist social relations, what Marxists term the capital–labor relation, seem only "natural." They punish deep dissent and deep critique.

Concerning the traditional morality aspect of neoconservatism, this varies in space and time, from country to country, and at different periods. It generally, but not always, includes a veneration of the family and heterosexual and married relationships. Conservative politicians and theorists vary over such matters as conservative social morality. Thus, for example, David Cameron, the current British prime minister, is socially liberal, not socially conservative. This is in contrast to his "Victorian morality" enthusiast predecessor, Margaret Thatcher, and, in other countries, for example in Turkey's Reycep Erdogan, the current, conservatizing prime minister of Turkey who is seeking to soft-Islamicize Turkey by banning kissing on the Metro, limiting birth control and alcohol availability, and bringing back and encouraging more conservative forms of dress for women, in particular the *hijab* (veil that covers the hair). As with Thatcher in the 1980s, Erdogan is marrying this morally conservative policy with neoliberalism.

However, a second aspect of conservatism and neoconservatism is that, universally, it involves and seeks to enforce an acceptance of elitism and hierarchy—and of one's place in that hierarchy. That hierarchy is raced and gendered, a racial hierarchy and a gender hierarchy as well as a social class hierarchy (D. Hill, 2013a). It is, as with the Tea Party and social conservatives in the US and as with Erdogan's governments in Turkey, also based on appeals to religion.

In the US, the prime exponents of neoconservative values are the Tea Party, with their ultrapatriotism, ultranationalism, and its proclaimed adherence to strict forms of personal and religious morality (see Martin, 2013; Robin, 2013).

The main aspects of neoconservatism as they relate to education can be seen as:

1. Control of Curricula: of schools, teacher education, universities, the removal of dangerous content
2. Control of Pedagogy: teaching methods, pedagogic relations between teacher and students
3. Control of Students: through debt and through actual or fear of unemployment
4. Control of Teachers and Professors: through surveillance, a culture of having to meet targets, punishment of dissidents and union

activists, dismissals and closures of schools, closures of university departments
5. Brute Force and the "Security State" Within Schools: with the use of tear gas, sound grenades, stun grenades, beatings, prosecutions, draconian sentencing, and, in some countries, imprisonment and killings (e.g., murders of trade union activists in Colombia)

Obama's National Defence Authorization Act gives powers to the state to imprison, deny legal representation to, and deny family access, on an unprecedented level, for those it deems suspected of terrorism ("Obama Versus Civil Liberties," 2012).

The Relationship Between Neoliberalism and Neoconservatism

The strength of the neoliberal alliance with (neo)-conservatism, with conservative forces, is particularly strong in the US and in Turkey. In the US the nexus, the alliance, between social conservatives and economic conservatives is pronounced and has been intensively analyzed by writers such as Michael W. Apple, for example in his *Educating the Right Way: Markets, Standards, God, and Inequality* (2006), where he charts and analyzes the "conservative restoration," whereby millions of US citizens actually vote against their own objective economic self-interest—such as support for Obamacare, for more protection of benefits and economic rights than offered by the Republicans and the Tea Party element. They do this because they believe that, or are persuaded to believe that, what people do in bed and with whom is more important an issue than improving the material conditions of people's lives. Such social conservatives believe that antigay, antiliberal, antisecular, antiabortion, anti-gun-control social morality is more important than their own economic self-interest. Of course, many also believe that "rolling back the state" or having a flat-rate tax, the same rate for the richest as for the middle and working classes, and cutting welfare budgets is also in their own economic self-interest.

The antiliberal, 'exceptionalist' (i.e., the US as the beacon of liberty and the chosen nation) neoconservativism is summed up as follows by Bill Reynolds:

> We now have political parties (most notably the Tea Party) who applaud at high rates of capital punishment, cheer at the concept of people left to die without health care, and, because of their homophobia, boo a gay serviceman risking his life for his or her country. This cruelty is accompanied by an avid anti-intellectualism as these same Tea Party pundits and their candidates propose deep cuts in education and criticize teachers and their unions. And most recently there has been a legislative attack on women's health care rights. (Reynolds, 2013, p. 207)

In Turkey, the Erdogan government is very nakedly pushing forward with Islamicization of society and the education system, and with brute use of the repressive apparatuses of the state, as seen in the summer 2013 national police brutality against the Gezi Park resistance movement, killing eight protesters and bystanders. Thus, in Turkey, neoliberalism is accompanied by traditionalist, Islamic conservativism in and through the ideological state apparatuses of the media, the mosque, and the education system, accompanied by the naked use of the repressive state apparatuses—such as the bullets, tear gas, and chemically treated water cannon used across Turkey through summer 2013 (Gezgin, İnal, & Hill, 2014; D. Hill, 2013d).

And in Britain in 2014, the centenary of the start of the First World War, the neoconservative (and neoliberal) secretary of state for education, Michael Gove, is trying to insist that schoolchildren be taught that the war was a grand patriotic war fought to "protect little Belgium" from German aggression. He decried the antiwar sentiments of television programs such as *Blackadder* and films such as *Oh What a Lovely War* that showed the war as senseless slaughter resulting from a quarrel between the ruling families of Europe, tied in with a clash of imperialisms and imperialist expansionism, particularly in Africa.

In this century we have been experiencing both neoliberalization and neoconservatization in the US, in the UK, in Europe generally, in Turkey, and globally. There are, of course, resistances within neoliberalized states. There are also isolated states resisting neoliberalism, such as the governments and states of Cuba and Venezuela, and, within the Anglo-Saxon neoliberal capitalist countries, and procapitalist countries in general, millions of liberal-left, socialist, and Marxist educators, and (often the same people) antiracist and antisexist activists, LGBT activists, and proindigenous and eco-activists, resisting both neoconservative and neoliberal schooling, university education, and control.

The UK and the US, and the international organizations of capitalism, such as the World Bank, the International Monetary Fund, and the European Bank, have been centers of this neoliberal transformation of economy, society, and education.

Neoliberalism is not everywhere accompanied by neoconservatism. In the UK, sections of the Conservative Party and government are in support of neoconservative return to Victorian values, are strongly promonarchy and royal family, want schools to teach classic proimperial and pro-British versions of history in schools, oppose women priests and homosexuality, and support law and order, hierarchy, and a respect for elites.

However, this neoconservatism is sometimes in tension with neoliberalism. For example, with respect to schools, neoconservatives want government control of the schools' curriculum (to shut out contrarian liberal, socialist, and anarchist versions of history, civics, and literature, for example). However, neoliberals want there to be a complete competitive market in schools, with each school having and developing its own brand of curriculum.

Another area of disagreement between neoconservatism and neoliberalism is that, for neoliberals, profit is the overriding goal. Thus there is less respect for traditional elites, more an attitude of "We don't care if a prospective employee is Black or White, straight or gay, male or female, as long as they can do the job." UK prime minister from 1979 to 1991, Margaret Thatcher, broke or substantially reduced the power not only of trade unions but also of traditional elites controlling access to the higher professions. For Thatcher, the importance of competition overrode the importance of the elitist status quo.

It is important to make clear that neoliberalism is simply the latest stage of capitalism. It is current capitalism. This chapter is written as a critique of neoliberal capitalism and its (neo)-conservative allies. But, importantly, this critique is, *in essence*, a critique of capitalism itself, of capitalist economic relations, of capitalist social relations, of the capital–labor relation. Removing neoliberalism and (neo)-conservatism, for example through social democratic reforms, may lead to a more compassionate society with some valuable welfare, workers' rights reforms, and even a slight equalization of income and wealth and power in society. But such reforms, while, to repeat, hugely valuable, will not remove class exploitation by the capitalist class of the labor power of the working class.

THE NEOLIBERAL AND NEOCONSERVATIVE EDUCATION REVOLUTION IN ENGLAND, IN THE US, AND GLOBALLY

In this section I want to show how schooling and education has been neoliberalized and neoconservatized in England, and to draw parallels with the US and elsewhere globally. I draw the parallels, even though the names, the terminology may be different, to show the main features of the neoliberal–neoconservative revolution in education. I wrote at greater length on this in a report published by the ILO, the United Nations-based International Labour Organisation (D. Hill, 2006).

Education and other public services in Britain have been subject to neoliberalization since the Margaret Thatcher (Conservative Party) governments of 1979–1990, in particular with the Education Reform Act of 1988. This established classic neoliberal policies of prompting the marketization of schooling (through so-called parental choice and through "league tables" of schools, whereby the exam results and academic test results of each school are published in league table format). It also (together with the 1986 Education Act and subsequent legislation) changed the composition of school-governing bodies, adding "business" governors and reducing the numbers and influence of governors appointed by locally democratically elected councils. And under the "Local Management of Schools" (LMS) section of the 1988 act, local authority/school district influence was further weakened, when most budgetary control was handed to school head teachers/principals and governing bodies (Ball, 1990; D. Hill, 1997, 2001).

Since Margaret Thatcher's governments of 1979–1990, successive Conservative (1990–1997 under John Major), New Labour (1997–2010 under Tony Blair and Gordon Brown), and Conservative–Liberal Democrat Coalition (2010–present under David Cameron) governments have intensified the neoliberalization of schools and of universities dramatically, alongside cuts in funding.

One notable recent cut in public expenditure was (from September 2011) that of education maintenance allowances (EMAs) paid to young people aged 16–19 from poor families, of (usually) £30 a week, to encourage them to stay on at school. I benefited from a similar scheme in the 1960s; one of my grandsons received an EMA, 2006–2009. For university students, the free university education that I, for example, received has been replaced by the imposition of annual university tuition fees of (usually, currently) £9,000 per annum (see D. Hill, 2010a). The New Labour government of Tony Blair abandoned free university education and introduced university tuition fees in 1998.

Ideologically, these neoliberal developments such as marketization and the introduction of new public managerialism (management methods drawn from private enterprise) can be interpreted as "the businessification" of education (Rikowski, 2002, 2003, 2007), the softening up, the preparation for the wholesale privatization of schools, vocational colleges (called, in Britain, further education colleges), and universities.

Currently (2014), there are only two private universities in the UK, but degree-awarding powers have been granted to a number of other organizations, and the current (2010–present) Conservative–Liberal Democrat coalition government in Britain is planning more private universities. It is indeed likely that in the fairly near future, some currently public/state universities in Britain will become private, bought and sold on international stock markets by transnational corporations and hedge funds. Ball (2012) is very clear on such developments regarding schools, colleges, and universities, detailing such developments in Britain and globally. Rikowski (2003) and Hirtt (2004) foresaw this development. Hirtt warned, in 2004, about state education provision and state health provision being "the last great El Dorados" for capitalist privatization and profit from public-sector-provided services.

MARKETIZATION/COMPETITION/CHOICE: "PARENTAL CHOICE," LEAGUE TABLES, AND HIGH-STAKES TESTING

Let me now go into more detail about some of the main aspects of neoliberalism, marketization, and privatization/preprivatization in schools and universities in the UK (or, to be more precise, England; Wales, Scotland, and Northern Ireland have a degree of autonomy/self-government regarding education policy and provision) and relate these to developments in the US and elsewhere.

With schools there is now a system of market competition between individual schools. Under the 1944 Education Act, which the Thatcher 1988 Education Act replaced, local authorities and school districts, which were directly elected, had allocated children/students to schools, sometimes taking into account a degree of parental choice, but sometimes attempting to ensure that within a largely comprehensive or all-ability intake of students, there was a mix of students of all "bands" of ability or attainment (D. Hill, 1997, 2001), what in the US is termed all "tracks" of students.

The conservative governments in Britain, those of Thatcher (1979–1990) and of John Major (1990–1997), introduced and extended what they termed "school choice," or, more specifically, "parental choice." However, in such systems it is not the parents who choose; it is the (more prestigious, high-attaining) schools that choose the children/students, the "preferred" children/students being those with high test scores and "acceptable" (high status, "middle class") cultural capital (Gewirtz, Ball, & Bowe, 1995; Gillborn & Youdell, 2002; Sellgren, 2013; Weekes-Bernard, 2007). This has led to considerably increased hierarchy and elitism within the state education system, elitism that is social class based and also based on ethnicity (Weekes-Bernard, 2007).

This leads to much increased hierarchy and elitism within the state education system, elitism that is "raced" and social class based. The Academies Commission Report of January 2013, *Unleashing Greatness* (Academies Commission, 2013), says it has received numerous submissions suggesting that "academies are finding methods to select covertly," that some academies may covertly select pupils by using extra information on families or holding social events with prospective parents (Sellgren, 2013). The report says it has received evidence that some popular schools, including academies, attempt to select and exclude pupils—despite the fact that the government admissions code says that schools cannot interview children or parents or give priority to children whose parents offer financial or practical support (Sellgren, 2013).

That is one aspect of the neoliberalization in schooling, a class-based increased hierarchicalization of schools. And this choice is facilitated by the creation of the league tables of schools and of universities, schools of schools and universities sorted by high-stakes exam results. It needs noting that this discussion is about state schools, that is, publicly funded schools. In the UK, 93% of school students attend state schools, with 7% attending private schools.

Neoliberalism requires that in a market, it is necessary to be able to test the efficiency and value of the products. In England there is now a very rigid system of testing children at different ages, even when they first enter the schools. That could be at either age four or five. As result of the exam results of the children, of the assessment results of the children, there becomes a league table in every municipality; in every part of the country, in every area, there are league tables of schools. It is middle-class parents who have the means, the cars, the ability to pay transport costs, to take the children to the schools that have higher results, which may be some distance away.

As a result of parental choice and published public league tables, there has been a notable increase in differentiation between the high-achieving schools and low-achieving schools. In Britain 13% of children have "free school meals" (FSM); the poorest 13% have free dinners at school. I did when I was a boy. If we look at two maps in England, the map showing who receives free school dinners and the map of exam results, the maps are very similar. The map showing assessments at tests and exams, the map of high and low attainment in school tests, substantially mirrors the map of the existing income inequality, though schools and local authorities can have an impact.

PRIVATIZATION/PREPRIVATIZATION OF SCHOOLING: CHARTER SCHOOLS (STATE-FUNDED SCHOOLS MANAGED AND CONTROLLED BY CORPORATE CHAINS OF SCHOOLS OR OTHER PRIVATE CONTROL)

In the US, the system of charter schools has gone further than in Britain. In the US, many charter schools are run by for-profit organizations; many too are not-for-profit. In England, there are not yet any for-profit academies. In Britain, the government is engaging with schools on a program of preprivatization, setting up a so-called academy system (and some "Free Schools") where numerous state schools remain state funded and within the state system, but are redesignated as academies.

Thus, in the school sector, state-funded schools are actually being handed over to private companies, to chains of schools, to a variety of religious organizations, to become academies, formerly known as City Academy Schools (Beckett, 2007; see also Anti-Academies Alliance, n.d., and Benn, 2011). Currently, more than 3,444 schools—including more than half of secondary schools—have taken on academy or free-school status (Syal, 2014). Since the Conservatives came to power in 2010, "they have given away over 3000 schools to unaccountable private sector interests for free. That is over £10 billion [$16.4 billion USD] of publicly owned property given away for free to unaccountable pseudo-charities, several of them operated by Conservative party donors" (Clarke, 2014).

Increasing numbers of primary or elementary schools as well as secondary or high schools are taken away from democratically elected local authority or school district control and residual funding to become quasi-independent schools, actually receiving their funding directly from central government. At the stroke of a ministerial pen they could easily, at some stage, become fully independent, fully private schools, offered for sale on the market.

An academy school is where government gives any religious group—Muslim, Jewish, Christian—or any rich businessmen or businesswomen, the power to rename a school, for example after their business or company; to appoint a majority of the governors, the people who run the school, and the people who oversee the head teacher, or principal; and to change the contracts of the teachers; to decide the skill mix of staff, that is, the numbers of fully qualified teachers, and the numbers of less-well-qualified (and much-lower-paid) teaching assistants; to change the length of the school day; and to change the curriculum. Some fundamentalist religious groups, or capitalists, introduce more religious teaching.

Academy schools are an aspect of preprivatization. At the moment all academies in England are not-for-profit organizations. At the moment, in England, those who control schools cannot make a profit themselves from actually running schools. But the new owners can pay themselves inflated salaries and award contracts for services such as cleaning services to their friends and business associates. (See D. Hill, Lewis, Yarker, & Maisuria, 2013, and Clarke, 2014, for details on this.) Academy schools, such as those run by the E-Act chain, which runs 35 schools, are characterized by "extravagant expenses claims, first-class rail travel and 'a culture of prestige venues' for meeting" (Clarke, 2014). A high-profile example is Academies Enterprise Trust (AET) (which pays six figure salaries to 20 of their staff, paying some of them more than the British prime minister, and salaries far in excess of those in the state nonacademy sector, and "which has been procuring 'services' from their own directors and trustees to the tune of half a million pounds, none of the contracts agreed under competitive tender" (Clarke, 2014).

Syal (2014) comments that "taxpayer-funded academy chains have paid millions of pounds into the private businesses of directors, trustees and their relatives, documents obtained from freedom of information requests show." To take one example, in July 2013 the UK's "largest taxpayer funded chain, the Academy Enterprise Trust, came under fire following revelations of almost £500,000 worth of payments made to private businesses owned by its trustees and executive" (Syal, 2014).

In the US, where there are charter schools, some are "for profit," with multinational and national capital companies/corporations making profits from running state schools. As Bryant (2014) notes:

> Charter schools have been relentlessly marketed to the American populace as a silver bullet for "failed" public schools, especially in poor urban communities of African-American and Latino/a students. Politicians in both parties speak glowingly of these schools—which, by the way, their children seem never to attend.

As Faith Agostinone-Wilson notes, "The whole argument for charter schools is wrapped in the language of civil rights and uses anti-government rhetoric aimed at a population who has indeed been let down by the government." She continues, "Much of the anti-public school stuff comes from libertarians who want to abolish the Department of Education" (Agostine-Wilson, 2014; see also Moore & Cohen, 2014).

Bryant (2014) continues:

> Huge nationwide chains—called education management organizations (EMOs)—now run many of these charters. A recent study by the National Education Policy Center found, "Students across 35 states and the District of Columbia now attend schools managed by these non-government entities." These for-profit and nonprofit EMOs—such as K12 Inc., National Heritage Academies, Charter Schools USA and KIPP—now account for nearly half of the students educated by charter schools. More than one in twenty students nationwide in the USA now attend Charter schools.

Agostinone-Wilson (2014) notes that "within the U.S. somehow charter schools can receive taxpayer funding AND exclude kids who have learning disabilities and other conditions without facing charges of discrimination."

NEOCONSERVATISM IN EDUCATION IN ENGLAND

Neoliberalism is often, but not always, accompanied by neoconservatism. Because the capitalist class, and the governments they control, have to make sure that this freedom in the market is controlled, in Britain the Thatcher government in the 1988 Education Reform Act instituted a national curriculum. Prior to 1988, schools and local education authorities (LEAs)/school districts had considerable autonomy over curriculum design and also teaching methods/pedagogies. However, the national curriculum for state schools—and the accompanying assessment—are quite rigid, and it is a conservative curriculum. Margaret Thatcher herself looked at some of the curriculum proposals and said, "No, that is too liberal." She herself changed the curriculum (D. Hill, 1997). That is an element of state control, control of the free market: an example of where neoliberalism, "free choice," is accompanied by state supervision/control and a rigid control of the curriculum for state schools. Not, interestingly, for private schools. They decide their own curriculum. (In Britain, the 7% of children who go to private schools are overwhelmingly middle class and upper class. Almost 100% of the ruling capitalist class send their children to elite private schools.)

For teachers and schools, the (privatized) school inspection system, the Office for Standards in Schools, Ofsted, has changed from its (pre-1988) role of "light touch"/supportive school inspection to its current, feared, draconian role with regularly used powers to close what it regards as "failing" schools and/or force them to become academies—often against the wishes of parents, teachers, and governors (Anti-Academies Alliance, n.d.; Benn, 2011; Local Schools Network, n.d.).

And for radical and critical educators in general, those of us trying to engage in "deep critique" (Rikowski, 2008) of capitalism, of capitalist economic, social, and political relations, and how these operate within schools and universities, there is often marginalization, nonpromotion, dismissal, pressure to conform to, to comply with procapitalist norms in ideology. And there is the pressure of performativity, of the endless form filling and surveillance and control of teachers.

NEOCONSERVATISM IN TURKEY

The Islamicization of Turkey's social and education systems may be described, in relation to jihadi Islamicization in Pakistan, Afghanistan, Somalia, Mali, and Egypt, for example, as "soft Islamicization." There are no beheadings, amputation of limbs, or widespread killings of religious minorities.

But for those choking on tear gas in Istiklal Street and Gezi Park in Istanbul, or in Kezilaye in Ankara (as I was, accompanied by brave comrades from leftist movements in Turkey), or for those tragically killed and blinded by Turkish police in recent demonstrations, there is nothing soft about the state repression of dissent by the Turkish government. In Turkey, neoliberalism is accompanied by a conservatization of society and education, backed up by police batons. It may not be of the same nakedness and institutionalized brutality as during the Turkish military dictatorship (1980–1983). But what is happening now is perhaps even more dangerous. In schools for example, the new curriculum, introduced by the AKP government, including, for the first time since the Kemalist revolution nearly a century ago the study in schools of two hours a week on the Koran, and two hours a week on the life of Muhammed is, for leftists and secularists (and liberals), very worrying. It is very convenient for capitalism if major sections of the population start to become more religious, more subservient to the afterlife, more subservient to conservative morality as opposed to Marxist collectivist morality.

I am also very well aware that leftists in schools and universities in Turkey feel pressures—not so much in the largest, most prestigious universities, but in small universities. Numerous comrades have told me of the increasing official pressures on/against them because of their Marxist/communist beliefs. In the small universities, I have comrades who are saying it is much more difficult for them to teach critical pedagogy, for them to teach Marxist analysis of society. This is a dangerous, repressive development. Fevziye Sayilan and Nuray Turkmen describe and analyze in detail this neoliberal and neoconservatism in Turkish society and education (Sayilan & Turkmen, 2013):

> In the last decade, Islamic conservatism has left its mark.... Public education has evolved dramatically under siege by both religion and market. While on the one hand the subsidy for public education has been gradually reduced, private schools and universities are encouraged and as a result, education and schools have accorded with the class and status structure of capitalism more clearly than the previous period. On the other hand, the content/ curriculum and structure of education have been Islamized. Today the integration of Turkish capitalism with global capitalism has been largely completed. The economy has been restructured to provide the terms of the expansion of capital accumulation. Over a period of more than thirty years, schools and universities have been the most affected areas by all of these changes.... In this process, the basis of relatively democratic society, which was formed on the basis of the relationship between the state, market and society, has also dissolved. Accordingly, the modernist ideology (scientific, secular and co-educational) that created a historically dominant philosophy of education in Turkey is also undergoing a major change.

Fevziye Sayilan and Nuray Turkmen continue:

> As in the rest of the world, marketization of education was realized in both hidden and open ways (see Ball and Youdell, 2007). Privatization and commercialization policies in education have openly focused on reducing state subsidies for the financing of public schools, using the subsidies, instead, in favour of private schools1, and charging families for education at every level under the name of "contribution" (Ercan, 1998; Gök, 2004; Sayılan, 2006; İnal, 2012). The education share of national income continued to decrease (Ercan, 1998; Kurul, 2012).

Sayilan and Turkmen further continue:

> The other face of educational inequality is the growing inequalities between schools. Insofar as much as the financing of schools and education is left to the families, the inequality between the elite state schools and ordinary state schools with regard to the quality of education and the learning environment has also increased. Furthermore, private schools, because of their having infrastructure, proper learning environment and social facilities, cause the increase of inequality between private schools and ordinary state schools. As a result of these policies, the schools became ever more openly characterized by their social class characteristics. So neoliberalism consolidates the reproduction of capitalist social relationships through education and schools.

It is of course what the US government and transnational/national capitalist classes want. The US and multinational capitalism are very happy now to work with probusiness, pro-neoliberal, what they regard as "moderate Islamic," states. The US has clearly seen Turkey as a possible future model for Egypt and Libya. It is noticeable in Egypt, where the strong trade unions and workers' organizations have a long history, that one of the first acts of the so-called democratic new Egypt was to attack to trade union rights and attack to trade unionists, a policy continued by the new post-Morsi military dictatorship. For the US, for capitalism, nothing must get in the way of the reproduction of capitalist social relationships and capitalist economic relationships.

SCHOOLS AND UNIVERSITIES AS IDEOLOGICAL STATE APPARATUSES: STIMULATING INDIVIDUALISTIC COMPETITIVE ENTREPRENEURSHIP IN SCHOOLS AND UNIVERSITIES

In many countries, there is now in schools and in universities an emphasis on designing, applying, and updating education and school teaching programs that seek to develop and stimulate students to develop very specific values/value systems. In some states of the US, these values are Christian fundamentalist, socially illiberal, economically individualistic. In Turkey, religion plays a similar role. While the values are Islamic and specifically Turkish and Islamic conservative, the same partnership thrives—the partnership between social illiberalism and conformity with economic individualism. In Britain, the hold of religion is very weak; it is a far more secular society than the US or Turkey. The specific value system being advanced by governments is for students to become individualistic, entrepreneurial, competitive. For example, some British universities now have institutional targets such as "at least 7% of students will go on to set up their own business."

This is a very good demonstration of what Louis Althusser (1971) wrote about education being one of the major ideological state apparatuses. The major ideological state apparatuses are the capitalist-controlled mass media and the (again, capitalist-controlled, through governments of political parties bankrolled by capital) state education systems. In every capitalist country, and in England, capitalists have an ideological agenda. Children are told to be competitive, individualistic; children are told to set up businesses, to value moneymaking and "the spirit of enterprise." This is against leftist notions of collectivity, solidarity, public service, and public good.

EFFECTS OF NEOLIBERALISM AND CONSERVATISM ON TEACHERS IN SCHOOLS: MANAGERIALISM, SURVEILLANCE, AND CONTROL

Neoliberalism is enforced through increased forms of surveillance and control in society, such as, for example, by the importation into public services such as education of "new public managerialism"—more brutalistic, finance-driven, authoritarian forms of management (Beckmann & Cooper, 2004; Beckmann, Cooper, & Hill, 2009; Deem, 1998). Public services such as schools and universities are increasingly run in accordance with the principles of "new public managerialism . . . based on a corporate managerialist model imported from the world of business. As well as the needs of Capital dictating the principal aims of education, the world of business also supplies the model of how it is to be provided and managed" (Beckmann & Cooper, 2004).

Stevenson (2007), writing of schools in England but analyzing a situation readily recognized by teachers in the US, is one of many analysts (see also Lewis, Hill, & Fawcett, 2009) who note that:

> A key feature of current school-sector reform in England is the restructuring of teachers' work and the increased use of support staff to undertake a range of activities previously undertaken by teachers. Supporters speak of a new teacher professionalism focused on the "core task" of teaching. Critics fear deprofessionalization through a process of deskilling, work intensification, and labor substitution.

Stevenson continues:

> [In] relentless drive to raise productivity, teachers have often found themselves the victims of unwelcome change in which they have had their professional judgment curtailed, witnessed the increasing managerialization of the educational process, and been subjected to ever more forensic scrutiny of their work by external agencies (Ball, 2003). . . . These developments have inevitably affected the work pressures on teachers and resulted in an intensification of the labor process of teaching. (Smyth, Dow, Hattam, Reid, & Shacklock, 2000)

In the section below I use some primary research about "teachers' work" carried out between September 2012 and January 2013 by James Lloyd Hill, who has worked in four different secondary (high) schools in England (J. L. Hill, 2013). James quotes a colleague as follows:

> [She] summarised her view of being a teacher as "you're not a teacher anymore, you're someone who works in a school"—she's been teaching 6 months, and was backed up by another colleague in the room with 12 years teaching experience behind her. The same teacher also said "I didn't get into teaching to deliver lessons which are already pre-planned for me which I have to follow, or teach subjects which I never trained for and to only deliver other peoples' resources, I wanted to inspire them to learn History" (her subject).

James's view is that:

> It seems to me the ability (time/insight) to inspire is taken up with filling in tracking data, data in-putting, filling in spreadsheets when homework has been set, making sure your room is not untidy for fear of senior management noticing and "having a word". The extra work that teachers now have to do has very little to do with the delivery of lessons, but ticking the boxes which senior management feel they should have ticked, in case Ofsted come calling. There is a lot of talk among heads of department about "how can we show this?" and "where's our evidence for that?", and as a result, we don't hear as much of "I think I'm going to try this with that group of students".

This view exemplifies research carried out by McBeath in 1995 (p. 12), not long after the National Curriculum and its testing and surveillance regime came into operation. McBeath quotes a student teacher as saying, "I used to feel that this school cared about how well I was doing. Now I just think it cares about how well *it's* doing."
James continues:

> I'm not suggesting that as teachers we are not accountable for students' attainment in our lessons, but there is a limit on our ability to be accountable, and certainly a limit on how that accountability is tracked; lesson plans, intervention documentation by teachers—what have you done about student x, y and z? Why are they still failing?! Documentation on each student, and each aspect of a student accounted for on your lesson plan (such as average reading age; SEN status; Gifted and Talented status; preferred learning style [VAK], learning goal; current grade).

James talks not just of the intensification of accountability, but of a managerial culture of control and fear:

> The voices of the Unions are quieter than they once were in schools, there are still those brave enough to speak out on behalf of those who must not be named to senior management, even though they do ask "and who thinks that?" but more recently it has had to be a case of safety in large numbers. We had a Joint Union meeting of the NUT ' (National Union of Teachers) and NASUWT (National Association of Schoolmasters/Union of Women Teachers) where we agreed on "work to rule" principles the unions had set out, but the added pressures being placed on staff meant that we signed a petition. One member of staff set it up, and had to guarantee at least 60 signatures before he would show it to the head. Staff feel they can be got rid of so easily now. Having spoken to a Union leader in the school, she said staff are just too afraid to speak out now, because they know that if senior management want rid of you, they can do it now.
>
> Senior management can observe you with their performance management duties (in some schools this may be once a year, in this, once

every term). There are the "learning walks" where they can "pop into" your lesson (for how ever long they choose—this may have a different label, but it has the same effect on their view of your teaching, and your anxiety levels). There are also "book looks", which have always been done, but now they must be standardised (making sure there are comments on how students can improve, and asking a "Learning Development Question", which the students must answer. This is to tick another box in case Ofsted arrive). And the over-riding view of the reasons for many of these quality initiatives, is that if Management want you out, they will force you out with the amount of pressure they will place on you from the observations, or you will slip up in an observation, which can then be used against you.

I was observed on a learning walk by a member of senior management, she came in as the class were doing an activity, there was music on in the background, I was sat at my desk looking over a student's book. The member of staff left after a few minutes. At the end of the day I received an email from my head of department, who had received an email from the senior management observer. It was a complaint that I hadn't got up and gone over to greet her at the door. She didn't see the reason why I was playing that music and so therefore thought it questionable. The fact I was sat at my desk also gave her cause for concern, especially as another member of staff had also seen me sat at my desk once when they had walked past my classroom and looked inside through the window in the door.

This type of micro management is something you may expect from working in a cubicle in an office. How teachers relate to students, how they engage them, is being written out in a memo, so Ofsted can tick it off.

McBeath (1995) is among many who note that:

> Inspections carry high stakes for schools and teachers and where the press for accountability overshadows the improvement motive. It also assumes that inspectors are able not only to "see" schools as they are but are able to tell the story in ways that depict the complexity, vitality and dynamic of a school's character. Snapshots are by nature limited by both frame and focus.

James continues:

> You hear they're (Ofsted) in the area, you panic. They call, you plan like you've never planned before (because it's impossible to do that amount of planning for 9 different teaching groups who you see at least 2/3 times a week, with the amount of detail the school thinks Ofsted require). They observe your lesson, the students are amazing, because

there's a new person in the room who looks important. Your nerves are hanging by a thread because you don't know if you've demonstrated 3 levels of progress in the 15 minutes the inspector has been in your room (possibly not, because they came in right in the middle of the activity). By the end of the lesson, the students may have learnt something, but if it hasn't been measured by the inspector, you're not a "good" teacher. So you'll be observed again, and again, and again.

NEOLIBERALISM AND (NEO)-CONSERVATISM AND THE NATURE AND POWER OF THE RESISTANCE

The paths of neoliberalization and (neo)-conservatism are similar in many countries. But each country has its own history, has its own particular context; each country has its own balance of class forces, its own level of organization of the working class, and levels of confidence within the working class and within the capitalist class. In countries where resistance to neoliberalism is very strong, as in Greece, then the government has found it actually so far very difficult to engage in large-scale privatization. When the Greek government tries to privatize public sector activity, the ports, the buses, the trains, the museums, and so on, these efforts are met with general strike. In Greece, working-class consciousness and class organization, in a situation of naked class war from above, are highly developed.

But in some countries, where trade union resistance and working-class organizations' resistance are historically very weak, for example, Ireland, the US, then neoliberalism and the capitalist class have an easier path. There has been little resistance even to extreme measures taken by, for example, in the US, in 2011, the Wisconsin state government passing a law that made it illegal to negotiate with trade unions. In other words, it has said there would be no more collective bargaining with trade unions. There were major demonstrations and trade union protests—but the law passed, even if it did electrify the left and the trade union movement in the US.

To leftists in Britain this was incredible, in the sense of it being hard to believe. Although there has been as succession of neoliberal and neoconservative governments in Britain, both Conservative and New Labour, the trade unions still have great strength. The Trade Unions Congress (TUC) in Britain has around 6 million members. On October 20, 2012, 150,000 of us went on the march in London against austerity. That followed on from the student and worker marches against education cuts of 2010 and 2011.

When the organized working class wakes up, then we can take very strong action. But some trade union leaders sometimes live comfortable lives; sometimes they have good relations with the government and are incorporated into the (capitalist) state apparatuses. Not all the trade union leaders are radical. However, some union leaderships are Marxist. In Britain, the Communist Party of Britain has some power in unions at the top level; so does the Trotskyist group called the Socialist Party, the Committee for a Workers International, and so does the Socialist Workers Party. And of course, socialists and Marxists are very active within the membership of trade unions, pushing the leaderships into more radical action. The power of the organized working class, if spurred into action, can have very considerable impact. We hope in Britain to have a general strike against "austerity capitalism." We (Marxists, activists) are working towards that. This would be only the second general strike in British history, the first since 1926.

Levels of resistance vary in different countries. In Portugal, for example, recently (June 2013) there were 1 million on strike, 1 million in demonstrations. That is in a small country of 8 million people. In Ireland, there are very small demonstrations. The most noteworthy action in Ireland against austerity and neoliberalism was one worker driving his big digger truck into the gates of parliament.

Levels and types of resistance against neoliberalism and austerity capitalism in the US, England and Wales (Canaan, Hill, & Maisuria, 2013), Greece, Ireland, and Turkey (İnal & Öztürk, 2013) are described and analyzed in great detail from a Marxist perspective in the country by country chapters on "resistance" in *Immiseration Capitalism and Education: Austerity, Resistance and Revolt* (D. Hill, 2013b).

RESISTANCE, CRITICAL EDUCATION, AND CRITICAL EDUCATORS

Critical Education, Critical Educators

In schools, colleges, and universities, many radical and Marxist critical educators try to affect four aspects of learning and teaching, asking questions about (at least) four aspects (see D. Hill, 2012b, 2012c). These questions are common to many types of radical educator, not simply Marxists.

Some critical educators question the teacher-centered *pedagogy*, the pattern of teaching and learning relationships and interaction, and try to use democratic participative pedagogy, which breaks down patterns of domination and submission and listens to children's, students', and local communities' voices—but not uncritically. This is no uncritical, postmodernist, or liberal acceptance of polyvocality. Critical Marxist educators engage in critique that frames educational experiences within the conditions of capitalism and its current neoliberal form. Critical Marxist educators also attempt to utilize different types of pedagogy in teaching, to engage in nonhierarchical, democratic, participative teaching and research, while by virtue of their role in actually teaching, may maintain an authoritative stance where appropriate. Such approaches are rooted in social constructivist Vygotskyan understandings of learning and are also aimed both at producing colearning, by teachers as well as taught, and at overtly welcoming and valuing more cultures than are commonly valued in a transmission mode of teaching. Vygotsky, as a Marxist, was inspired by Marx's *dialectic* in that it rejects top-down and bottom-up accounts of the learning process—these unidirectional models originate in class-based societal relations, which Marxists reject.

Of course critiques of overdominant teacher-centered pedagogy are not restricted to Marxist educators. They are also made by liberal-progressive, child/student-centered educators and by some conservative educators, concerned about teaching effectiveness and preparation for the workplace.

But critical education is about far more than pedagogy (D. Hill, 2014). Indeed, it takes place outside schools and universities as well as inside (D. Hill, 2012a, 2013a,), as the rise of alternatives to the English university indicates (Canaan, Hill, & Maisuria, 2013; D. Hill, 2013b). There is educational resistance outside the state-controlled education structures, in connection with the teach-ins at "tent cities," a free-university movement, and through oppositional media and cultural workers, as well as within trade union and student groups.

A second question Marxist and other critical educators can and should ask is about the *curriculum*—who selected the content and how rigid is it? Even where the curriculum is very tightly controlled, even where it is very rigidly prescribed, there are, as Gramsci taught us, always spaces, little spaces for us to infiltrate, to use, to colonize. For example, this can be seen in the teaching schools, prisons, youth clubs, universities, and vocational colleges and in "tent cities," teach-ins and teach-outs, and emergent alternatives.

Marxist educators, indeed critical educators in general, can, with students, look at the curriculum and ask, "Who do you think wrote this?" "Who do you think decided on including this in the curriculum?" "What do you/we think should be in the curriculum that is currently absent?" "Why do you think it is absent?" "Who do you think benefits and who loses from this curriculum?" "What is the ideology behind this book/task/lesson/curriculum piece?" These questions can be asked with 10-year-olds, 16-year-olds, 40- or 70-year-olds.

However limited the spaces are, within a school, university, or educational site, within a curriculum, we can always find some possibility to question and to encourage the children/students to do this as well so that they are, in effect, developing an awareness of what can be called "ideology critique" (Kelsh & Hill, 2006). And then we can suggest, and seek from students, an alternative, perhaps even if only for five minutes in a lesson/session. We can question existing versions of history. We can ask, "Is there a different version or view of the past, the present, or the future?" So, looking at the work of Marxist and communist teachers and critical educators, we can affect the content of curriculum, or, if that is, at any particular time/space, almost impossible, we can seek to develop ideology critique, an understanding of the capital–labor relation, of capitalism and its relationship to education systems, of ideological and repressive state apparatuses, and of how schools and universities are shaped and controlled into producing politically and ideologically quiescent and hierarchically organized and rewarded labor power. Where Marxist educators and revolutionary critical educators (McLaren, 2005; McLaren & Jaramillo, 2010) differ from more social democratic and liberal critical educators is in the emphasis placed on resistance and socialist transformation (D. Hill, 2014; Kelsh & Hill, 2006; Skordoulis & Hill, 2012).

A third question in education that critical and Marxist educators can and should ask is about *organization of the students*. How should children of different social class, gender, and ethnic backgrounds and different sexual orientations be organized within classrooms, within institutions such as schools and universities, and within national education systems? Are some groups, such as girls, such as ethnic minorities, such as the poorer sections of the working class, in fact systematically labeled, segregated, divided, demeaned? In some countries, virtually all children go to the same *type* of school. But children tend to go to schools where their own class predominates. There is also a question of how the education system inculcates a differentiated sense of class awareness in working-, middle-, and ruling-class students. And it tries to keep the working class as a working class that is obedient, subservient, individualistic, interested in only themselves, not in collectivity, not in community. Marxist and other egalitarian educators clearly prefer and work for what in Britain is called "comprehensive" schools, and in India, for example, is called "the common school." But then, even where this happens (as in Finland, where there are only a single handful of private schools, where students up to the age of 16 are taught in common/comprehensive schools in "mixed-ability" classes), there are internal informal mechanisms, the hidden curriculum of differentiation ("raced," "gendered," and "sexually oriented" expectations and responses to different cultural capitals) (D. Hill, 2009; Reay, 2006).

A fourth question Marxist and other critical educators ask is about *ownership and control of schools* (and, indeed, universities). Who should own, control, and govern schools, further education (vocational) colleges, and universities? Of course we cannot change the law at a stroke, but we can lead a movement that at some stage—in 2 years' time, 10 years' time, 20 years' time—the ownership and governance of schools can be changed, made democratic and secular, and can attempt to be egalitarian. Instead of, as in some countries, schools, colleges, and universities being run by a religious state, by transnational corporations (Ball, 2012), or by religious organizations themselves, by "for-profit" private companies, by companies that are in theory and public discourse "not-for-profit" (but that reward handsomely their executives and their friends), or schools that are run and governed by rich businessmen or women. Marxist educators (and others, of course) believe that schools, colleges, and universities should be run democratically, with education workers and students, as well as elected representatives of local communities, having powers in and over those education institutions, within a secular, democratic national framework. Explicit in this is the assertion that education is a public good and a public right that should not be distorted and corrupted by private ownership—there should be no private schools, colleges, or universities. (For an attempt to address these various aspects of education in developing a socialist policy for education, see D. Hill, 2010b.)

MARXIST EDUCATORS

What is specifically Marxist about these four questions is that while Marxists work for and willingly embrace reforms such as are implicit in the above, we are committed to three things, three forms of analysis and action, that radical liberals, or radical democrats, or non-Marxist feminists, or non-Marxist antiracists or non-Marxist Queer activists are not.

What defines Marxists is firstly our belief that reforms are not sustainable under capitalism and that therefore what is needed is a revolution to replace, to get rid of, the capitalist economic system with its capitalist economic relations of production and its capitalist social relations of production—the ownership by capitalists of the wealth and the power in society. Revolutions can be violent (ruling classes do not often give up their power peacefully), or it might, possibly, be through the ballot box, or a combination of the two. The ballot box alone cannot bring about revolution because state institutions in capitalism are not democratic. A congress or parliament or president or prime minister has limited power over these institutions. An elected socialist government would not be able to bring about much change that went against the interests of the capitalist class because the military, judiciary, police, and corporate hierarchy are not democratic. The national (and transnational) capitalist class uses state violence to stop socialist, revolutionary change. But a socialist revolution is necessary so that there comes *into power* (not just *into government*) an egalitarian, socialist economic, political, and education system.

The second point of difference between Marxist and non-Marxist radicals is that in order to replace capitalism, Marxists have to work to organize for that movement, for that action, through political parties, social movements, workforces, trade unions.

The third point is the salience of class as compared with other forms of structural oppression and discrimination and inequality. Marxists, Marxist feminists, Marxist antiracists, and Marxist Queer theorists stand together with social movements, anti-racist, anti-sexist, anti-homphobic and civil rights campaigners. But they go further, into economic rights. And further than that, into the recognition that full social rights cannot be achieved under a capitalist economic system, but only under a socialist or democratic Marxist system.

Furthermore, it is only the organized working class (Black-White; male-female; straight-LGBT) that can organize to and succeed in replacing the capitalist system. These are the major points of difference between Marxists and other radical liberals and leftists, such as separatist feminists and separatist black nationalists.

EDUCATE, AGITATE, ORGANIZE: A MARXIST ANALYSIS

We Marxists seek to serve and advance the interests of the working class. We, as teachers, as educators, are working class too; we sell our labor power to capitalists and to the apparatuses of the capitalist state, such as schools and universities. We have to consistently and courageously challenge the dominant ideology, the hegemony of the ruling class, the bourgeoisie, the capitalist class. We are in a battle for dominance of our ideas; there are "culture wars" between different ways of looking at/interpreting the world. We have to contest the currently hegemonic control of ideas by the capitalist state, schools, media, and their allies in the religions.

But the situation we face is not just a war of ideas, an ideological war; it is also a class war, where the social and economic conditions and well-being of the working class are threatened and undermined by the ruling class and its capitalist state (Campagna, 2013). David Blacker (2013) goes even further and argues that contemporary and future capitalist onslaughts will result in deaths for "superfluous" workers and sections of the nonworking industrial reserve army (such as elderly people, e.g., the 13,000 extra deaths of old people in the winter months in the UK due to lack of affordable heating). If we sit and do nothing, if their ideas are not contested, then capitalism will continue to rule, to demean, to divide, to impoverish us and the planet.

At certain times in history, and in certain locations, the disjunction—the gap, the difference—between the material conditions of workers' existence on the one hand, our daily lived experience, and, on the other hand, what the newspapers and the media and the imam and the priest and the rabbi say/preach, that gap becomes so stark, so obvious, that workers' subjective consciousness changes. This is particularly likely when workers with more advanced revolutionary consciousness succeed in bringing about a widespread and more evenly distributed consciousness among the class as a whole, where there is intense class polarisation, as in Greece, the European country worst affected by immiseration/ austerity capitalism.

At this moment—now—in some countries in the world, the gap between the "official" ideology that "we are all in it together" and that "there is no alternative" (to austerity), or, in schools and universities faced by commodification and managerialism and (pre)-privatization—that gap becomes so large that the ruling party, and the ruling capitalist class, and capitalism itself, loses legitimacy. And so, as in Greece now, and in Portugal, in Spain, in Turkey and Brazil, and in other countries such as Britain, we Marxists are necessary. Necessary in leading and developing changes in consciousness, a change in class consciousness, and in playing a leading role in organizing for the replacement of capitalism.

PROGRAM

In 1938 in *The Transitional Programme*, Trotsky addressed the types of programs moving the discussion beyond the *minimum program* (minimum acceptable reforms, such as those to protect and improve existing rights and entitlements, such as rights at work, social and political rights) and the *maximum program* (socialist revolution, with the type of society ultimately envisaged by Marx, a socialist noncapitalist/postcapitalist society) that were advanced by late 19th- and early 20th-century social democrats and by communists of the Third International and articulated a new type of program: the *transitional program*. Trotsky, with a distinct resonance to today's struggles, wrote:

> The strategic task of the next period—prerevolutionary period of agitation, propaganda and organization—consists in overcoming the contradiction between the maturity of the objective revolutionary conditions and the immaturity of the proletariat and its vanguard (the confusion and disappointment of the older generation, the inexperience of the younger generation. It is necessary to help the masses in the process of the daily struggle to find the bridge between present demand and the socialist program of the revolution. This bridge should include a system of transitional demands, stemming from today's conditions and from today's consciousness of wide layers of the working class and unalterably leading to one final conclusion: the conquest of power by the proletariat.
>
> Classical Social Democracy, functioning in an epoch of progressive capitalism, divided its program into two parts independent of each other: the minimum program which limited itself to reforms within the framework of bourgeois society, and the maximum program which promised substitution of socialism for capitalism in the indefinite future. Between the minimum and the maximum program no bridge existed. And indeed Social Democracy has no need of such a bridge, since the word socialism is used only for holiday speechifying. The Comintern has set out to follow the path of Social Democracy in an epoch of decaying capitalism: when, in general, there can be no discussion of systematic social reforms and the raising of the masses' living standards; when every serious demand of the proletariat and even every serious demand of the petty bourgeoisie inevitably reaches beyond the limits of capitalist property relations and of the bourgeois state. (Trotsky, 1938)

Trotsky continued:

> Under the menace of its own disintegration, the proletariat cannot permit the transformation of an increasing section of the workers into

chronically unemployed paupers, living off the slops of a crumbling society. The right to employment is the only serious right left to the worker in a society based upon exploitation. This right today is left to the worker in a society based upon exploitation. This right today is being shorn from him at every step. Against unemployment, "structural" as well as "conjunctural," the time is ripe to advance along with the slogan of public works, the slogan of a sliding scale of working hours. Trade unions and other mass organizations should bind the workers and the unemployed together in the solidarity of mutual responsibility. On this basis all the work on hand would then be divided among all existing workers in accordance with how the extent of the working week is defined. The average wage of every worker remains the same as it was under the old working week. Wages, under a strictly guaranteed minimum, would follow the movement of prices. It is impossible to accept any other program for the present catastrophic period.

. . . The question is not one of a "normal" collision between opposing material interests. The question is one of guarding the proletariat from decay, demoralization and ruin. The question is one of life or death of the only creative and progressive class, and by that token of the future of mankind. If capitalism is incapable of satisfying the demands inevitably arising from the calamities generated by itself, then let it perish. "Realizability" or "unrealizability" is in the given instance a question of the relationship of forces, which can be decided only by the struggle. By means of this struggle, no matter what immediate practical successes may be, the workers will best come to understand the necessity of liquidating capitalist slavery. (Trotsky, 1938)

The "decay, demoralization and ruin" Trotsky speaks of are, for many millions of workers' families—including what in the US and elsewhere are called "middle-class" workers—an everyday reality in this current era of capitalism, neoliberal capitalism, or "immiseration capitalism." The precise organization and characteristics of the resistance to the depredations is a matter for strategic and tactical considerations, relating to the current balance (strength, organizations, [dis]-unity) of class forces in specific local and national contexts. What is clear, though, is that the problematic regarding capitalism, for Marxist activists and educators, is not just to reform it—welcome though such reforms, such as "minimum program," are, and active in campaigning for and to protect such reforms we must be. But, regarding capitalism, our task is to replace it with democratic Marxism.

ACKNOWLEDGMENTS

This is to thank Faith Agostinone-Wilson, Gail Edwards, and Glenn Rikowski for their comments on a draft of this chapter, and to James Lloyd Hill for carrying out a series of semistructured interviews and personal ethnography in relation to the intensification and managerialization of teachers' work. Responsibility for the final version is mine.

REFERENCES

Academies Commission. (2013). *Unleashing greatness: Getting the best from an academicised system.* London: RSA and Pearson. Retrieved June 12, 2014 from http://www.thersa.org/__data/assets/pdf_file/0020/1008038/Unleashing-greatness.pdf

Agostinone-Wilson, F. (2014). Comments on a draft of this chapter. Unpublished.

Althusser, L. (1971). Ideology and state apparatus. In L. Althusser, *Lenin and philosophy and other essays.* London, England: New Left Books. Retrieved June 12, 2014 from http://www.antiacademies.org.uk/

Apple, M. W. (2006). Educating the" right" way: Markets, standards, God, and inequality. Abingdon, England: Taylor & Francis.

Ball, S. (1990). *Politics and policy-making in education: Explorations in policy sociology.* London, England: Routledge.

Ball, S. (2003). The teacher's soul and the terrors of performativity. *Journal of Education Policy, 18*(2): 215–228.

Ball, S. (2012). Global Education Inc.: New policy networks and the neoliberal imaginary. London, England: Routledge.

Ball, S. J., & Youdell, D. (2007). *Hidden privatisation in public education.* Preliminary Report. Education International 5th World Congress. July 2007.

Beckett, F. (2007). *The great city academy fraud.* London: Continuum.

Beckmann, A., & Cooper, C. (2004). "Globalization", the new managerialism and education: Rethinking the purpose of education. *Journal for Critical Education Policy Studies, 2*(1). Retrieved June 12, 2014 from http://www.jceps.com/index.php?pageID=article&articleID=31

Beckmann, A., Cooper, C., & Hill, D. (2009). Neoliberalization and managerialization of "education" in England and Wales—a case for reconstructing education. *Journal for Critical Education Policy Studies, 7*(2). Retrieved June 12, 2014 from http://www.jceps.com/index.php?pageID=article&articleID=170

Benn, M. (2011). *School wars: The battle for Britain's education.* London, England: Verso.

Blacker, D. (2013). *The falling rate of learning and the neoliberal endgame.* Winchester, England: Zero Books.

Bryant, J. (2014). The truth about charter schools: Padded cells, corruption, lousy instruction and worse results. [Web log message] Retrieved June 12, 2014 from: http://www.salon.com/2014/01/10/the_truth_about_charter_schools_padded_cells_corruption_lousy_instruction_and_worse_results/

Campagna, F. (2013). *The last night: Anti-work, atheism, adventure.* Winchester, England: Zero Books.

Canaan, J., Hill, D., & Maisuria, A. (2013). Resistance in England. In D. Hill (Ed.), *Immiseration capitalism and education: Austerity, resistance and revolt.* Brighton, England: Institute for Education Policy Studies.

Chrysochou, T. (2014) Teachers in Times of Crisis. *Journal for Critical Education Policy Studies,* 12(2).

Clarke, T. G. (2014). Michael Gove's Ideological Vandalism of the Education System. [Web log message]. Retrieved June 12, 2014 from: http://anotherangryvoice.blogspot.co.uk/2014/01/michael-gove-ideological-vandalism.html

Deem, R. (1998). "New managerialism" and higher education: The management of performances and cultures in universities in the United Kingdom. *International*

Studies in Sociology of Education, 8(1). Retrieved June 12, 2014 from http://www.tandfonline.com/doi/pdf/10.1080/0962021980020014

Ercan, F. (1998). 1980'lerde Eğitim Sisteminin Yeniden Yapılanması: Küreselleşme ve Neo Liberal Eğitim Politikaları [Restructuring of the education system in the 1980s: Globalization and neoliberal education policies]. *75 Yılda Eğitim, 75,* 23–38. Türkiye İş Bankası yayını. İstanbul.

Fraser, S., & Gertsle, G. (2005). *Ruling America: A history of wealth and power in a democracy.* Cambridge, MA: Harvard University Press.

Gamble, A. (1988). *The free society and the strong state.* Basingstoke, England: Macmillan.

Gewirtz, S., Ball, S., & Bowe, R. (1995). *Markets, choice and equity in education.* Milton Keynes, Bucks., England: Open University Press.

Gezgin, U. B., İnal, K., and Hill, D. (Eds.). (2014). *The Gezi revolt: People's revolutionary resistance against neoliberal capitalism in Turkey.* Brighton, England: Institute for Education Policy Studies.

Gillborn, D., & Youdell, D. (2002). *Rationing education: Policy, practice, reform and equity.* Milton Keynes, Bucks., England: Open University Press.

Giroux, H. (2004). *The terror of neoliberalism: Authoritarianism and the eclipse of democracy.* Boulder, CO: Paradigm.

Gök, F. (2004). Eğitimin Özelleştirilmesi [Privatization of education]. In *Neoliberalizmin Tahribatı: 2000'li Yıllarda Türkiye,* pp. 94–110. 2. Cilt. Metis Yayınları. İstanbul.

Harvey, D. (2005). *A brief history of neoliberalism.* Oxford, England: Oxford University Press.

Hill, D. (1997). Equality in primary schooling: The policy context of the reforms. In M. Cole, D. Hill, & S. Shan (Eds.), *Promoting equality in primary schools* (pp. 15–47). London: Cassell. Retrieved June 12, 2014 from http://www.ieps.org.uk/papersdh.php

Hill, D. (2001). Equality, ideology and education policy. In D. Hill & M. Cole (Eds.), *Schooling and equality: Fact, concept and policy* (pp. 7–34). London, England: Kogan Page. Retrieved June 12, 2014 from http://www.ieps.org.uk/papersdh.php

Hill, D. (2003). Global neo-liberalism, the deformation of education and resistance. *Journal for Critical Education Policy Studies, 1*(1). Retrieved June 12, 2014 from http://www.jceps.com/index.php?pageID=article&articleID=7

Hill, D. (2006). Education services liberalization. In E. Rosskam (Ed.), *Winners or losers?: Liberalizing public services* (pp. 3–54). Geneva, Switzerland: ILO. Retrieved June 12, 2014 from http://www.ieps.org.uk/PDFs/DaveHill-2006-EUCATIONSERVICESLIBERALIZATION.pdf

Hill, D. (2009). Theorising politics and the curriculum: Understanding and addressing inequalities through critical pedagogy and critical policy analysis. In D. Hill & L. Helavaara Robertson (Eds.), *Equality in the primary school: Promoting good practice across the curriculum.* London, England: Continuum. Retrieved June 12, 2014 from http://www.ieps.org.uk/PDFs/Ch20HillandRobertson2009.pdf

Hill, D. (2010a). Students are revolting—and quite right too. *Radical notes.* Retrieved June 12, 2014 from http://radicalnotes.com/journal/2010/12/03/students-are-revolting-education-cuts-and-resistance/

Hill, D. (2010b). A socialist manifesto for education. *Socialist Resistance.* Retrieved June 12, 2014 from http://socialistresistance.org/?p=905

Hill, D. (2012a). Immiseration capitalism, activism and education: Resistance, revolt and revenge. *Journal for Critical Education Policy Studies, 10*(2). Retrieved June 12, 2014 from http://www.jceps.com/index.php?pageID=article&articleID=259

Hill, D. (2012b). Fighting neo-liberalism with education and activism. *Philosophers for change.* March 1. Retrieved June 12, 2014 from http://philosophers.posterous.com/fighting-neo-liberalism-with-education-and-ac

Hill, D. (2012c). The role of Marxist educators against and within neoliberal capitalism. *Socialist Resistance*. February 26. Retrieved June 12, 2014 from http://socialistresistance.org/3184/the-role-of-marxist-educators-against-and-within-neoliberal-capitalism

Hill, D. (2013a). Class struggle and education: Neoliberalism, (neo)-conservatism, and the capitalist assault on public education. *Critical Education*. Retrieved June 12, 2014 from http://ojs.library.ubc.ca/index.php/criticaled/article/view/ 184452

Hill, D. (Ed.). (2013b). *Immiseration capitalism and education: Austerity, resistance and revolt*. Brighton, England: Institute for Education Policy Studies.

Hill, D. (2013c). *Marxist essays on education: Class and "race", neoliberalism and capitalism*. Brighton, England: Institute for Education Policy Studies.

Hill, D. (2013d). Gezi Park and Taksim Square: Reflections and reactions: Islamic conservatism, predatory neoliberalism and the continuing courage of the resistance. *Socialist Resistance*. September 29. Retrieved June 12, 2014 from http://socialistresistance.org/5509/gezi-park-and-taksim-square-reflections-and-reactions

Hill, D. (Ed.). (2014). *Critical education, critical pedagogies, Marxist education*. Unpublished manuscript.

Hill, D., & Kumar, R. (Eds.). (2009). *Global neoliberalism and education and its consequences*. New York, NY: Routledge.

Hill, D., Lewis, C., Yarker, P., & Maisuria, A. (2013). Capitalism and education in Britain. In D. Hill (Ed.), *Immiseration capitalism and education: Austerity, resistance and revolt*. Brighton, England: Institute for Education Policy Studies.

Hill, D., & Rosskam, E. (Eds.). (2009). *The developing world and state education: Neoliberal depredation and egalitarian alternatives*. New York: Routledge.

Hill, J. L. (2013). Interview and personal ethnography research data gathered on secondary school teachers' perspectives on and reactions to the intensification and managerialization of teachers' work. Unpublished.

Hirtt, N. (2004). Three axes of merchandisation. *European Educational Research Journal*, 3(2), 442–453. Retrieved June 12, 2014 from http://www.wwwords.co.uk/eerj/

İnal, K. (2012). The educational politics of the AKP: The collapse of public education in Turkey. In K. İnal & G. Akkaymak (Eds.), *Neoliberal transformation of education in Turkey* (pp. 17–32). New York, NY: Palgrave Macmillan.

İnal, K., & Öztürk, H. T. (2013). Resistance in Turkey. In D. Hill (Ed.), *Immiseration capitalism and education: Austerity, resistance and revolt*. Brighton, England: Institute for Education Policy Studies.

Jones, B. (2009, April 30). Using "civil rights" to sell communism. *Socialist Worker*, 696. Retrieved June 12, 2014 from http://socialistworker.org/2009/04/30/using-civil-rights-to-sell-privatization

Kelsh, D., & Hill, D. (2006). The culturalization of class and the occluding of neoliberalism consciousness: The knowledge industry in/of education. *Journal for Critical Education Policy Studies*, 4(1). Retrieved June 12, 2014 from http://www.jceps.com/index.php?pageID=article&articleID=59

Kurul, N. (2012). Turkey under AKP rule: Neoliberal interventions into the public budget and educational finance. In K. İnal & G. Akkaymak (Eds.), *Neoliberal transformation of education in Turkey* (pp. 83–94). New York, NY: Palgrave Macmillan.

Lewis, C., Hill, D., & Fawcett, B. (2009). England and Wales: Neoliberalised education and its impacts. In D. Hill (Ed.), *The rich world and the impoverishment of education: Diminishing democracy, equity and workers' rights* (pp. 106–135). New York, NY: Routledge.

Local Schools Network. (n.d.). Retrieved June 12, 2014 from http://www.localschoolsnetwork.org.uk/campaigns/transparency-academies-freeschools/page/3/

Luxemburg, R. (1971). What does the Spartacus League want? *Monthly Review Press*. Retrieved June 12, 2014 from http://www.marxists.org/archive/luxemburg/1918/12/14.htm (Original work published 1918)

Luxemburg, R. (2013). Barbarism and socialism. YouTube presentation. Retrieved June 12, 2014 from http://www.youtube.com/watch?v=uRzb0FqgBf0

Malott, C., Hill, D., & Banfield, G. (2013). Immiseration capitalism. *Journal for Critical Education Policy Studies*, 11(4). Retrieved June 12, 2014 from http://www.jceps.com/index.php?pageID=article&articleID=311

Martin, I. (2013). *Rich people's movements: Grassroots campaigns to untax the one percent*. New York, NY: Oxford University Press.

McBeath, J. (1995). Self-evaluation and inspection @ a consultation response, for the National Union of Teachers. London: National Union of Teachers. Retrieved June 12, 2014 from www.teachers.org.uk/.../Future_of Inspection-MacBeath_response.d

McLaren, P. (2005). *Capitalists and conquerors: A critical pedagogy against empire*. New York, NY: Rowman & Littlefield.

McLaren, P., & Jaramillo, N. (2010). Not neo-Marxist, not post-Marxist, not Marxian, not autonomist Marxism: Reflections on a revolutionary (Marxist) critical pedagogy. *Cultural Studies<—>Critical Methodologies*, 20(10), 1–12.

Moore, K., & Cohen, R. (2014, January 22). Unmasking the Chicago charter scam. Retrieved June 12, 2014 from http://socialistworker.org/2014/01/22/the-chicago-charter-scam

Picketty, T. (2014) *Capital in the Twenty-First Century*. Cambridge, MA: Harvard University Press.

Reay, D. (2006). The zombie stalking English schools: Social class and educational inequality. *British Journal of Education Studies*, 54(3), 288–307.

Reynolds, W. M. (2013). Iron man democracy: Militainment and democratic possibilities. In A. Abdi & P. Carr (Eds.), *Educating for democratic consciousness: Counter-hegemonic possibilities* (pp. 206–218). New York: Peter Lang.

Rikowski, G. (2002). *Globalisation and education*. Paper prepared for the House of Lords Select Committee on Economic Affairs, Inquiry into the Global Economy, January 22. Retrieved June 12, 2014 http://www.leeds.ac.uk/educol/documents/00001941.htm

Rikowski, G. (2003). The profit virus: The business takeover of schools. Retrieved 12 June, 2014 http://www.flowideas.co.uk/?page=articles&sub=The%20Profit%20Virus%20-%20The%20Business%20Takeover%20of%20Schools

Rikowski, G. (2007, June 3). The confederation of British industry and the Business takeover of schools. Retrieved 12 June, 2014 from http://www.flowideas.co.uk/?page=articles&sub=The%20CBI%20and%20the%20Business%20Takeover%20of%20Schools

Rikowski, G. (2008). The compression of critical space in education today. Retrieved 12 June, 2014 from http://www.flowideas.co.uk/?page=articles&sub=Critical%20Space%20in%20Education

Robin, C. (2013). *The reactionary mind*. New York, NY: Oxford University Press.

Saad-Filho, A. (2011). Crisis in neoliberalism or crisis of neoliberalism? *Socialist Register*, 47.

Sayılan, F. (2006, November–December). Küresel Aktörler (DB ve GATS) ve Eğitimde Neoliberal Dönüşüm [Global actors and the neoliberal transformation in education]. *TMMOB Jeoloji Mühendisleri Odası. Aylık Bülten Eğitim Dosyası*, pp. 44–51.

Sayılan, F., & Turkmen, N. (2013). Austerity capitalism and education in Turkey. In D. Hill (Ed.), *Immiseration capitalism and education: Austerity, resistance and revolt* (pp. 73–91). Brighton, England: Institute for Education Policy Studies.

Sefla, L. (2012). *The Democrats: A critical history*. Chicago, IL: Haymarket Books.
Sellgren, K. (2013, January 10). Academies could "fuel social segregation." BBC. Retrieved 12 June, 2014 from http://www.bbc.co.uk/news/education-20960500
Skordoulis, C., and Hill, D. (Eds.). (2012). Introduction. In *Proceedings of the First International Conference on Critical Education*, 2011. Athens, Greece: University of Athens.
Smyth, J,. Dow, A., Hattam, R., Reid, A., & Shacklock, G. (2000). *Teachers' work in a globalizing economy*. London, England: Falmer Press.
SocialistWorker (2012) Obama versus civil liberties. (2012, January 4). Retrieved June 12, 2014 from http://socialistworker.org/2012/01/04/obama-versus-civil-liberties
Stevenson, H. A. (2007). Restructuring teachers' work and trade union responses in England: Bargaining for change? *American Education Research Journal*, 44(2), 224–251. Retrieved 12 June, 2014 from http://aer.sagepub.com/content/44/2/224.full
Syal, R. (2014, January 12). Revealed: taxpayer funded academies paying millions to privatefirms. *The Guardian*. Retrieved 12 June, 2014 from http://www.theguardian.com/education/2014/jan/12/taxpayer-funded-academy-paying-millions-private-firms-schools-education-revealed-education
Trotsky, L. (1938). *The death agony of capitalism and the tasks of the Fourth International: The transitional program*. Retrieved 12 June, 2014 from http://www.marxists.org/archive/trotsky/1938/tp/tp-text.htm#m
Weekes-Bernard, D. (2007). *School choice and ethnic segregation: Educational decision making among Black and ethnic minority parents*. London: Runnymede Trust. Retrieved 12 June, 2014 from http://www.runnymedetrust.org/uploads/publications/pdfs/School%20ChoiceFINAL.pdf
Wilkinson, R., & Pickett, K. (2009). *The spirit level: Why more equal societies almost always do better*. London, England: Allen Lane.

4 Debunking the Myth of Standardized Education to Promote Equity and Rigor

Debra A. Root

INTRODUCTION

This chapter considers how standardized education has failed in its promise to provide equity and rigor for students. Many teachers in today's schools feel powerless to create engaging educational experiences and by default become complicit in the political and corporate "webs" related to standardized education (Hamel & Ryken, 2010; Louis, Febey, & Schroeder, 2005; Olsen & Sexton, 2009). For the purpose of this chapter, standardized education refers to the practice of creating discipline-specific standards and accountability through testing to assure that teachers indeed teach the prescribed standards. Often teachers express concern that they have little time to venture into the messiness of reflective and evaluative curriculum and give in to the bifurcated system of "right" and "wrong" answers under the pressure to perform well on standardized tests (Ravitch, 2010; Taubman, 2009). Teachers tend to focus on "covering" large amounts of content with little depth in order to achieve favorable test scores (Louis, Febey, & Schroeder, 2005). To debunk the myth that standardized educational reform ensures equity and rigor, I will use the symbolic interactionism model proposed by Snow (2001) to analyze the results from my recent case study on standardized education.

Snow's (2001) work on symbolic interactionism was used to discuss the historical development and acceptance as well as the current reality of reform based on accountability and standardization. The historical reality of *who* drove reform in Texas (business elites, not educators) and the infusion of language that invokes images of corporate control (accountability, administration, and data management) became apparent during the analysis of the data, from the analysis of the historic record through the words of the three teacher participants.

The number of participants in this case study was small in order to promote a curricular discussion among the teachers and was held in a small conference room at a local university near the school sites. The study focused on how teachers made sense of their role as curriculum professionals, and the theme of standardization emerged as a dominant topic. The recent history of educational reform movements, particularly those initiated in Texas, has been founded on rhetoric that includes a commonsense notion that standardized education would provide rigor and equity in education (Gunzenhauser, 2006; Hursh, 2005). Analysis of the transcripts and historical documents in this study included an explanation of the web of interactions between the recent history of political activity of leading business executives, the reality of living educational policies in Texas, school and the implementation and accountability actions between district administrators, and teachers as viewed through a symbolic interactionism critical lens (Snow, 2001).

This chapter first highlights a short history of standardized reform that considers the imposition of corporate models on education. Included in the chapter is a review of the literature related to teachers' understanding of the reality of corporate-style, standardized educational reform to contextualize the study. Next, I discuss the data from my recent (2012–2013) case study of three high school social studies teachers from economically challenged school districts in a large city in Texas using a symbolic interactionism critical lens (Snow, 2001). Data for the case study were collected through three focus groups and follow-up interviews during the fall of 2012, after the implementation of the new STAAR system of standardized assessment. The study was designed to examine the ways of thinking of teachers who are required to implement standardized reforms by using Snow's (2001) symbolic interactionism model. The study provides an opportunity to consider how these corporate-style reforms impact the curriculum work of teachers in economically challenged schools.

Lastly, the chapter suggests ways that human agency by teachers is required to push back against top-down reforms to provide students, including those in impoverished areas, with a critical curriculum that encourages students to affect future changes in society. At the end of the chapter are questions to promote discussion related to the topic.

THE ROOTS OF EDUCATIONAL REFORM IN TEXAS: A CONTEXTUALIZED PHENOMENON

The roots of reform in Texas's recent history can be traced to a select committee appointed by Governor Mark White in the early 1980s. Earlier, a national report, *A Nation at Risk* (ANAR), proclaimed that American schools were falling behind in the world according to standardized test score comparisons. Further, ANAR warned that schools were placing equity concerns over high standards and questioned the ability of the educational system to compete on a global scale (Hanna, 2005). Rhetoric following the ANAR report insisted that "rigor," which loosely referred to the ability to achieve well on tests but was never clearly defined, dominated the popular press (Hanna, 2005). Dallas businessman H. Ross Perot was appointed to chair a committee to find a way to fund increases in teachers' salaries in Texas (Hobby, 2010). The select committee, the Special Committee on Public Education (SCOPE), seized the opportunity to reform education to become more competitive and to be poised for globalization. The committee applied a "best practices" approach to teacher funding; that is, they wanted to ensure that the public would receive a good return on their investment for raising teacher salaries (Haney, 2000).

SCOPE attempted to reform public education using a business approach to school management to ensure accountability through implementing standards and testing on those standards (Haney, 2000). No educators were included in the committee; only influential businessmen and policy makers were appointed by the governor (Salinas & Reidel, 2007). The SCOPE committee approached their commission from the governor as a mandate to reform the educational system in Texas. The businessmen on the committee viewed standards and assessment as a type of educational reform that would produce economic benefits for society by producing a suitable workforce for business and industry (Salinas & Reidel, 2007).

The resulting reform bill of 1984 mandated sweeping changes in public schools (Haney, 2000). The language of education evolved to incorporate "corporate" terms such as "management," "accountability," and "efficiency" (Haney, 2000; Salinas & Reidel, 2007). According to Salinas and Reidel (2007), the business "best practice" model lingo became the language of educational reform. The law mandated assessment measures tied to curriculum standards (Booher-Jennings, 2005). In this reform system, teachers and schools were accountable to taxpayers through the use of an assessment system that tested students' ability to recall knowledge as prescribed by the curricular standards. The law institutionalized a standardized curriculum called the Essential Elements in reading, math, science, and social studies, and these reforms were imposed on all public school districts in Texas (Haney, 2000).

Additionally, the Texas legislature produced SB 994, in 1987, to reconstruct teacher preparation programs in Texas. No longer would teachers major in education but either in a content area or in an interdisciplinary studies program (Funkhouser, 1988). The emphasis on content rather than on educational theory related to curriculum and pedagogy fostered an assumption that knowledge in a discipline is more important for teaching than learning about the art of teaching (Funkhouser, 1988). Such teacher training programs created a perception of teachers as implementers of curriculum, not creators of curriculum.

In an effort to standardize Texas school test results for comparison so that parents could be informed "consumers" of education, the Texas Education Agency (TEA) began labeling schools in 1993 (TEA, 2011). According to the TEA website, "Exemplary" reflected the highest standard a school could achieve on testing results. "Recognized" or "acceptable" reflected schools that are performing at measures that can be considered offering appropriate education (TEA, 2011). "Low performing" schools were at risk of being sanctioned through funding and revocation of local management (TEA, 2011).

A series of performance-based testing based on a standardized curriculum has existed in Texas for the last 30 years (Martinez & Martinez, 2002; Salinas & Reidel, 2007). Texas's State Accountability System continued to evolve through a variety of testing measures: from the TABS to the TAAS, to the TAKS to the STAAR. More recently in Texas public education history, exit exams were required for student graduation (Salinas & Reidel, 2007). The initial "objective" measure of student preparedness in Texas, the End of Course (EOC) exams, required 12 exit exams for high school students to pass in order to graduate. This latest round of standardization and testing met with challenges from state high schools and parents. The "commonsense" notion of standards and testing became burdensome in high schools, and the number of EOC exams required for graduation has been reduced (TEA, 2013).

No discussion of recent educational history is complete without a mention of the *No Child Left Behind Act* (NCLB) of 2001. This revision of the Elementary and Secondary Education Act (ESEA) of 1964 was a cornerstone of President Johnson's War on Poverty. The latest iteration of the law proposed to build upon the original goal of the legislation to provide equity in education and rigorous curriculum. This rhetoric incorporated the recommendation of the ANAR report to supply "rigor" with the intended goals of the original legislation that pushed for desegregation and equity in education for all children. This bipartisan, seemingly objective bill was the highlight of President George Bush's educational policy and transplanted the "Texas Miracle" to the national level (Haney, 2000; Salinas & Reidel, 2007).

Haney (2000) referred to the "miracle" as a "myth," citing many factors indicating that reforms were not truly effective. He pointed to low graduation rates, unchanged scores on the SAT, failing National Assessment of Educational Progress (NAEP) testing juxtaposed to rising scores of Texas schools, and the high number of minority and impoverished students identified as "special education" to avoid state-mandated testing. Texas students were not performing better and were experiencing high rates of high school dropouts in poverty areas (Haney, 2000).

LITERATURE REVIEW: THE PROBLEM WITH CURRENT REFORM

A review of the literature paints a picture of standardized education as a narrowed, simplistic view of curriculum that changes teacher pedagogy and their perception of curriculum work, particularly in the context of economically challenged schools (Au, 2007; Craig, 2009; McNeil, 1988). The use of standardized education in schools challenges the traditional role of teachers as curriculum professionals and results in students from "at-risk" schools being spoon-fed standards containing bits of historical information with little critical consideration in social studies classes (Au, 2009).

Much has been published about the effects of educational reform and the curriculum work of teachers. The heart of education, according to Null (2011), is curriculum work. Research into effects of standardized content-knowledge assessment reveals that the teacher's role as curriculum intellectual has been diminished (Root, 2013). Teachers have been subject to disciplining forces from administrators and politicians, and teachers are abdicating their role of curriculum intellectual. Teachers perceive their role as technicians destined to carry out a standardized curriculum.

Curriculum scholars realize the importance of context as an influence on education. An example of the practical paradigm for curriculum work articulated by Schwab (1983) proposed four common "spaces" as a framework for understanding curriculum. Years ago, Schwab (1971) asserted that curriculum theories do not neatly solve practical problems, but teachers should employ multiple theories for curriculum work. Schwab (1983) proposed that practical measures for education depend on the context of individuals, groups, societies, cultures, and structures of learning and teaching, what he called the "Practical 4" (Schwab, 1983). The "Practical 4" involve four, equal "common places" of: the teacher, the students, the accepted bodies of knowledge, and the consideration of the milieu of teaching and learning. The purpose of education is often situated by society and is part of the teaching and learning milieu.

John Dewey (1916) explained that the purpose of education was a journey of learning, not a particular destination. Dewey condemned the view of education as a means to an end such as getting a specific job. Dewey viewed education as a time for young curiosity to grow, investigations to flourish, and understandings of society to develop (Dewey, 1916). However, in today's educational reform era, passing standardized tests has become the perceived purpose of education for teachers (McNeil, 2000; Salinas & Reidel, 2007). McNeil (2000) illustrated that teachers who once created relevant curriculum for students of color in poverty areas of Houston changed their affective and cognitive processes after the implementation of the standardized testing. Soon teachers abandoned their role as curriculum creators and became implementers of prescribed, irrelevant activities and lessons (McNeil, 2000).

Curriculum, as a thoughtful, intellectual, and ethical consideration, contextualizes learning and creates a bond between the learner and knowledge (Eisner, 2003). Many view curriculum work as a process that is conceptualized through inquiry and reflection with an eye to transformation (Joseph, 2011). However, a standardized curriculum fails to consider the contextual considerations that educators, students, and context bring to the classroom (Schwab, 1983). Far from an objective, prescribed list of knowledge to be doled out to students, curriculum must be relevant for students, researched by teachers, and delivered in a manner and sense of timing that best suits the needs of the students (Schwab, 1983).

Further, the tension between educational purposes of reform measures of those who have the power and authority to dictate school policy and those who perform the curriculum work in urban schools for economically disadvantaged students is a contemporary issue for teachers in public education (Hamilton et al., 2007; Holme & Rangel, 2011; Sleeter, 2008). Taken-for-granted knowledge assumes that schools in Texas that meet the minimum standards are offering a rigorous curriculum. Many educators have fallen in line with the performance-based goals of testing and fail to question the rigor of reform and the equity of a performance-based model of success (Au, 2007; Ryan & Weinstein, 2009). A failure to challenge the accountability and standardization model of reform resulted from the rhetoric of equity and rigor that undergirded the justification of educational reform in states such as Texas in the early years of reform.

Craig (2009) conducted a 10-year qualitative study in Houston, Texas, schools that considered teacher perceptions of their curricular work through the increasing pressure to have students from low-income schools perform well on standardized accountability measures (tests). She and her team chronicled how teachers who once created stimulating, relevant curriculum shifted their focus to adapting to a scripted version of curriculum that did not engage students because teachers worried about what the people in the "suits" would think of their teaching (Craig, 2009). Craig's research painted a picture of experienced teachers who resented being told what to teach and how to teach. The teachers felt that they had turned their back on their commitment to a rigorous and equitable curriculum under the pressure to conform to a dry, scripted curriculum that was framed by rhetorical promises but no practical means to deliver on those promises (Craig, 2009).

Au (2007) conducted a meta-synthesis of research into the effects of standardization of curriculum. He found the biggest effects of standards and testing to be: (a) a narrowing of curriculum to tested subject areas, (b) content that is fragmented and lacking conceptual understanding related to chronology and cause and effect, and (c) changes in teacher pedagogy towards teacher-centered lecture rather than student-led discussions, reflective and evaluative assignments, and development of curiosity and inquiry skills (Au, 2007). In other words, the structure of the test had the greatest impact on curriculum over teacher knowledge, student needs, or the context in which lessons were taught.

Other studies conducted in schools with large number of "at-risk" students, those who have English as a second language or are from low-income areas, indicate that standardization of education has limited opportunities for students (Achinstein & Ogawa, 2011; Fenwick, 2012). Students labeled "at risk" were more likely to receive remedial lessons focusing on minimal standards rather than rich, engaging opportunities to learn, according to Achinstein and Ogawa (2011) and Fenwick (2012).

METHODOLOGY

In this study, I used primary and secondary sources to detail the history of standards and reform in Texas and the country at large. No Child Left Behind (2001) became the focus of a case study to contextualize the words of three teachers who implemented the reforms in their classrooms. According to Lather (2006), the case study approach afforded the opportunity to make critical connections between the complexities and contradictions of the intended goals of reform and the daily experiences of the teachers. The transcriptions of three focus groups and individual follow-up interviews describe in detail (using the teachers' own words) the processes used in sense making and curriculum work. I chose to organize my research in this manner due to the complexity of the data and the need to go beyond surface explanations of the teachers' thinking about curriculum. In the study the teachers formed one case by virtue of their commonalities, and additionally, each participant in the study was considered a case due to the differences in experience and perspective.

The context for this research was a large, urban city in Texas. One of the school districts in which two of the teachers worked has over 90% of its students listed as Hispanics and roughly 80% of its students identified as economically disadvantaged (TEA, 2012). Two school districts and three schools were represented in this study, and all schools reflected an "at-risk" population due to poverty guidelines.

Recruitment for the study was purposeful sampling. I selected participants that were likely to be "information-rich" with respect to the purpose of the case study (Gall, Gall, & Borg, 2010). The requirement to participate in the study included having three years of teaching experience in social studies in this particular large, urban Texas city. Recruitment for the study was through announcements in graduate education courses at a particular university, but only one of the participants was actually a student at the university. Enrolled students referred the other two participants. Upon explanation of the Institutional Review Board (IRB) documents, the three participants (two women and one man) agreed to participate. The participants chose their own pseudonyms and committed to meet for three focus groups and a follow-up interview at the university outside of school hours.

Data were collected from four data sources: historical documents, focus groups, interviews, and my research diary. Historical documents included articles from the TEA, newspaper articles, and other secondary sources related to legislation. The three focus groups lasted about one and one-half hours each over the course of six weeks. The follow-up individual interviews were semistructured and intended to clarify remarks made by the participants during the focus groups. The research diary included my thoughts, questions, and analysis of the data.

The method used to analyze data was constant comparative qualitative research, and this recursive process enabled me to focus the data using emerging categories (Glaser & Strauss, 1967). As new data were collected from each focus group and interview, I continued comparisons until no new categories were detected. Data analysis included both within-case and across-case analysis of commonalities and differences among the participants.

Frequently in the focus groups, the themes of "rigor" and "equity" emerged as a symbol of NCLB and as commodities in the classroom. Through my note taking and analysis, I realized that the participants often described working within the webs of interaction between the different social levels of their work. District expectations, state testing scores, state rating systems, and site administrators played an important part in the teachers' perceptions of their curriculum work.

SYMBOLIC INTERACTIONISM AND REFORM

Upon reflection of the connected webs described by the participants in this study, I chose to use Snow's model of symbolic interactionism to understand how these teachers thought about corporate-style standardization to reform education and their understanding of the reality of "equity" and "rigor" in their classrooms. Snow (2001) expanded on earlier concepts of symbolic interactionism to include the following dimensions: interactive determination, emergence, symbolization, and human agency. I applied this model of symbolic interactionism approach to analyze the data from the case study.

Snow (2001) explained that a phenomenon in society (in this case standardization of education) cannot be considered without including the first facet of his model, *interactive determination.* Whether perceived or actual, individuals, groups, and institutions involved in the phenomenon anticipate its effects and react accordingly. Strategic measures, such as educational reform, induce a reaction from those involved, namely teachers, parents, students, administrators, and district personnel. Rather than being proactive and feeling in control of the situation, those involved tend to react based on their anticipation of the effect of the phenomenon (Snow, 2001).

Second, Snow's (2001) model includes the development of *symbolism* that incites an emotional response from interested parties. The acceptance of the symbolic terms or rhetoric becomes part of the taken-for-granted knowledge of the public, and the symbol is used to "frame" the phenomenon. In this example, "rigor" and "equity," terms that are taken for granted but loosely defined, become the symbol for standardization and reform. The public accepts the symbols of the phenomenon because they appeal to them at an emotional level. How could one challenge the need for rigor and equity in schools? An assumption of rigor and equity dominates public perception and frames action related to reform.

The next facet of Snow's (2001) model considers the *emergence* of webs formed between the players involved in the phenomenon. Such webs effect people to make cognitive and affective changes such as those teachers in the Craig (2009) study who conformed to scripted curriculum despite their prior success with an enriched curriculum. Those involved in the webs of relationships begin to operate in new and different ways seeking clarification and questioning the requirements of the change. In the current era of educational reform, district personnel make explicit demands of teachers to meet the goals of standardized assessment in their curriculum work. Teachers make changes to the pedagogy and curriculum design to accommodate (or challenge) the changes related to their role in the phenomenon of reform.

The fourth and last facet of the Snow (2001) model of symbolic interactionism is that of *human agency*. This is human action taken, either individually or collectively. Social and cultural restraints may limit the degree of human agency that the individual or group may perceive is possible. It also shapes the form of human agency. Perceptions of the webs of interactionism may cause overt or covert action to effect changes depending on social and cultural restraints. Human agency includes teachers' curriculum work and their understanding of educational purposes. If teachers feel that their students, their school, and they would benefit from high test scores, this becomes a focus of curriculum work. If teachers feel empowered to go beyond their scripted lesson plans, they can effect change in their curriculum.

RESULTS

The data from historical documents and teachers' insights in this study support the notion that reform measures were to be the champion of "rigor" and "equity" for all children, hence the label "No Child Left Behind," an updated iteration of the Elementary and Secondary Education Act. The dominance of top-down management style and the infusion of a one-size-fits-all, best practices mind-set sets the stage for teachers to react to the pressure to conform despite their personal judgment and understanding of curriculum.

Interactive Determinism and the Teachers' Words

The first facet of Snow's model, interactive determinism, details how perceptions by stakeholders in the process of curriculum reform perceive change and react to change. Curriculum reform can best be understood when analyzing the intersection of the "webs" connected to curriculum. Teachers in the case study felt caught in the webs surrounding the standardization of education and pulled in many directions. The teachers lamented that many, including themselves at times, react to the pressure of standardization by conforming to the expectations of delivering high test results out of fear or shame. These teachers commented that high test scores was what mattered in their district. The first participant, Claudia, worked with low-income women of color and took pride in embracing true rigor and promoting equitable opportunities for her students, but admitted to feeling uneasy about not always conforming to standardized, scripted curriculum.

Claudia *(Focus Group 1):* Sometimes when you hang out there, all by yourself, you get really tired, you get tired. And you feel alone. And then you feel like, like if you deviate at all from your [test results] scores, then they say well you know that's because you're not doing this [the district's prescribed curriculum]. And so we know you're stuck between a rock and a hard place. You know that it's not right not to go there [with the mandated curriculum based on standards], but if you do [deviate from the curriculum], and you have some wingnut kid on that day, on testing day that decides he doesn't feel like doing it, and then your testing numbers are off because of it ... then they're like, "Well you shouldn't have been doing what you were doing. You need to stick with exactly what the curriculum is."

The teachers in the study reflected that teachers feel ashamed if their students do not have a high passing rate for tests. Further, the teachers believed that high school graduation was the only chance for their economically challenged students to escape poverty; failing tests prevented students from graduation. The teachers likened this quandary to emotional blackmail because either they had to conform or their students may suffer.

Interactive determinism illustrates how the web of interested parties affects standardized education. Politicians perceived that teachers needed to be held accountable for implementing standards, and so they instituted tests to gauge how well educators teach the standards. Publishing companies created and marketed preparation materials in anticipation that teachers and schools would make time to prepare students for standardized tests. Curriculum specialists in school districts spent time preparing efficient lesson plans to cover material that would be tested to increase test scores. School district administrators monitored teachers' test scores to maintain a positive school rating. Parents and students expect that much time will be devoted to test preparation. Students question relevancy of curriculum but know they must pass tests. Teachers react and attempt to balance their ideas of appropriate curriculum with fears of failure on standardized tests.

Each of the three teachers in the case study described their attempts to "make sense" of the often conflicting discourses of the "webs" of standardization. Teachers in this study wanted to make the content for social studies rigorous for students and integrate different ways of teaching such as Problem Based Learning to promote equity, but feared the results if their students did not perform well on tests. The high school social studies teachers explained how this web of control influences many teachers to choose to teach to the test.

Symbolic Conceptual Framework

The rhetoric related to "rigor" and "equity" underlies a complex, symbolic conceptual framework that situates measurable results (test scores) as a justification for the need for a top-down style of accountability to keep teachers in line with reform efforts. The second facet of Snow's model exemplifies how the symbolic rhetoric of "rigor" and "equity" undergird corporate style of educational reform. Commonsense thinking would indicate the need for rigor and equity in schools as a positive goal; however, teachers questioned if the methods of standardization actually met the stated goals. The teachers spoke about "equity" as a selling point of reform, but reflected that in reality the symbolic justification of "equity" revealed a sort of "anti-equity" that was undemocratic for their low-income students who received a remedial approach to curriculum.

Further, the rhetoric of "rigor" in testing and accountability systems delivered inverse results in light of the discipline of social studies and negated the inherent authenticity of the discipline. Rather than empowering students as members of a democratic society with access to an equitable system, students in these economically challenged schools were relegated to pseudo-intellectual experiences formed by scripted curricula and powered by lower-level thinking skills. The resulting data from the teachers in the study reveal that the reality of "at-risk" (economically challenged) students incorporates a "tracking" mechanism that sorts students and robs many of opportunities for rich curriculum.

The taken-for-granted notion surrounding standardized education is that the standards will provide a "rigorous" course of study for students, and testing would "shine a light" on the performance of "at-risk" groups of students (Lauen & Gaddis, 2012). Terms such as "rigor" and "accountability" became symbols of the benefits of a standardized education. By testing all students on a standardized body of knowledge, reform was framed as a measure to reassure the public that teachers are providing an equitable and rigorous education for all students. A teacher in the case study criticized the use of the word "rigor" when connected to the standardized curriculum. No Child Left Behind promised rigorous standards. Anyone who argued against the rigor of standardized testing would appear to limit a student's right to an appropriate education. But largely, "rigor" became a symbolic term and did not play out in the implementation of standardized education.

Xraju *(Focus Group 1):* I think the state of Texas has developed a curriculum to make our students stupid. And it really doesn't teach them any critical thinking. A lot of our, and I'm sure you heard it from the other teachers, people are just teaching to the test. They're teaching kids how to test, they're not teaching any of the actual skills [of the discipline]. They keep telling us. They keep throwing that work rigor, rigor, rigor, and then you look at the test, then there's no need for rigor there.

Xraju *(Focus Group 2):* As rigorous the standards as the state claims they are, they're not. And if you look at all their vocabulary, it's all "define," "describe," "identify." If you look at Bloom's Taxonomy, I mean that's low-level Bloom's [Bloom's Taxonomy]. And the only problem with our TEKS [Texas state standards] is that the scope of it is so large, but, the skills it's requiring to do are basic.

This teacher wanted to provide a rigorous curriculum that promoted a sense of critical and historical thinking, but thinking of that sort is not promoted in the social studies curriculum in Texas, he felt. When the Texas social studies standards were revised in 2010, the popular press and even conservative think tanks condemned the standards as simplistic and lacking a variety of historical perspectives (Robelen, 2010; Stern & Stern, 2011; Williams, 2010). This teacher, Xraju, admitted to focusing only on information that would be tested, even if students demonstrated an interest or asked probing questions outside of the standards for the social studies class. Claudia spoke to this concern as well.

Claudia *(Focus Group 3):* If you can't read and write, you can't function in this world period. Period. You can't do any of your science or math. And I said so, that is the most important thing that we teach at that school. It is the most important thing that is taught in each and every solitary school. And it's not taught. It's shoved, it's regurgitated ... [later in the same focus group] You never have to think for yourself. So they graduate never having had to construct their own thoughts.

Claudia relates higher-order thinking skills as important to rigor, but explains that the scripted curriculum merely requires "regurgitation" with no real opportunities for authentic thoughts or reflection.

Emergence

Emergence, the third facet of Snow's symbolic interactionism, refers to the affective and cognitive changes by teachers related to the standardization of curriculum. The emergence facet of symbolic interactionalism theory frames the standards as important knowledge that all students should know. Terms in education have changed since the inception of standardized education. Terms previously found only in business have become the vernacular of education and frame the process of top-down pressure to conform to standardized knowledge sets.

Principals are now administrators. Parents and students have become consumers of education. Tests have become tools for teacher accountability, and learning goals in curriculum target measurable objectives. Teacher efficacy has been reduced to quantifiable data, test scores. Evaluation refers to students' ability to meet minimum standards as measured on tests given on a certain day of the year.

The more conforming teacher in the study, Xraju, admitted to teaching flawed standards and having students bored and resentful. His responses in the follow-up interview demonstrated the difficulty of being emerged in the phenomenon of standardization of knowledge. Xraju was the most "successful" teacher in the district on standardized exams and winner of the social studies department teacher of the year award for his district.

Xraju *(Follow-up interview):* The Texas TEKS, it's somewhat racist what they teach, and a lot of historians and a lot of scholars, argue with what politicians and others want them to have in the TEKS and so. Umm, I can agree with this, the dominant group in our society does want our students to learn a certain amount, or have a certain knowledge. And they're the ones who get to determine what that knowledge is. So, how do you remedy that? You help the kids pass the exam that they need to, but then you supplement, supplement, and supplement. Because you know my class is used as a breaking class [for advanced placement], and I hate to admit it, but that's what it is. It's used as a breaking class. Their sophomore year, they hate me. I, I am monster; I am everything that you can imagine. Every cuss word is used in their mind somewhere . . . But by the time they're seniors, the ones that have survived are like, well you're not a jerk.

Xraju explained how he covers the required standards, yet he confessed that he tries to "weed out" students to move them out of the Advanced Placement classes because there are very few spots. This forces students into being tracked in lower-level classes with fewer academic and cognitive demands.

Kelly talked about changes in her affective and cognitive views of teaching regarding teaching students in order to pass the TAKS. Although she says she did not teach exactly to the test, she did use the scripted curriculum when she taught in the regular education program.

Kelly *(Focus Group 1)*: I remember being too terrified that some of my kids who were ELL [English Language Learners], or you know, I had a very high special ed population, I worried that they would not pass the TAKS test, and it's not that I taught to the test . . . I didn't want that to be something that kept them from graduating high school. I couldn't imagine having some of those kids like not being able to leave the school because like they couldn't pass the US history TAKS test. So I think I probably had less freedom to stray from the TEKS and the curriculum in that course because I felt that in the end it would potentially be a disservice to those kids.

Now that Kelly is teaching in a magnet school, she admits that she has freedom to teach beyond the TEKS (standards) to provide a thoughtful, rigorous curriculum. She laments that the mandated curriculum is a whitewashed, prescribed series of activities and lessons. When Kelly shared concerned about marginalized groups being ignored, Claudia asserted that she would have to go beyond the standards to include marginalized groups because the standards do not fairly address all persons who contributed to American history, including women.

Claudia *(Focus Group 1)*: Any marginalized group . . . is pretty much gone, that's correct. And I teach in an all girls school! How can I sit there, and I can't do it. I couldn't do it with a good conscious . . . I tell you right now I would openly defy what the state's TEKS are and I would teach the course the way it should be taught.

Claudia shared concern that her students, nearly 100% students of color, would not find the standards relevant to them. Further, she believed that the standards do not encourage students to challenge current social systems that discriminate against marginalized groups.

Human Agency

Kumashiro (2012) wrote insightfully of how the movement to standardize teachers has created the image of the "bad teacher" as a scapegoat for school failure. The human agency facet of the Snow symbolic interactionism model of analysis offers teachers a choice to conform to or rebel against standardized education. Some teachers strive to present relevant courses of study and challenge standardized knowledge as presented by the state. But others fall in line with the curriculum in order to have their students pass tests and make the teacher look "good." Claudia does not consider herself or her students as a failure, but blames other teachers for failing students.

Claudia *(Focus Group 1):* These kids [in her magnet school] are the same neighborhood kids that go to every other school in River City District . . . if you tell me that those kids can't do what mine just did. They come from the same neighborhood. They get on the same bus, and they change places at the same depot. That's crap. It's the teachers who don't want to do it.

Claudia falls into the trap of blaming teachers in low-income area schools for their students' failure. She fails to consider that *her* students may come from the same neighborhoods as students in neighboring tradition schools, but her students' parents demonstrate that education is a priority in the household by bringing their students to the magnet school.

Xraju also blamed teachers for poor school performance. Further, he gauged his success by getting kids to pass standardized tests.

Xraju *(Final follow-up interview):* So you know what does make a good teacher. Who makes a good teacher? I don't even know if I'm a good teacher. Sometimes I think, that lesson sucked, I was even bored in my class. I was bored hearing myself talk. But it's like you know, I don't even know who would make a good teacher . . . There's a group of teachers that nicknamed me the "Golden Boy." 'Cause I was the successful one. And it's like oh there he is doing everything that he needs to do to get his kids pass. And working hard to get his kids passed.

Teachers seem to have difficulty judging "bad" and "good" when it comes to their teaching due to the conflicting demands of meeting the requirements for testing and the demands of teaching from a social justice perspective.

To varying degrees, however, the teachers in this study did feel a sense of agency to incorporate intellectual skills and critical analysis into their social studies curriculum. Now that Kelly is teaching at a magnet school, she feels a sense of agency to question the institutional knowledge that is prepackaged in the state-mandated standards.

Kelly *(Final follow-up interview):* Because it's this institutional knowledge that they [people who create the standards] were afraid, if I didn't do it, didn't do it the right way, kids wouldn't really know. Wouldn't really know what? And there's this really interesting thing [counternarrative], and I think it's a social justice issue. Like I must carry on this institutionalized knowledge that is wrong. And incorrect, and actually really bad . . . And I think kids appreciated that when I brought that [counternarrative] to their attention. Most of my kids would say like, "Yeah, why have they been . . . lying to us this whole time . . . And that actually piques their interest in that there's all this new knowledge out there that's not new. They just have never ever been taught that [counternarrative].

Xraju also explained that in his higher-level classes, he did take time to develop varying perspectives related to history. He included journals, headlines, and other texts that presented Adolf Hitler as a positive force for the quality of life of Germans in the context of post–World War I reconstruction. Claudia discussed a lesson she conducted in racism; she explained how she allowed students to consider context as an important factor in history. The three teachers admitted that their advanced classes did have some opportunities for critical thought and relevant curriculum. Yet all three teachers admitted that doing so was a balancing act between test performance and authentic, rigorous learning about historical skills such as perspective.

CONCLUSION

The study participants (all three teachers) told of their fear of blame and shame if test scores were to fall. They felt conflicted about teaching students to perform well on tests at the expense of teaching to promote transformative goals for students. The teachers, to varying degrees, discussed their balancing act between complicit participation in the standardized education movement, and their push-back measures to infuse democracy into their social studies curriculum through providing critical lesson approaches (rigor) that challenge social narratives and systems (equity). This angst illustrates how the webs of symbolic interactionism in corporate-style reform (Snow, 2001) bind teachers through fear of failure and reprisals and call for teachers to exercise their sense of human agency to effect change.

Further, the historical analysis of the present corporate style of educational reform has its roots in committees with business executives developing rhetorical concepts of "rigor" and "equity" with little understanding from an educational perspective on how those goals could be defined and implemented. The teachers in the study believed that the resulting reform actually produced a less than rigorous curriculum, especially for students of color who live in poverty. The resulting curriculum has little relevance for their students and results in their students being tracked into remedial classes. In these classes, students are preparing to take tests, not preparing to enter into society on a level standing. Further, the standardized curriculum reinforces the social narrative that subjected these students to a life of poverty and discrimination (Martinez & Martinez, 2002). Often these students drop out of school, and even if they graduate, have little preparation for college (Ogawa, Sandholtz, Martinez-Flores, & Scribner, 2003).

Corporate-style educational reform, according to the teachers in this study, impoverishes critical thinking skills, weakens the traditional approach of social studies as a study of existing social structures, and binds teachers to a watered-down, biased version of history through intimidation and reprisals. These teachers, though they perceived a lack of agency, demonstrated varying levels of desire to be curriculum intellectuals and go beyond established educational standards. Xraju tended to follow the district's expectations most of the time and admitted that earning high passing rates often led to bored and resentful students. Claudia presented a more critical, thoughtful curriculum, but worried about reprisals if her students' test scores fell. Only Kelly, upon transferring to a magnet school, felt freedom to teach her students to be critical thinkers. Only through a relevant curriculum will teachers encourage students to think deeply about social studies and the implications for their lives (Schwab, 1983).

REFERENCES

Achinstein, B., & Ogawa, R. T. (2012). New teachers of color and culturally responsive teaching in an era of educational accountability: Caught in a double bind. *Journal of Educational Change, 13*(1), 1–39.

Au, W. (2007). High-stakes testing and curricular control: A qualitative metasynthesis. *American Educational Research Journal, 36*(5), 258–267.

Booher-Jennings, J. (2005). Below the bubble: "Educational triage" and the Texas accountability system. *American Educational Research Journal, 42*(2), 231–268. doi: 10.3102/00028312042002231

Craig, C. J. (2009). The contested classroom space: A decade of lived educational policy in Texas. *American Educational Research Journal, 46*(4), 1034–1059.

Dewey, J. (1916). *Democracy and education.* (Original work published Retrieved April 1, 2012, from Macmillan Co. website: http://www.ilt.columbia.edu/publications/dewey.html

Eisner, E. W. (2003). Questionable assumptions about schooling. *Phi Delta Kappan, 84*(9), 648–657.

Fenwick, L. (2012). Limiting opportunities to learn in upper-secondary schooling: Differentiation and performance assessment in the context of standards-based curriculum reform. *Curriculum Inquiry, 42*(5), 629–682. doi: 10.1111/j.1467-873x.2012.00609.x

Funkhouser, C. (1988). For the record: An editorial review of Senate Bill 994. *Teacher Education & Practice, 5*(1), 31–41.

Lauen, D. L, & Gaddis, M. S. (2012). Shining a light or fumbling in the dark? The effects of NCLB's sub-group specific accountability on student achievement. *Educational Evaluation and Policy Analysis 34*(2), 185–208. Retrieved November 11, 2013, from http://epa.sagepublcom/content/34/2/185

Glaser, B. G., & Strauss, A. L. (1967). *The discovery of grounded theory: Strategies for qualitative research.* Chicago, IL: Aldine.

Gunzenhauser, M. G. (2006). Normalizing the educated subject: A Foucaultian analysis of high-stakes testing. *Educational Studies (American Educational Studies Association), 39*(3), 241–259.

Hamel, F. L., & Ryken, A. E. (2010). Rehearsing professional roles in community: Teacher identity development in a school-university partnership. *Teacher Development, 14*(3), 335–350.

Hamilton, L. S., Stecher, B. M., March, J. A., McCombs, J. S., Robyn, A., Russell, J. L., Naftel, S., & Barney, H. (2007). *Standards-based accountability under No Child Left Behind: Experiences of teachers and administrators in three states.* Santa Monica, CA: RAND Corporation.

Haney, W. (2000). The myth of the Texas miracle in education. *Education Policy Analysis Archives, 8*(41). Retrieved October 15, 2012 from http://epaa.asu.edu/ojs/article/view/432

Hanna, J. (2005). The Elementary and Secondary Education Act: 40 years later. *President and Fellows of Harvard College.*

Hobby, W. (2010). Bill Hobby on the 1984 education reform battle. *The Texas Tribune.* Retrieved June 2012 from http://www.texastribune.org/texas-legislature/texas-legislature/bill-hobby-on-the-1984-education-reform-battle/

Holme, J. J., & Rangel, W. S. (2011). Putting school reform in its place: Social geography, organizational social capital, and school performance. *American Educational Research Journal, 20*(10), 1–27. doi: 10.3102/000283110.3102/0 002831211423316

Hursh, D. (2005). Neo-liberalism, markets and accountability: Transforming education and undermining democracy in the United States and England. *Policy Futures in Education, 3*(1), 3–15.

Joseph, P. B. (2011). *Cultures of Curriculum* (2nd ed). New York: Routledge.

Kumashiro, K. K. (2012). *Bad teacher!: How blaming teachers distorts the bigger picture.* New York, NY: Teachers College Press.

Lather, P. (2006). Foucauldian scientificity: Rethinking the nexus of qualitative research and educational policy analysis. *International Journal of Qualitative Studies in Education, 19*(6), 783–791.

Louis, K. S., Febey, K., & Schroeder, R. (2005). State-mandated accountability in high schools: Teachers' interpretations of a new era. *Educational Evaluation and Policy Analysis, 27*(2), 177–204.

Martinez, T. P., & Martinez, A. P. (2002). The lowdown on dropouts, in Texas and elsewhere: Interesting findings from Texas media, IDRA and other researchers. *Hispanic Outlook in Higher Education, 12*(18), 11.

McNeil, L. M. (1988). Contradictions of control, part 2: Teachers, students, and curriculum. *The Phi Delta Kappan, 69*(6), 432–438.

McNeil, L. M. (2000). *Contradictions of school reform: Educational costs of standardized testing.* New York, NY: Routledge.

Null, W. (2011). *Curriculum: From theory to practice.* Lanham, MD: Rowman & Littlefield.

Ogawa, R. R., Sandholtz, J. H., Martinez-Flores, M., & Scribner, S. P. (2003). The substantive and symbolic consequences of a district's standards-based curriculum. *American Educational Research Journal, 40*(1), 147–176. doi: 10.3102/00028312040001147

Olsen, B., & Sexton, D. (2009). Threat rigidity, school reform, and how teachers view their work inside current education policy contexts. *American Educational Research Journal, 46*(1), 9–44. doi: 10.3102/0002831208320573

Ravitch, D. (2010). *The death and life of the great American school system.* New York, NY: Basic Books.

Robelen, E. (2010). Civil rights groups file complaint over Texas standards. Retrieved May 2011 from http://blogs.edweek.org/edweek/curriculum/2010/12/texas_naacp_files_federal_comp.html?qs=texas+social+studies+standards

Root, D. A. (2013). *Purpose, policy, and possibilities: Social studies teachers' sensemaking of curriculum* (Order No. 3563234, University of Texas at San Antonio). *ProQuest Dissertations and Theses.* Retrieved November 25, 2013 from http://search.proquest.com/docview/1412353216?accountid=7122 (1412353216)

Ryan, R. M., & Weinstein, N. (2009). Undermining quality teaching and learning: A self-determination theory perspective on high-stakes testing. *Theory and Research in Education, 7*(2), 224–233. doi: 10.1177/1477878509104327

Salinas, C. S., & Reidel, M. (2007). The cultural politics of the Texas educational reform agenda: Examining who gets what, when, and how. *Anthropology and Education Quarterly, 38*(1), 42–56.

Schwab, J. J. (1971). The practical: Arts of eclectic. *The School Review, 79*(4), 493–542.

Schwab, J. J. (1983). The Practical 4: Something for curriculum professors to do. *Curriculum Inquiry, 13*(3), 239–265.

Sleeter, C. (2008). Equity, democracy, and neoliberal assaults on teacher education. *Teaching and Teacher Education, 24*(8), 1947–1957.

Snow, D. A. (2001). Extending and broadening Blumer's conceptualization of symbolic interactionism. *Symbolic Interactionism, 24*(3), 367–377.

Stern, S. M. Stern, J. A. (2011). The state of state U. S. history standards 2011. from Thomas B. Fordham Institute: Advancing Educational Excellence. Retrieved November 12, 2012 from http://ritter.tea.state.tx.us/rules/tac/chapter113/index.html

Taubman, P. M. (2009). *Teaching by numbers: Deconstructing the discourse of standards and accountability in education.* New York, NY: Routledge.

Texas Education Agency. (2011). Social Studies TEKS. Retrieved May 3, 2012 from http://www.tea.state.tx.us/index2.aspx?id=3643

Texas Education Agency. (2012). STAAR Resources. Retrieved December 2, 2013 from http://www.tea.state.tx.us/student.assessment/staar/

Texas Education Agency. (2013). End of Course (EOC) Assessments. Retrieved November 2, 2013 from http://www.tea.state.tx.us/index3.aspx?id=3302

Williams, J. K. (2010). God's country: Religion and the evolution of the social studies curriculum in Texas. *American Educational History Journal, 37*(2), 437–454.

5   An Inquiry into the Myth of Neutrality
Curriculum and Pedagogy in an Age of Terrorism

Jessica A. Heybach

INTRODUCTION

The dilemma of neutrality, as both a form of teacher identity and a curricular demand, has persisted since the inception of public schooling in America. Where does the concept and demand for neutrality come from, *really*, and what end is sought in the creation of an educational experience predicated on neutrality, and a pedagogy conceived in "neutral" terms? These questions have puzzled social foundations of education scholars since the early 20th century for sure, but could plausibly be traced to Socrates's decision to "banish the poets." Education's role in indoctrination, influence, political manipulation, and the shaping of souls has always garnered intense attention; however, contemporary standardization and the "scripting" of an entire profession now pose new challenges in terms of deconstructing the myth of teacher neutrality.

This chapter seeks to expose the mythological character of teacher neutrality by exposing the nationalistic neoliberal corporate ideology lurking in discussions of curriculum in the post-9/11 and post-NCLB (No Child Left Behind) context (see Ravitch, 2013, for a discussion of neoliberal corporate school reform). Beyond the mandates of corporate reforms such as efficiency, accountability, competition, and an unrelenting economic imperative, this ideology is predicated on a hypernationalistic rhetoric that has enveloped educational discourse regarding what is appropriate for American children to know about the world they inhabit. At the same time, a discourse of fear has settled deep into the marrow of teachers' identity as they take the blame for countless social ills (e.g., school shootings, bullying, escalating obesity rates, the mental health status of our children, academic failure, and an unprepared global workforce). With these factors in mind, my argument begins with the assumption that both neoliberal corporate rhetoric and a discourse of fear—both in education and in issues of difficult knowledge—buttress the myth of neutrality. Thus educational critics are left to wonder: Who benefits from the persistent myth of neutrality in teacher education and the resulting obedience that follows such an ideology? Before proceeding with this argument, however, I'd like to qualify my use of the word "myth."

Roland Barthes (1957/1972), semiotician and philosopher, describes myth as a type of speech propagated with a social use in society: "Everything can be a myth provided it is conveyed by a discourse" (p. 109). This definition helps to reveal how teacher neutrality has been reinforced again and again, so much so that educators often feel neutrality to be a de facto mandate. Thus I want to focus on the aspect of "naturalization" as described by Barthes:

> The naturalization of the concept [is] the essential function of myth . . . In a first (exclusively linguistic) system, causality would be, literally, natural: fruit and vegetable prices fall because they are in season. In the second (mythical) system, causality is artificial, false; but it creeps, so to speak, through the back door of Nature. This is why *myth is experienced as innocent speech*: not because its intentions are hidden—if they were hidden, they could not be efficacious—but because they are naturalized. (p. 131, emphasis added)

If Barthes is correct and myths are experienced as forms of seemingly "innocent speech" and subsequently normalized, then this may help to explain why teachers cling to the notion of neutrality as a desired identity—that is, as an unquestioned a priori—without the recognition that a "neutral" curriculum created by corporate textbook publishers and venture philanthropists is in fact not neutral at all. I want to suggest that the imaginary of this apparent neutrality poses a greater danger to democracy than educators tend to realize.

Rather than tracing the discrepancies between educational corporatization and the demand for teachers to be neutral (how could corporate-driven, economic imperatives ever be seen as neutral?), I will describe how assumptions of neutrality influence how teachers themselves experience controversial content in the teacher education classrooms with particular attention to issues of human rights regarding the recent war in Iraq. The omission of controversial content regarding American identity and policies, in the wake of 9/11, has been well documented and need not be rehearsed in these pages (Apple, 1999; Evans, 2004; Hess & Stoddard, 2008). This study explores how teachers consciously and unconsciously omit difficult knowledge regarding issues of human rights and the Iraq War from the classroom. Adopting a neutral posture regarding such issues generally has become everyday practice and a commonsense attitude among many educators who claim these topics are inappropriate for school-aged children, or that such knowledge disrupts more comforting views of American identity.

A QUALITATIVE INQUIRY INTO THE VISUAL CULTURE OF WAR AND DIFFICULT KNOWLEDGE

This present inquiry is a part of a much larger qualitative study regarding critical aesthetic pedagogy in teacher education that investigated teacher neutrality via the public and private discourse of teachers concerning recent American military actions (See Freedman [2003] for a complete discussion of visual culture in education). The study began by asking participants to respond to representations of the Abu Ghraib prison scandal. In particular, participants were asked to view the artwork of Malaquias Montoya and the photographic history of the 2004 Abu Ghraib prison scandal that occurred during the early years of the Iraq War. The aim of this aesthetic content was to purposely push participants out of their comfort zone and challenge the commonsense logic that has enveloped the war in Iraq as being necessary and just, given the events of 9/11 (Garoian & Gaudelius, 2008; Mitchell 2011). The study was conducted at a large regional public institution of higher education in multiple foundations of education classrooms, both undergraduate and graduate levels. The participants consisted of preservice and in-service teacher education students as well as students in school support staff roles (counseling, coaching, para-professional, etc.).

Before classroom discussions began, participants completed a questionnaire regarding their background in education, their reasons for wanting to be an educator, and their familiarity with the Iraq War and the issue of state-sponsored torture. A sample of participant responses to the question "Why do you want to be an educator" can be summarized with the following comments: "I feel morally obligated to teach our future leaders"; "I enjoy helping children discover new information and new ways of learning"; and "I want to spark the genius in each young individual I meet." Many participants reported a desire to "be a positive influence in students' lives," as well as "prepare students to be critical thinkers."

The survey questions regarding the Iraq War showed that few considered themselves "well-informed" on the topic unless they were married to or related to a member of the military, and even fewer were familiar with the issue of state-sponsored torture and the Abu Ghraib prison scandal. However, there were blanket statements such as "I don't agree with torture," or "It is not right" expressed by participants even though they claimed unfamiliarity with the particularities of the Abu Ghraib prison scandal. All of the classrooms visits were purposefully arranged so that I had not previously met the participants, nor was I their instructor of record. These choices were made to avoid my influence over their responses. Before examining these testimonials, however, I want to provide some brief biographical and historical context into the content of the study.

WHO IS MALAQUIAS MONTOYA?

Malaquias Montoya is an American artist, born in Albuquerque, New Mexico. Montoya came of age in the 1960s and was a significant catalyst in the Chicano civil rights movement. The central purpose of his work is the utilization of art to expose social injustices and to shape a social-justice-oriented consciousness. Deeply influenced by an indigenous spirit and relationship to the disenfranchised voices in American society, Montoya's (n.d. a) self-description is:

> Through our images we are the creators of culture and it is our responsibility that they are of our times. My work depicts honesty and promotes an attitude towards existing reality; a confrontational attitude, one of change rather than adaptability—images of our time and for our contemporaries . . . This form allows me to awaken consciousness, to reveal reality and to actively work to transform it. What better function for art at this time? A voice for the voiceless. (Bienvenidos section, para. 1–2)

Montoya offers his "confrontational attitude" to the world as a social commentary that blends art, aesthetics, and politics in a deliberate and meaningful way to "reveal reality." His work has been described by Peter H. Selz and Susan Landauer (2006) as the art of "relevance and power" (p. 176). The core of his work is a critical reflection of his own experiences growing up in the cultural malaise of 1960s American society.

Montoya's childhood of strife and considerable difficulty helped fuel his desire to change the circumstances of the lives of Chicano Americans. In 1957, Montoya enlisted in the US Marine Corps and spent three years in the military. He credits this experience with influencing his realization that politically motivated, often profit-driven, public policy impacts the individual in often socially unjust ways. Military service afforded him, via the G.I. Bill, the opportunity to attend the University of California–Berkeley and realize a different life beyond the fields of California. In 1968, he cofounded the Mexican-American Liberation Art Front and has been considered "arguably the most influential Chicano artist in the movement" (Terezita, 2011, p. x).

Montoya's aesthetic expression draws attention to issues of human rights that seem to exist only on the fringe, or in the lives of those who are victimized by various systems of oppression. Artists that engage in this brand of social critique are often criticized for being too ideological and strident. Montoya (n.d. b) answers this charge by replying: "I must say my work is often referred to as propaganda art. I don't mind being labeled as such since I feel all work is propagandist in nature; it just depends who you want to propagandize for" (Objectives section, para. 1). In the wake of the American invasion of Iraq, Montoya found himself again working to expose the human impact that precipitates from military aggression and unchecked global power. In 2007, his exhibition *Globalization and War: The Aftermath* opened for audiences and spent the next several years on display at various galleries throughout the US. Before getting to the participants' reactions, a brief historical record of the events that led to Montoya's artwork will follow.

A BRIEF HISTORY OF ABU GHRAIB AND STATE-SPONSORED "TORTURE"

QUESTION: Mr. Secretary, a number of times from the podium you've said U.S. troops do not torture individuals. There was a joking colloquy one time here about the iron maiden, remarks—I mean, does this report undercut your notion that the U.S. doesn't torture, this is—is one of those rare exceptions here that torture took place?

SEC. DONALD RUMSFELD: I think that—I'm not a lawyer. My impression is that what has been charged thus far is abuse, which I believe technically is different from torture . . . Just a minute.

QUESTION *(Off mike)*: SEC. RUMSFELD: I don't know if the—it is correct to say what you just said, that torture has taken place, or that there's been a conviction for torture. And therefore I'm not going to address the torture word.

—*Defense Department Operational Update Briefing, May 4, 2004*

The moment the photographs that gave rise to the Abu Ghraib prison scandal were splashed across the evening news, the frequently obscured face of American power had been exposed—globally—and quickly the line distinguishing liberator from terrorist was blurred for many paying attention to these events in the spring of 2004.

Clearly the invasion of Iraq was always controversial and never particularly "popular"—the British Broadcasting Company (2003) reported that "between six and 10 million people are thought to have marched in up to 60 countries . . . the largest demonstrations of their kind since the Vietnam War" (para. 3). Yet despite popular opposition, the memory of 9/11 was repeatedly used to justify military action in Iraq. The media-induced confusion regarding the "truth" and the redefining of such concepts as "war," "torture," and "human rights" did much to confuse the American public's understanding of what constituted acceptable international behavior. By the time the images depicting torture at the hands of American troops appeared on *60 Minutes II*, significant damage—in the form of desensitization—had already been done to American perceptions regarding war, terrorism, and the human consequences of violence.

The images of the Abu Ghraib prison scandal depict acts of torture and violence that defy imagination. The now-famous Taguba Report (2004) described:

> That between October and December 2003, at the Abu Ghraib Confinement Facility (BCCF), numerous incidents of sadistic, blatant, and wanton criminal abuses were inflicted on several detainees. This systemic and illegal abuse of detainees was intentionally perpetrated by

several members of the military . . . The allegations of abuse were substantiated by detailed witness statements (ANNEX 26) and the discovery of extremely graphic photographic evidence. (Specific Finding of Facts #5 & #8)

The Taguba Report (2004) leaves little to the imagination and explicitly describes what occurred in fine detail. I have chosen not to paraphrase, or summarize, but rather invite the reader to remember what exactly occurred in the Abu Ghraib prison as a result of American's new policy of "enhanced interrogation" and torture:

> Punching, slapping, and kicking detainees; jumping on their naked feet. Videotaping and photographing naked male and female detainees. Forcibly arranging detainees in various sexually explicit positions for photographing. Forcing detainees to remove their clothing and keeping them naked for several days at a time. Forcing naked male detainees to wear women's underwear.
> Forcing groups of male detainees to masturbate themselves while being photographed and videotaped.
> Arranging naked male detainees in a pile and then jumping on them.
> Positioning a naked detainee on a MRE Box, with a sandbag on his head, and attaching wires to his fingers, toes, and penis to simulate electric torture.
> Writing "I am a Rapest" [sic] on the leg of a detainee alleged to have forcibly raped a 15-year old fellow detainee, and then photographing him naked.
> Placing a dog chain or strap around a naked detainee's neck and having a female Soldier pose for a picture.
> A male MP guard having sex with a female detainee.
> Using military working dogs (without muzzles) to intimidate and frighten detainees, and in at least one case biting and severely injuring a detainee.
> Taking photographs of dead Iraqi detainees. . . .
> Breaking chemical lights and pouring the phosphoric liquid on detainees.
> Threatening detainees with a charged 9mm pistol.
> Pouring cold water on naked detainees.
> Beating detainees with a broom handle and a chair.
> Threatening male detainees with rape.
> Allowing a military police guard to stitch the wound of a detainee who was injured after being slammed against the wall in his cell.
> Sodomizing a detainee with a chemical light and perhaps a broom stick.

These facts are undeniably horrific, but the governmental officials at the time chose to deny the moral atrocity of such acts. American citizens were repeatedly spoon-fed the story of a "few bad apples" to explain away these actions

(Sanchez & Philips, 2008, pp. 276–278). Consequently, a "few bad apples" reinforces the idea that these actions are the result of morally corrupt individuals and not that of institutions and official military policy sanctioned by various levels of government oversight. Conservative commentator Rush Limbaugh (2004) likened the acts to "boys being boys"—a fraternity prank to "blow some steam off" in the dead of night (para. 3). Shockingly, the only military personnel who were charged with any crimes were the low-ranking soldiers who *literally* committed the acts; to date, no commanding officer has been charged with any crime (Hersh, 2004). In a telling statement, at the close of the April 2004 Article 23 hearing for Sergeant Frederick, defense attorney Capt. Robert Shuck argued that the Army was "attempting to have these six soldiers atone for its sins" (as cited in Hersh, 2004, p. 28).

Prior to the release of the Abu Ghraib images, public discourse was riddled with the problem of redefining one important word—"torture"—because of the growing concern over the treatment of detainees in Guantanamo Bay, Cuba. It is worth noting in this regard how exactly Jay S. Bybee (2002), head of the Justice Department's Office of Legal Counsel (currently a federal judge on the Ninth Circuit Court of Appeals), understood the meaning of the word "torture":

> Certain acts may be cruel, inhuman, or degrading, but still not produce pain and suffering of the requisite intensity to fall within [a legal] proscription against torture ... we conclude that for an act to constitute torture ... it must inflict pain that is difficult to endure. Physical pain amounting to torture must be equivalent in intensity to the pain accompanying serious physical injury, such as organ failure, impairment of bodily function, or even death. (para. 2)

Such state-sponsored redefining of commonly understood words to suit the needs of those in power, to morally justify the unjustifiable, is dystopian indeed.

Prior to 9/11, the accepted meaning of "torture" at the state level was derived from the United Nation's Convention Against Torture (1984), which defined torture as follows:

> [Torture is] any act by which severe pain or suffering, whether physical or mental, is intentionally inflicted on a person for such purposes as obtaining from him or a third person information or a confession, punishing him for an act he or a third person has committed or is suspected of having committed, or intimidating or coercing him or a third person, or for any reason based on discrimination of any kind, when such pain or suffering is inflicted by or at the instigation of or with the consent or acquiescence of a public official or other person acting in an official capacity. It does not include pain or suffering arising only from, inherent in or incidental to lawful sanctions. (Part I, Article 1)

The UN document, ratified by the United States in 1994, states that *"no exceptional circumstances whatsoever*, whether a state of war or a threat of war, internal political instability or any other public emergency, may be invoked as a justification of torture" (Article 2, #2, emphasis added). Beyond the UN Convention Against Torture document, the US was and is legally bound to the Geneva Conventions (although the complicated history of this document will not be taken up in this chapter). What appears lost in the legal debates over definitions of torture is what I believe to be an unstated public pedagogy and visual culture of dystopia that induces a citizenry's tacit support of such acts. Moreover, this largely implicit cultural overlay operated to condition American citizens to normalize behavior that is in fact criminal.

In this connection, Susan Sontag (2004) argues that "to refuse to call what took place in Abu Ghraib—and what has taken place elsewhere in Iraq and in Afghanistan and at Guantánamo Bay—by its true name, torture, is as outrageous as the refusal to call the Rwandan genocide a genocide" (Section I, para. 3). Furthermore, Sontag (2004) argues that the Abu Ghraib images are particularly disturbing because the perpetrators in the photos are smiling, with their thumbs up, posing, as if they are showing the world their exceptionally good work:

> If there is something comparable to what these pictures show it would be some of the photographs of black victims of lynching taken between the 1880's and 1930's . . . The lynching photographs were souvenirs of a collective action whose participants felt perfectly justified in what they had done. So are the pictures from Abu Ghraib. (Section II, para. 2)

Clearly, this historical example serves as a reminder of the criminality that becomes possible when justification for such actions are collectively felt by a majority of a citizens. In hindsight, many Americans find it difficult to imagine that the lynching photos from late 19th- and early 20th-century America were not met with immediate collective action to stop such acts; a similar shock is expressed by those theorizing and paying attention to the Abu Ghraib prison scandal: Why did the images of prisoner abuse do so little to move American citizens to action?

VOICES FROM THE CLASSROOM: DIFFICULT KNOWLEDGE AS INAPPROPRIATE PEDAGOGY?

Although most of this study's participants did seem to reach a consensus that the use of images, in general, offer classrooms a powerful impetus for critical thinking and reflection, Montoya's artwork remained deeply controversial and outside the boundaries of acceptable classroom content. One participant exemplified this attitude with the comment: "I think using images is a very powerful educational tool and I think it's good for kids to be exposed to this, but I feel that this is slightly pushing an agenda too far, you know." Although I often recorded this type of opinion, in this instance, I felt the desire to push the issue and have participants explain what *exactly* was controversial about the artwork:

Researcher: And what is controversial about this work?
Alexandra: I just think that part of the controversy is that the author, the artist has a point of view and it is a solid point of view, that the killing and the war is affecting and destroying many innocent people. So there's two sides to that argument, but this artist is just portraying one . . . This is pretty extreme, so I guess that's why it is controversial.
Sophie: Well it is showing some very ugly things that we sometimes do what [we have] to do.

As someone who has devoted significant time and energy on issues of social justice within the classroom, I found myself frustrated by the repeated articulations of the idea that there should be "another side" to Montoya's work. Even though participants agreed that social studies and history curriculum "sugar-coats" reality and misleads students regarding the "truth" of American actions, participants still remained committed to the idea that Montoya was manipulating and exaggerating the view of America as an unjustified aggressor. As Alexandra stated above, "The artist has a . . . solid point of view, that the killing and the war is affecting and destroying many innocent people. So there's two sides to that argument, but this artist is just portraying one." Thus participants repeatedly advocated that there was "another side" to what occurred in the Abu Ghraib prison. The clear suggestion, then, was that this other side, if brought out and explored, would justify the actions Montoya was committed to critiquing.

The theme of "another side" to human rights violations became a preoccupation of my personal reflections throughout this study. I wrote the phrase "blaming the victim" on the transcripts and found myself often bothered by the direction of the conversations. Participants asserted the "other side" argument as if it had been established as fact, and few participants were willing to challenge this assumption once it was spoken in the classroom discussions. This sentiment is aptly reflected in the following participant comment:

> I don't think the people that were being tortured maybe deserved it, but they were obviously in that prison for a reason. Most of those people were caught trying to kill soldiers. That's why they were there in the first place. I'm not saying they should have been tortured, but they were by no means completely innocent by standards stuck in a prison.

The issue of innocence and lack thereof, as related to responsibility, helps to construct the understanding that the abuses at Abu Ghraib are of no real concern because the prisoners deserved it for "trying to kill soldiers." Another participant added, "I think in some ways, I don't know, some of these pictures made it seem like it was, I don't know, it was democracy, it was the way our country went about causing this violence ... all these atrocities." Yet, she quickly inserted, "But it wasn't just that, I mean there was like horrible, you know, stuff going on in Iraq long before we entered that country and there was horrible things being done to people, people lived in fear of their dictators, people were killed on a regular basis."

As participants began to express apprehension regarding Montoya's artwork and his exposure of "very ugly things," I probed students to tease out the difference between including a curriculum centered on the atrocities of the past and the controversial images of today's conflict:

Researcher: Does anyone feel that it's completely inappropriate even to bring up today's war? Some of you have mentioned that you teach about the Holocaust with images right, [and] it's state law ... that we teach about genocide, but many times I have heard people say I don't think it's appropriate for this [war in Iraq/Abu Ghraib] to be talked about now, so am I understanding this correctly?

Patricia: I think it would be inappropriate to in some degree to show images that would be of innocent people being harmed, because and even for older students because they have relatives or they have friends that are in the war right now and I think it would be almost too close to try to have that discussion with older students too close to them, that it could be more damaging than good.

Certainly, the audience for such images should be considered, but these images are already in the perpetual internet stream that our students consume daily. Thus what is the effectiveness of teacher-sponsored censorship? My effort to engage students to articulate what, precisely, made Montoya's images inappropriate did not elicit many meaningful responses. Rather, a deafening silence fell on the classroom, which, upon reflection, is quite meaningful in and of itself. Although I did not always probe directly given the emotional tone of these moments, this experience signals that the direct probing of difficult knowledge in a classroom does not necessarily produce the desired type of dialogue that is often favored by educators (Fieldnotes, June 2011). However, had I been the classroom teacher in this attempt to draw participants out, I may have been more successful. Fortunately, the participants' written journals did explore these ideas much more substantively than they were willing to articulate in a public discussion with peers.

PROTEST ART AS ANTI-AMERICAN PROPAGANDA?

The concern that Montoya was anti-American appeared at times throughout the classroom discussions. One participant wrote: "We are looking at

An Inquiry into the Myth of Neutrality 97

one side . . . anti U.S. . . . . I've seen movies where U.S. soldiers are buried alive as a form of torture . . . [the] Iraq people have no values, need no respect." This comment was by far the sharpest offered, revealing how deep these sentiments and emotions run. Furthermore, the comment highlights how these emotions are often connected to an image—"movies where U.S. soldiers are buried alive"—thus revealing that many do construct understandings of others based on powerful images, images often meant to exploit our emotions rather than critically interrogate our assumptions. Furthermore, there were participants who were concerned that Montoya's use of the American flag in the artwork was itself anti-American: "I find the use of the American flag very offensive," and "The American flag . . . has always had such positive symbolism (by how I was raised). Using it as binding and restraining someone is the opposite of how I view it." Moreover, some participants revealed their attachment to the image of the flag as a symbol of American identity rooted in notions of unquestioned goodness.

Another participant wrote about the theme of anti-Americanism and began by questioning the legitimacy of Montoya's perception of the war: "How much knowledge does this artist truly have about the conditions/conflict in Iraq?" As previously seen, these types of questions appeared often and seem emblematic of a desire to deflect the content of Montoya's artwork by attacking his integrity. This participant continued her journal with the following:

> [I] feel like this artwork is definitely portraying an agenda—Anti-American sentiment, which I don't agree with. It is good to not forget the human aspect of war and violence, and to show the suffering of those affected. I wish it could be done without pointing a finger—which this artist clearly did.

Based on my observations, it seems evident that the desire to suspend judgment and condemnation applied fairly readily when American actions were being deliberated. However, in many journal entries judgment and condemnation against other nations' actions (i.e., the Holocaust, Saddam Hussein, or Montoya) were rarely suspended or withheld. Thus participants seemed more at ease with critiquing the actions of "others" than with critiquing military actions done in the name of America.

The belief that the victims of Abu Ghraib must have been imprisoned for justifiable reasons was reflected quite frequently within the study. I initially coded these statements as "desires to believe," because there is very little factual evidence that the overwhelming majority of prisoners at Abu Ghraib engaged in anything that could be classified as "terrorism" (Jehl, Zernike, & Cushman, 2004; Taguba, 2004). Yet many participants seemed deeply invested in this belief. One participant wrote:

> Men were being tortured in the Abu Ghraib prison and treated inhumanely, but these men were also guilty of acts of terrorism against the

98   *Jessica A. Heybach*

> people who were trying to free them and their country from a cruel and ruthless dictator. They were by no means "innocent" of any wrong doing. Should they have been subjected to acts of torture in the manner they were, I think no, but if they were not carrying out acts of terrorism in the first place that never would have happened to begin with. Also, they were more likely to have been tortured by Saddam if he continued to rule Iraq without any trial or justification for being tortured.[1]

This, and similar passages, speak to the sophisticated reasoning that buttresses comments shared during the classroom dialogue. In much the same vein, another participant wrote, "September 11th changed a lot and the thought of raising children in the world makes me want the government to do what it can to make it safe." Another participant wrote regarding Montoya's artwork, "It seems that those that have died in the war were completely innocent victims. Though I don't believe that to be true. Of those that have died sure there have been some innocent victims, but how many have been terrorists?"

Many participants described the artwork as "one viewpoint," "[a] limited view of what happens in Iraq," and "one man's opinion." Of course, this is true given that we viewed only the work of Montoya; however, participants used these statements as an indicator that the artwork need not be taken as seriously because it was *just* "one man's opinion." For example, one participant wrote: "I do not care for the artwork. This is one man's opinion on war. War will always bring tragedy and success for both sides. His images focus solely on innocent victims of war and the tragedy and violence they endure."

Participants returned to the theme of "other side" of the images that Montoya was leaving out—the "other side" that would explain why such military actions were warranted. One participant wrote:

> I agree with the comment that it is one man's opinion of what goes on in Iraq in regards to this war. I too was not a big fan of these pictures ... I do believe it happens, but it seemed to point to the conclusion that all soldiers and figures of power in war act this way and I really disagree with that.

I'm not sure Montoya is pointing "to the conclusion that all soldiers and figures of power in war act this way"; rather Montoya is asking citizens to recognize that soldiers are forced to commit crimes because of distant policies that the American public sustain in our daily obedience to the status quo. Furthermore, participants expressed unease as to the intent of Montoya's work, as one participant wrote: "I wonder if some artists create such strong images to gain the attention of other people, and I wonder if these images represent their true feelings or if they are meant to promote their names and careers." Thus there appeared, in many of these entries, an expressed degree of distrust for Montoya that clearly "informed" their interpretation of his artwork.

In their written testimonies, participants consistently articulated the idea that Montoya was unfairly judging military actions (and soldiers in particular). One participant wrote: "It is one thing to shine a spotlight on abuses by the US and another thing to paint it as if the US systematically murders innocent people. In my opinion he takes it too far." The blurring of "victim" and "victimizer" is certainly achieved in Montoya's work and appears to be of concern—thus, given the high level of ambiguity and critique embodied in Montoya's images, it is much easier to dismiss, deny, repress, and adhere to notions of neutrality and commonsense notions of appropriateness (See Butler (2009) for a discussion of the larger issue of grieving for other's lives that are portrayed as less than human).

DIFFICULT KNOWLEDGE AND NEOLIBERAL CURRICULAR "NEUTRALITY"

Deborah Britzman (1991, 1998, 2000a, 2000b) has long argued that learning to teach often requires the abandonment of long-held beliefs that occur at both the conscious and unconscious levels, and the resulting radical modification of one's identity contains the hallmarks of "difficult knowledge." Bonnell and Simon (2007) describe the theory of difficult knowledge as what "happens when one's conceptual frameworks, emotional attachments, and conscious and unconscious desires delimit one's ability to settle the meaning of past events" (p. 68–9). Clearly, the artwork in this study called into question many of the participants' long-held beliefs regarding the ethics of American actions and the nature of what it means to be a teacher in a post-9/11 context (war, terrorism, uncertainty, etc.). Specifically, participants were unable to recognize the contradiction between their desire to "create critical thinkers" and "spark genius," while at the same time believing that Montoya had no right to question American actions whatsoever. Their repeated desire to uphold the standard of classrooms as neutral spaces might be necessary, practically speaking (i.e., pressure from school administration), but must be renegotiated to uncover how antidemocratic this practice actually is as it obscures reality and deadens civic connections from taking root.

Confronting the difficult knowledge embedded in Montoya's artwork and images of torture found many participants hiding behind notions of neutrality and age appropriateness. The repeated commitment to show "all sides" and the "other side" of torture, I believe, is meant only to neutralize Montoya's critique and render his questions irrelevant to classroom life. How many teachers, in equal part, include a substantive inquiry into Holocaust deniers in their curricular exploration of the events of World War II? I assume not many, because this would be viewed as absurd given the enormous number of verifiable facts and images that command our attention regarding Nazi concentration camps. Yet the same logic does not seem to be applied to contemporary wars and conflicts. Of course, there are moral considerations in showing the *actual* photographs of the Abu Ghraib prison scandal to students, and differences surrounding the inclusion of Montoya's images in elementary classrooms as opposed to high school classrooms (Parsons 1987a, 1987b); however, why are teachers in near universal agreement with showing images of the Holocaust or past atrocities that found America on the right side of history, and not images that question America's role in current global events?

Until American educators realize that teacher neutrality as an identity supports only the curricular demands of corporate-owned textbook publishers, the aim of critical thinking will remain irrelevant and detached from the lived experience of our students in classrooms. Doyle (2011), a high school teacher, recently wrote in regard to the omission of the wars in Iraq and Afghanistan in school curriculum that "in my school, and hundreds like it, students are isolated from firsthand accounts and the formal study of events that textbooks will one day proclaim as defining experiences of their generation" (p. 20). This should be a significant universal concern of educators who seem committed to "creating critical thinkers" and concerned that students should be prepared for the world they meet after K–12 schooling. Doyle (2011) continues his argument by stating: "Schools tend not to teach many, perhaps most, headline-making problems: climate change, debt crises, the national and international polarization of wealth, revolutions in the Middle East, and oil dependence. No wonder we commemorate 9/11 without teaching it as historical cause and effect. Students can graduate from many, perhaps most, high schools today and remain tragically naïve about the public history of their own times" (p. 21). How can this be? How has "historical cause and effect" come to be seen outside the boundaries of a classroom, or further yet, as anti-American?

In the wake of 9/11, and in the unending wars that followed, many educational researchers scrambled to make curricular sense of these events—events in real time—that do not have the benefit of historical distance. Although the events of the Abu Ghraib prison scandal are rarely spoken of in the current study of curriculum and educators appear to not take seriously the demand for textbooks to reveal difficult realities to students, I want to take a cue from the empirical work regarding 9/11 and terrorism in textbooks that has been systemically investigated. Hess and Stoddard (2007) embarked on a look at 9/11 and terrorism in textbooks and have argued that textbook publishers suffer from a desire to mobilize 9/11 as symbolically important and terrorism as a corollary event that impacts America, but they do so by repeatedly oversimplifying the complexity of such events. Hess, Stoddard, and Murto (2008) write:

> Texts fail to treat events deemed controversial in society as such, and fail to provide students with the tools to successfully analyze and deliberate

the few issues about which they ask students to think intensely. Consequently, in the main, the textbooks fait to help young people do what is most needed during extremely troubling times—which is to think deeply and hard. (p. 221)

Not surprisingly, curriculum regarding 9/11 has championed the creation of a nationalistic sympathy while at the same time has been written as if its readers already know what happened (Hess, Stoddard, & Murto, 2008). Also, there exists significant confusion *across* textbooks regarding how to define terrorism and what qualifies as an act of terrorism (Hess, Stoddard, & Murto, 2008). Yet, within a single textbook volume, the topic of terrorism tends to be tidy and settled, with little room for authentic negotiation. This seems to a lesser degree to remind me of the contestation over the word "torture" and suggests that something is gained or lost in complicating the reality all children since 2001 have been born into—a world at war. Finally, it appears that the educators in this study possess the same naïve narrative that occupies our textbooks and are willing to defend such an analysis.

Perhaps a better means to achieve a citizenry capable of "critical thinking" would be to include ideas, images, and concepts that actually compel students to *become thinkers* by questioning and allow students to inquire into the state of reality. But first, teachers themselves must reconsider their adherence to standardized forms of curriculum propagated by corporations with a neoliberal agenda that profits from textbook-sponsored confusion regarding the nature of America. Furthermore, only a teacher identity that recognizes the unethical logic at heart in the demand for neutrality will be able to truly meet the demands of a 21st-century schooling experience. Rather, the 24-hour news cycle and the proliferation of electronic information could easily, and does in some quarters, allow teachers to construct their own curriculum regarding current events. Only by creating critical curricular experiences that call into question what it is students think they believe, rather than the perpetuation of the long-criticized "standardized" curriculum and a teacher identity that supports only those in positions of economic power—corporations—can educators ever hope to create the "critical thinkers" for whom they long.

NOTES

1. Had I been the classroom teacher, I could have reminded this participant that American military policy has led to the indefinite detention of detainees at the Guantanamo Bay Detention Camp without trial that continues to date.

REFERENCES

Apple, M. (1999). *Official knowledge: Democratic education in a conservative age*. New York, NY: Routledge.

Barthes, R. (1957/1972). *Mythologies* (Annette Lavers, Trans.).New York, NY: Hill and Wang.

Bonnell, L., & Simon, R. (2007). 'Difficult' exhibitions and intimate encounters. *Museum and society, 5*(2) 65–85.

Britzman, B. (1991). *Practice makes practice: A critical study of learning to teach.* Albany, NY: SUNY Press.

Britzman, B. (1998). *Lost subjects, contested objects.* New York, NY: State University of New York Press.

Britzman, B. (2000a). If the story cannot end: Deferred action, ambivalence, and difficult knowledge. In R. I. Simon, S. Rosenberg, & C. Eppert (Eds.), *Between hope and despair: Pedagogy and the remembrance of historical trauma* (pp. 27–58). Lanham, MD: Rowman & Littlefield.

Britzman, B. (2000b). Teacher education in the confusion of our times. *Journal of Teacher Education, 51*(3), 200–205.

British Broadcasting Corporation. (2003, February 17). Millions join global anti-war protest. Retrieved Februrary 1, 2014 from http://news.bbc.co.uk/2/hi/europe/2765215.stm

Butler, J. (2009). *Frames of war: When is life grievable?* Brooklyn, NY: Verso.

Bybee, J. S. (2002). The Jay Bybee torture memo. Retrieved September 15, 2013 from http://www.uchastings.edu/facultyadministration/faculty/paul/class-website/docs/BybeeTortureMemo.pdf

Doyle, C. (2011). Iraq, Afghanistan, and teaching insurgencies in public schools. *American Educator, 35*(4), 18–21.

Evans, R. (2004). *The social studies wars: What should we teach the children?* New York, NY: Teachers College Press.

Freedman, K. (2003). *Teaching visual culture: Curriculum, aesthetics, and the social life of art.* New York, NY: Teachers College Press.

Garoian, C., & Gaudelius, Y. (2008). *Spectacle pedagogy: Art, politics, and visual culture.* New York, NY: State University of New York Press.

Hersh, S. (2004). *Chain of command: The road from 9/11 to Abu Ghraib.* New York, NY: Harper.

Hess, D. & Stoddard, J. (2007). 9/11 and terrorism: "The ultimate teachable moment" in textbooks and supplemental curricula. *Social Education, 71*(5), 230–236.

Hess, D., Stoddard, J., & Murto, S. (2008). Examining the treatment of 9/11 and terrorism in high school textbooks. In J.Bixby & J. Pace (Eds.), *Educating democratic citizens in troubled times: Qualitative studies of current efforts.* (pp.192–225) Albany, NY: SUNY Press.

Jehl, D., Zernike, K., & Cushman, J. H. (2004, May 30). The reach of war: Abu Grhaib; Scant evidence cited in long detention of Iraqis. *The New York Times.*

Limbaugh, R. (2004, May 4). It's not about us; this is war. *The Rush Limbaugh Show.* Retrieved July 1, 2013 from http://mediamatters.org/research/200405050003 (para. 3)

Mitchell, W. J. T. (2011). *Cloning terror: The war of images, 9/11 to the present.* Chicago, IL: University of Chicago Press.

Montoya, M. (n.d.-a). Malaquias Montoya. Retrieved March 1, 2013 from http://www.malaquiasmontoya.com/

Montoya, M. (n.d.-b). Malaquias Montoya Objectives. Retrieved March 1, 2013from http://www.malaquiasmontoya.com/objectives.php

Parsons, M. (1987a). *How we understand art: A cognitive developmental account of aesthetic experience.* Oxford, England: Cambridge University Press.

Parsons, M. (1987b). Talk about a painting: A cognitive developmental analysis. *Journal of Aesthetic Education, 21*(1), 37–55Ravitch, D. (2013). *Reign of error:*

The hoax of the privatization movement and the danger to America's public schools. New York, NY: Knopf.

Rumsfeld, D. H. (2004). Defense Department operational update briefing, May 4, 2004. Retrieved September 15, 2013 from http://www.defense.gov/transcripts/transcript.aspx?transcriptid=2973

Sanchez, R., & Phillips, D. (2008). *Wiser in battle: A soldier's story.* New York, NY: Harper.

Selz, P., & Landauer, S. (2006). *Art of engagement: Visual politics in California and beyond.* Berkeley, CA: University of California Press.

Sontag, S. (2004, May 23). Regarding the torture of others. *The New Yorker.* Retrieved September 15, 2013 from http://www.nytimes.com/2004/05/23/magazine/regarding-the-torture-of-others.html?pagewanted=all&src=pm

Taguba, A. (2004). Article 15–6 investigation of the 800th military police. Taguba Report. Retrieved July 1, 2013 http://news.findlaw.com/hdocs/docs/iraq/tagubarpt.html

Terezita, R. (2011). *Malaquias Montoya.* Los Angeles, CA: UCLA Press.

United Nations. (1984). A/RES/39/46. *Convention Against Torture and Other Cruel, Inhuman or Degrading Treatment or Punishment.* Retrieved March 1, 2014 from http://www.un.org/documents/ga/res/39/a39r046.htm

6 Deceptive Data
How the Corporate Reform Movement Uses Standardized Tests to Achieve the Neoliberal Agenda

David Hursh

High-stakes testing has been central to the corporate education reform movement that aims to harness education to serve the needs of corporations by transforming students into competitive entrepreneurs and consumers, and privatizing education by creating charter schools, taking over school management, or selling technology, tests, and texts (Hursh, 2008; Ravitch, 2013; Saltman, 2012). Standardized testing alters the ways in which we think about, discuss, organize, and practice education. Corporate reformers use, misuse, and manipulate test scores as evidence that their proposals are needed and are successful. For example, in New York, recent test scores on the Common Core standardized tests portray 69% of students as failing, with only 5% of students in Rochester—the district with the highest rate of poverty—passing. Therefore, we need to ask: What does high-stakes testing enable and accomplish? How does high-stakes testing transform how we talk about and practice education?

In this chapter, I focus on the increasing use of and importance given to standardized testing in New York State. I do so not because New York is the only or worst state when we consider standardized testing. Florida and Texas were earlier adopters than New York, and failing the tests often had harsher consequences (Nichols & Berliner, 2005). Moreover, the most egregious examples of districts cheating on tests have occurred in cities not in New York: Atlanta (Winerip, 2013) and Washington, DC (Strauss, 2013), to name a few.

However, New York provides an example of how the amount and consequences of standardized testing continue to increase, and has become central to efforts to portray the public schools, teachers, and students as failures, in need of corporate reform. Over the last two decades, elementary and secondary students in New York State have experienced an increasing number of standardized tests, subject areas tested, and grades examined. Further, as I will show, the tests have become high stakes not only for students but also for teachers, schools, and school districts.

The first increase in testing arose in the 1990s when the Board of Regents began requiring that high school students pass five standardized tests in four subject areas to graduate from high school. Then, in 2002, the federal government, under No Child Left Behind (NCLB), mandated that all 50 states use standardized exams in math and reading in Grades 3 through 8 to assess not only the students but also whether schools and school districts were making Adequate Yearly Progress. In 2011, New York State applied for and won $700 million under the Race to the Top (RTTT) competition. As winners, the state agreed to implement the Common Core State Standards and standardized testing for all subject areas and grade levels, with the test scores used to assess not only students and schools but also teachers (see Hursh, 2013, for an overview of the politics of testing in New York).

In this chapter, I will briefly describe the rise of testing and its impact on students, teachers, and schools in New York. However, we need to go beyond description, to analysis. Therefore I will also show how the practice and discourses around testing function

> in connection with other things, what it makes possible, the surfaces, networks and circuits around which it flows, the affects and passions that it mobilizes and through which it mobilizes. It is thus a matter of analyzing what counts as truth, who has the power to define truth, the role of different authorities of truth, and the epistemological and technical conditions for the production and circulation of truths. (Rose, 1999, pp. 29–30)

At the institutional level, I argue that testing is central to the "assemblage" of things that make up schooling (Ball, 2013; Burchell, 1996):

- Testing assigns an ostensibly objective value to students, teachers, and schools that become the basis for comparing them and turning people and institutions into object and commodities.
- Testing narrows teaching to the knowledge and skills likely to be tested. Because the tests are designed to be easily graded and administered to a set of students across the state, curriculum that focuses on the local, such as environmental issues or history, or that cannot be reduced to multiple-choice questions, such as writing or the arts, are omitted from tests.
- Testing transforms the relationship between students, teachers, administrators, and parents into what they can contribute to increasing test scores.

Consequently, we need to understand how standardized testing radically alters what counts as knowledge, the purpose of education, how we view teaching and learning, and how schools are organized.

Moreover, testing and test scores are used for political and economic ends, portraying public schools as failing and in the need of rescuing by the corporate reformers. As I will show, New York's Commissioners of Education intentionally raise and lower test scores to get the results they desire and, therefore, portray their efforts to raise standards through standardized testing as successful. Michael Bloomberg, the former mayor of New York City who asked for and was granted control over the public schools, used manipulated scores as evidence that the schools were improving and that he deserved reelection. Similarly, Bill Gates and heads of other conservative foundations claim that test results show that students, teachers, and teacher educators are failing (Hursh, 2011).

In what follows, I begin by dispelling the neoliberal argument that standardized testing provides the objectivity missing from teacher evaluations, and suggest that their real purpose is to portray public schools as failing so that education can be privatized, and to divert our attention from the primary cause of educational failure, the neoliberal policies themselves. The last four decades of neoliberalism have increased poverty through policies that have produced record profits for Wall Street but reduced median family income, and have reduced or eliminated welfare, health care, early childhood education, and public schooling.

PROMOTING STANDARDIZED TESTS AS OBJECTIVE AND SOCIALLY JUST

Proponents of standardized testing typically assert that standardized tests provide a more objective means of evaluating student learning than that provided by teachers and that objective test results help ensure that all students are provided with a quality education. For example, in New York, both the chancellor and commissioner of education responded to criticism of the new graduation requirement of passing five standardized tests by asserting that the state's curriculum standards were "objectively determined" and that standardized tests provided a valid and reliable means to assessing student learning. Such objective measures were required because teachers and administrators could not be trusted to assess students objectively and accurately (Hayden, 2001).

Portraying standardized tests as more objective than teachers is a common practice. In promoting NCLB, the Bush administration's *Parents Guide to NCLB* alleged that teachers often fail to give parents objective data about how "their children performed" and that standardized tests would rectify this (US Department of Education, 2003).

Furthermore, while criticizing teachers as self-interested and unreliable, proponents of testing portray themselves as interested only in doing what is best for children and fighting for children's civil rights, often invoking Martin Luther King, Jr., and the civil rights movement to justify standardized tests. Ten years ago, Bush's secretary of education, Rodney Paige, explicitly connected NCLB to the legacy of Martin Luther King, Jr., stating:

> Forty-four years ago, Dr. Martin Luther King, Jr., said, "The great challenge facing the nation today is to solve segregation and discrimination

and bring into full realization the ideas and dreams of our democracy." The No Child Left Behind Act does that. (Paige & Jackson, 2004)

More recently, both former New York mayor Michael Bloomberg and current governor Andrew Cuomo used separate 2012 observances marking Dr. King's birthday to assail teachers as the primary cause for the failures of the city's educational system and submit that high-stakes standardized testing responds to the vision of Martin Luther King, Jr. Bloomberg, who advocates improving education by firing half the teachers and doubling salaries and class size (Strauss, 2011), declared that he is "ready to fight for the kids: I'm ready to stand up to special interests," meaning, the teachers. Similarly, Cuomo advocated: "We have to realize that our schools are not an employment program. . . . It is this simple: It is not about the adults; it is about the children" (Kaplan & Taylor, 2012, p. A17).

While we have had three decades of neoliberal reform discourses and policies, the evidence from New York calls into question whether the policies have improved education outcomes and whether New York's standardized tests have provided a more objective measure of student learning. There is ample evidence from the rise and fall of scores on New York's tests and the decline by New York's students on the National Assessment of Educational Progress (NAEP) that educational outcomes have not improved.

In a recent review of the last 10 years of standardized testing in New York, Winerip (2011) recounts some of the more dubious outcomes of testing, which include administering tests that were poorly constructed, had misleading or erroneous questions, or used a grading scale that either overstated or understated students' learning. Critics have argued that an exam's degree of difficulty has varied depending on whether the New York State Education Department (NYSED) wanted to increase the graduation rate and therefore made the Regents exams easier, or wanted to appear rigorous and tough and therefore made the exam more difficult. The NYSED can raise or lower the passing rate on an exam by simply adjusting the cut score, turning a low percentage of correct answers into a pass or a high percentage of correct answers into a failure. In the paragraphs below, I offer only a small part of the available evidence.

In exams that students are likely to take as part of the graduation requirement to pass five Regents exams in four different subjects, the NYSED has made it easier for students to pass by lowering the cut score. For example, a decade ago the biology or "living environments" exam was criticized as being too easy, as students needed to answer only 39% of the questions correctly to earn a passing grade of 55% (Cala, 2003). The practice has not substantially changed over the last decade. A current analysis of the scoring rubrics on the NYSED website reveals that to pass, students need correct answers on only 47% of multiple-choice questions on the living environments exam and 53% correct on the algebra exam.

Conversely, the exams for the advanced, nonrequired courses, such as physics and chemistry, have sometimes been made more difficult. In 2003,

39% of students failed the physics exam, in order, critics charged, to make Regents testing appear more rigorous (Winerip, 2003). Commissioner Mills figured that since students did not need to pass the physics exam to graduate, a high failure rate would be of little concern to the students and their families. However, because most of the students who enroll in physics are academically successful middle-class students applying for university, and low or failing grades on the state physics exam harm their chances for admission, the students and their parents pressured the State Education Department to change the scoring. Commissioner Mills first defended the results as "statistically sound" (Dillon, 2003; Winerip, 2011, p. 27). But the test results were so dubious the State Council of Superintendents sent letters to universities urging them to disregard the test results. Finally, revelations on how the scores were manipulated and in response to public pressure, the commissioner relented (Winerip, 2003).

While the results on the secondary schools exams have fluctuated, the scores on the primary school exams have, until recently, steadily increased at rates of questionable validity. For example, in 2005, "New York City fourth graders made record gains on the state English test, with 59% scoring proficient, compared with 49% the year before." Similarly, in "2008 math scores for grades three through eight indicate that 89.7% are proficient, up from 72.7% in 2007" (Winerip, 2011, p. 27).

In the same way that scores on the Regents exams have been manipulated by raising or lowering the cut scores, the minimum scores necessary to reach increased levels of proficiency on the math and reading tests required under NCLB have consistently declined, therefore resulting in students' passing rates increasing. Ravitch, in *The Death and Life of the Great American School System: How Testing and Choice Are Undermining Education* (2010), points out how much easier it has become for New York's elementary students to score in the top three of four levels on the standardized tests. She notes:

> On the sixth-grade reading test in 2006, students needed to earn 36.2% of the points to attain level 2; by 2009, students in that grade need only 17.9%. In seventh grade math, students needed to earn 36.2% of the points on the test to advance to level 2 in 2006, but by 2009, they needed to earn only 22% The standards to advance from level 1 to level 2 dropped so low that many students could get enough correct answers to pass to level 2 by randomly guessing. (p. 79)

That these improvements in student learning are deceptive is also revealed when the results on New York State's tests are compared with New York State's students' scores on the more statistically rigorous NAEP English and math exams. The NAEP exams are administered every other year to statistically representative samples of students in 4th, 8th, and 12th grades and the results can be compared from year to year. In 2005, only 19% of the

New York City students were proficient on the eighth-grade reading test, compared to 22% two years before, and by 2009 the test results were the lowest in a decade. By November 2011, "New York [was] one of two states in the nation to post statistically significant declines on the National Assessment tests" (Winerip, 2011, p. 19). So, while a higher percentage of students are passing the New York State exams, a lower percentage are passing the NAEP exams, providing evidence that the improvements may be more of a mirage than real.

However, whenever questions are raised regarding the validity of the state tests, the commissioners and chancellors defend them as rigorous and statistically sound. In New York City, Mayor Bloomberg used the improving test results to successfully lobby the state legislature to renew mayoral control of the schools and to win reelection. However, finally, in June 2010 Merryl Tisch, the current chancellor of the Board of Regents, admitted that the state test scores were ridiculously inflated and should not be believed, and test scores were rescaled so that, for example, the 68.8% English proficiency rates was immediately rescaled to 42.4% (Winerip, 2011).

While Tisch's new realism seems to be an acknowledgment that standardized tests scores are unreliable, her rescaling the scores so that fewer students are proficient fits in with a pattern of lowering scores early in an administrator's tenure so that he or she can take credit for subsequent improvements (Linn, 2003). For example, in summer 2013 the scores on the new Common Core State Standards tests were published, with only 31% of the students in the state scoring as proficient. Urban districts, like the Rochester City School District (RCSD), had only a 5% pass rate, which was the lowest in the state.

Mayor Bloomberg, who took credit for improving test results, now describes the low percentage of city children classified as proficient as "some very good news" (Pallas, 2013). Amazingly, Tisch has already promised that the percentage of students scoring proficient will be higher, in part no doubt because they can just lower the cut score.

So, the scores are manipulated for political purposes, and politicians like Bloomberg can spin rising or falling test scores as "good news." What is their purpose? What does high-stakes testing do? In this section, I want to argue that standardized tests are intentionally used and misused to blame public (primarily urban) schools and school teachers for the shortcomings of education, so that corporate reformers can push privatizing schools (by either converting them to charter schools or turning over their management and operation to for-profit companies) and shift the blame for increasing inequality onto the schools rather than where it should belong: neoliberal economic and social policies (Apple, 1996).

We can see how this plays out in the RCSD. As noted above, only 5% of RCSD students were proficient on the recent Common Core assessments, which have ramifications for the teachers, students, schools, and school districts. First, in order to receive RTTT funding, the state agreed that teachers will be evaluated as failing ("ineffective" or "developing") or passing ("effective" or "very effective") based largely on their students' test scores as part of their Annual Professional Performance Review (APPR). Teachers who are determined to be failing will be required to develop a Teaching Improvement Plan (Strauss, 2011).

In an urban district like Rochester, the students' low test scores resulted in 922 of the 2,474 RCSD teachers (or 37%) receiving ratings of "developing" or "ineffective," all of whom now require a professional development plan; and according to the union's agreement with the State Education Department, if the teachers are rated as failing for two consecutive years, proceedings to terminate their employment can begin. Adam Urbanski, president of the Rochester Teachers Association, stated, "APPR was intentionally positioned to dismantle urban public schools—possibly to diminish union power—and allow for the growth of charter schools" (Macaluso, 2013b).

Urbanski's observation is backed up by two recent events regarding the school district's future. Soon after the test scores were made public, Governor Cuomo declared that low-scoring school districts might suffer the "death penalty." Subsequently, the current commissioner of education, John King, is "pushing for a bill that would allow the Board of Regents to take over schools districts with histories of low academic performance or financial problems" (Macaluso, 2013a).

Moreover, the low percentage of Rochester students reaching proficiency on the tests provides a rationale for increased privatization through charter schools. Joe Klein, who owns Klein Steel in Rochester and was a former board member of True North Rochester Preparatory Program, has created a nonprofit company to recruit charter schools to Rochester. He has used the low test scores to legitimize charter schools and developed a partnership with the Rochester Institute of Technology to operate charter schools. He recently stated, "In Rochester you get 5% proficiency rates. Obviously, it's not working. You can go to Rochester Prep and see those same kids thriving. I think you will start to see every university involved with a high-quality charter school" (Lankes, 2013, p. 5A).

The above discussion regarding the political manipulation to test scores and their use and misuse demonstrates how test scores can organize how we think about the world. Ball (2013) writes, "Discourse is related directly to power, to regimes of truth and grids of specification—the dividing, classifying, and relating together objects of discourse" (pp. 23–24). As we can see, the test scores serve to describe students as more or less successful, without any connection to what students were also learning. Similarly, 37% of urban teachers can be classified as failing, while few suburban teachers are classified as such. As Ball (2013) further describes:

> Here we see again the relations between the delimitation and constitution of a field of knowledge in relation to a form of expertise—statistics—that

> ... creates and legitimates new sites of truth. This "making up of people" consists of what Hacking (1995) identifies as five interactive elements—classification, people (the subject of measurement), institutions, knowledge, and expert. (p. 74)

Ball continues by describing how testing aims to "represent reality in terms of quantifiable and manipulable domains, and thus render reality as a field of government" (p. 74); that is, policies and practices are developed to improve test scores rather than to positively affect what occurs in classrooms and schools. Rather than discussing what is worth learning, whether teachers are developing curriculum and pedagogical practices that promote learning, how we can assess that learning, and its value to the community that consists of school, neighborhood, nation, and world, the conversation focuses on the so-called failure of teachers, students, and schools and how privatizing test development and scoring, school management, and whole schools as charters can remedy the problem.

Not only does high-stakes testing limit the ways in which we conceptualize schooling, it also limits how we conceptualize education within society as a whole. Again, Ball (2013) writes:

> This "grid of social regularities" constitutes "what becomes socially visible as a social problem and what becomes socially visible as a range of credible solutions" (Sheurich, 1994, p. 301)—the possible and the impossible (what actors do not think about)—and thus the objects, subjects, and concepts that policies form and regulate. (p. 23)

The focus on test scores promotes discourses that objectify students and teachers as failing and limit our ability to imagine what could be done to improve student learning. Such discourses also undermine our ability to focus on the factors that most affect educational outcomes: poverty and lack of jobs and social services, factors that have been exacerbated under neoliberalism.

TEST SCORES SERVE TO BLAME TEACHERS, PARENTS, AND STUDENTS FOR OUR INADEQUATE EDUCATIONAL OUTCOMES RATHER THAN WHERE THE BLAME BELONGS: OUR NEOLIBERAL POLICIES

Neoliberals aim to reverse the reverse the rise of social democratic liberalism that occurred under Franklin Roosevelt and for the quarter century after World War II. Social democratic liberalism produced Social Security, Medicare, state university systems, unions and welfare rights, and corporate regulations such as the Glass Steagal Act that limited commercial banking and the Federal Deposit Insurance Corporation that protects individual bank deposits. Instead, neoliberals aim to reduce government's role in society and transform our social interactions (such as attending school or choosing health care) into corporate market transactions. Specifically, neoliberals aim to reduce government's role in promoting equality, reducing poverty, and providing other social services, including education, arguing that these can best be provided through competitive markets and private corporations. Such policies, neoliberals advance, reduce governmental spending and therefore taxes, increasing the capital available for corporate investments. Neoliberal principles guide members of the Republican Party as they call for further cuts in state and federal funding. The current federal sequestration of funds has reduced funding for almost all federally funded programs, and resistance to funding the national debt is a result of the neoliberal rationality that governmental funding is contrary to corporate interests.

Consequently, neoliberals have, since the 1980s and the publication of *A Nation at Risk* (National Commission on Excellence in Education, 1983), portrayed public schools as failing with the goal of decreasing educational funding, introducing market rationalities into education, and turning over education to private corporations, as in replacing publicly governed schools with charter schools. The neoliberal portrayal of schools contradicts the available objective national assessments, such as the NAEP, that show continuing improvement in student learning and reductions in the achievement gap. Since the claims of neoliberals and corporate reformers contradict the evidence, Berliner and Biddle (1995) label the purposeful mis-portrayal of public schools as failing as a "manufactured crisis."

Ravitch, in her book, *Reign of Error: The Hoax of the Privatization Movement and the Danger to America's Schools* (2013), counters arguments by Bill Gates and other corporate reformers that our schools are broken. She shows that according to the NAEP data, "there have been significant increases in both reading and mathematics, more in mathematics than reading," a difference she attributes to our increasing number of immigrants who do not speak English as their first language. She notes that "the sharpest increases [in NAEP scores] were registered in the years preceding the implementation of NCLB, from 2000 to 2004" (p. 49).

The manufactured crisis continues today. For example, Joel Klein, former chancellor of the New York City schools under Bloomberg, and Condoleezza Rice, former secretary of state under George W. Bush, cochaired the report *Education Reform and National Security* (2012) from the US Council on Foreign Relations. In the report they asserted, echoing *A Nation at Risk* 30 years earlier, that the low quality of public schools places our nation at risk.

However, that our schools could do better is reflected in comparisons with other countries. But, like individual schools, our nation's schools are not on par with other nations' schools in large part, writes Berliner (2013), not only because of our high poverty rate, especially for children, but also because children living in poverty do not do as well as similar students in other countries. This difference can be partially attributed to low-income US students receiving inferior or nonexistent early childhood education, and health and dental care, and attending schools with a homogeneous population by income and culture. Berliner (2013) states:

> Out-of-school variables account for about 60% of the variance that can be accounted for in student achievement. In aggregate, such factors as family income; the neighborhood's sense of collective efficacy, violence rate, and average income; medical and dental care available and used; level of food insecurity; number of moves a family makes over the course of a child's school years; whether one parent or two parents are raising the child; provision of high-quality early education in the neighborhood; language spoken at home; and so forth, all substantially affect school achievement. (p. 5)

Moreover, the last 30 years of neoliberal policy has resulted in economic stagnation for most of the population and increasing economic inequality. Many (Ravitch, 2013; Sachs, 2011) have noted that since the 1970s, worker productivity has increased, but the real median earnings of full-time male workers have stagnated and income inequality is at its highest level since the 1920s. Even the so-called economic recovery since 2007 has produced increased income only for the top 1%. Lowrey (2013) reports that a recent study showed that for the top 1%, earnings rose by 11.2% since 2007, while for the other 99%, their earnings declined by 0.4%.

The real economic and educational gains that were made after World War II and before neoliberalism became dominant are being erased. Our manufactured crisis is being turned into a real crisis, with those who are causing the crisis—those demanding excessive testing, ranking, and privatization—promoting themselves as the saviors. Neoliberal education policies harm schooling and society as neoliberals focus on test scores to undermine our efforts to seriously examine and undertake to improve teaching and learning.

Further, over the last several decades we have seen curricular and pedagogical decisions shift from the local level towards first the state/provincial and then the national levels. Both state/provincial and the federal governments use standardized tests to steer local policy making from a distance (Ball, 1994), therefore attempting to avoid claims that they are undermining local control by imposing curriculum on schools.

At the same time that state/provincial and national governments are imposing policies on local schools, they are also teaming up with neoliberal foundations—such as the Bill and Melinda Gates Foundation and the Walton Foundation—and organizations created and funded by foundations—such as the National Governors Association—to make education policies. Furthermore, state education commissioners and federal secretaries of education are typically appointed and not elected. Therefore, while school policies were once created by locally elected school board members, they are increasingly created by unelected, unreachable, and unaccountable officials.

Neoliberals have already succeeded in gaining control over much of what occurs in schools. They have also handed over many administrative and teaching responsibilities to those in the private sector. Much of what was public about public education has disappeared over the last several decades. The debate over test scores has diverted our attention from the real issue we face in education.

However, parents, teachers, students, and the wider community are becoming critical of the use and misuse of testing. The public managed to reverse the commissioner's stand on the physics exam. More recently, thousands of teachers, parents, and students are providing critical testimony at public and legislative hearings on the Common Core standards and exams. Parents and teachers know that their schools are better than the 69% failure rate indicated by the recent Common Core exam results. They are also demanding that policy not be made in secret at provincial and national levels. The state teachers and administrative unions have called for a three-year moratorium on the curriculum and tests, raising many of the criticisms I have raised here. The neoliberal reforms may not be inevitable after all. We may be able to return to asking the essential question: How do we engage in building the kinds of schools and society that we need to improve students' learning and society?

REFERENCES

Apple, M. (1996). *Cultural politics and education.* New York: Teachers College Press.
Ball, S. J. (1994). *Education reform: A critical and post-structural approach.* Buckingham, England: Open University Press.
Ball, S. J. (2013). *Foucault, power, and education.* New York, NY: Routledge.
Berliner, D. C. (2013). Effects of inequality and poverty vs. teachers and schooling on America's youth. *Teachers College Record, 115*(12). Retrieved June 10, 2014 from http://www.tcrecord.org (ID no. 16889)
Berliner, D. C., & Biddle, B. (1995). *The manufactured crisis: Myths, fraud, and the attack on America's public schools.* Reading, MA: Addison Wesley.
Burchell, G. (1996). Liberal government and techniques of the self. In A. Barry, T. Osborne, & N. Rose (Eds.), *Foucault and political reason: Liberalism, neoliberalism, and rationalities of government* (pp. 19–36). Chicago, IL: University of Chicago Press.
Cala, W. (2003, October 22). Testimony before the New York Senate Standing Committee on Education, Roosevelt Hearing Room C, Legislative Office Building, Albany, New York. Retrieved June 10, 2014 from http://www.timeoutfromtesting.org/testimonies/1022_Testimony_Cala.pdf
Dillon, S. (2003, July 18). Outcry over Regents physics test. But officials in Albany won't budge. *The New York Times.* Retrieved June 10, 2014 from http://www.nytimes.com/2003/07/18/nyregion/outcry-over-regents-physics-test-but-officials-in-albany-won-t-budge.html?pagewanted=all&src=pm
Hacking, I. (1995). *Rewriting the soul: Multiple personalities and the sciences of memory.* Princeton, NJ: Princeton University Press.

Hayden, C. (2001, May 7). Letter to the Hon. Richard Brodsky and Hon. Richard Green, New York State Assembly.

Hursh, D. (2008). *High-stakes testing and the decline of teaching and learning*. Lanham, MD: Rowman & Littlefield.

Hursh, D. (2011). The Gates Foundation's interventions into education, health, and food policies: Technology, power, and the privatization of public problems. In P. E. Kovacs (Ed.), *The Gates Foundation and the future of U.S. "public" schools* (pp. 39–52). New York, NY: Routledge.

Hursh, D. (2013). Raising the stakes: High-stakes testing and the attack on public education in New York. *Journal of Education Policy, 28*(5), 574–588, doi: 10.1080/02680939.2012.758829

Kaplan, T., & Taylor, K. (2012, January 17). Invoking King, Cuomo and Bloomberg stoke fight on teacher review impasse. *The New York Times*, p. A17.

Lankes, S. (2013, September 9). Charter school, RIT join effort: College to work with new city high school. *Democrat and Chronicle*, pp. 1A, 5A.

Linn, R. (2003). Accountability: Responsibility and reasonable expectations. *Educational Researcher, 32*(7), 3–13.

Lowrey, A. (2013, April 28). Wealth gap among races has widened since recession. *The New York Times*, p. B1.

Macaluso, T. L. (2013a, August 16). Albany is going to fix urban schools . *City Newspaper*. Retrieved June 10, 2014 from http://www.rochestercitynewspaper.com/NewsBlog/archives/2013/08/16/albany-is-going-to-fix-urban-schools

Macaluso, T. L. (2013b, October 2). Hundreds of teachers appealing APPR. *City Newspaper*. Retrieved June 10, 2014 from http://www.rochestercitynewspaper.com/NewsBlog/archives/2013/10/02/hundreds-of-city-teachers-appealing-appr

National Commission on Excellence in Education. (1983). *A nation at risk: A report to the nation and the secretary of education*. Washington, DC: US Department of Education.

Nichols, S., & Berliner, D. (2005, March). *The inevitable corruption of indicators and educators through high-stakes testing*. Education Policy Studies Laboratory. Retrieved June 25, 2007, from http://epsl.asu.edu/epru/epru_2005_Research_Writing.htm

Paige, R., & Jackson, A. (2004, November 8). *Education: The civil-rights issue of the twenty-first century*. Hispanic Vista. Retrieved from http://hispanicvista.com/HVC/Opinion/Guest-Columns/1108Rod_Paige-Alponso_Jackson.htm

Pallas, A. (2013, August 8). The envelope please. *A sociological eye on education*. Retrieved June 10, 2014 from http://eyeoned.org/content/the-envelope-please_501/

Ravitch, D. (2010). *The death and life of the great American school system: How testing and choice are undermining education*. New York, NY: Basic Books.

Ravitch, D. (2013). *Reign of error: The hoax of the privatization movement and the danger to America's public schools*. New York, NY: Knopf.

Rose, N. (199). *Powers of freedom: Reframing political thought*. Cambridge, England: Cambridge University Press.

Sachs, J. (2011). *The price of civilization: Reawakening American virtue and prosperity*. New York, NY: Random House.

Saltman, K. J. (2012). *The failure of corporate school reform*. Boulder, CO: Paradigm.

Scheurich, J. J. (1994). Policy archaeology: A new policy studies methodology. *Journal of Education Policy, 9*(4), 297–316.

Strauss, V. (2011, December 7). Are half of New York's teachers really "not effective"? *The Washington Post*. Retrieved December 7, 2011 from http://www.washingtonpost.com/blogs/answer-sheet/post/are-half-of-new-yorks-teachers-really-not-effective/2011/12/05/gIQAhDXyaO_blog.html

Strauss, V. (2013, April 12). Why not subpoena everyone in the Washington cheating scandal—Rhee included? (update). *The Washington Post*. Retrieved April 12, 2014 from http://www.washingtonpost.com/blogs/answer-sheet/wp/2013/04/12/why-not-subpoena-everyone-in-d-c-cheating-scandal-rhee-included/

US Department of Education, Office of the Secretary. (2003). *NCLB: A parents guide to NCLB: What to know and where to go*. Washington, DC: Author.

Winerip, M. 2003. Passing grade defies laws of physics. The New York Times, March 12, A22 & B7. http://www.nytimes.com/2003/03/12/nyregion/on-education-when-a-passing-grade-defies-laws-of-physics.html?src=pm.

Winerip, M. (2011, December 19). 10 years of assessing students with scientific exactitude. *The New York Times*, p. A24.

Winerip, M. (2013, March 30). Ex-schools chief in Atlanta is indicted in testing scandal. *The New York Times*, p. A1.

7 Behind the Common Core Standards Movement
OECD'S PISA and Global Education Policy

Richard D. Lakes

A NEOLIBERAL IMAGINARY

Education policymakers in the US are advocating for a standardized common core curriculum in which students are prepared to attend college and train for jobs in the science, technology, engineering, and mathematics fields—the STEM subjects. The objective is to demand more from the schools, raising academic standards so that college-bound students will take their place in a high-skill economy as knowledge workers. The national priority for common core standards in public schools is due to growing concerns among school reformers—education and business leaders alike, such as CEOs and executive boards of major corporations, presidents of universities and community colleges, labor leaders and directors of industry trade groups and chambers of commerce, and the like—all powerful neoliberal elites desiring to restore America's standing as worldwide leader in college completion rates. Recent data show the US ranked 14th among 37 advanced industrial countries with a leveling off of postsecondary attainment in the past decade as compared to the rest of the field (Organization for Economic Cooperation and Development [OECD], 2012). Consequently, elected officials are pressured by elites to advance a public policy agenda that students accelerate their studies towards university graduation, thereby engendering normative assumptions that common core standards will raise the nation's competitive economic advantage in global markets through product innovation with advanced technology.

We should be concerned about the vocationalizing messages that education reformers offer these days. Few place an emphasis upon educating young people as future citizens devoted to maintenance of our public institutions through critical analysis and problem-solving skills, ones that strengthen community life, rebuild neighborhoods, and rectify injustices due to poverty and neglect. Yet adolescents are asked to think of themselves as do-it-yourself projects, fully engaged in self-management and responsibilization strategies for planning a life course in knowledge work. Individuals are policed to become enterprising selves making first-rate choices that promise to reposition oneself in the new economy (Rose, 1990). Neoliberal elites hope to wean people away from thinking about the commons on issues regarding what a democratic government can and should do to narrow the income gap through educational access and opportunity. Under new times, "the economic fates of citizens within a national territory are uncoupled from one another, and are now understood and governed as a function of their own particular levels of enterprise, skill, inventiveness and flexibility" (Miller & Rose, 2008, p. 96). Neoliberal elites make use of specific discourses around knowledge worker or high-skills nation that privilege free-market capitalism in the desire to stimulate economic and human capital development. Discourses such as *world-class education* act as social imaginaries, Fairclough (2010) noted, as "projections of possible states of affairs, 'possible worlds'. These imaginaries may be enacted as actual (networks of) practices—imagined activities, subjects, social relations etc. can become real activities, subjects, social relations etc." (p. 266).

Education reform rhetoric has heightened due to international comparisons of schooling via league tables on the Programme of International Student Assessment (PISA), sponsored by the OECD as a new model of global governance. Over the past decade this intergovernmental organization based in Paris has become a powerful policy think tank and influential broker of convergent education system reforms. Importantly, OECD's PISA influences the direction of *internal* state affairs "in which the very meaning of public education is being recast from a project aimed at forming national citizens and nurturing social solidarity to a project driven by economic demands and labor market orientations" (Meyer & Benavot, 2013, p. 10). Education ministers compare published benchmarking data in their continuous drive to gain an edge in global economic performance. By measuring the longitudinal changes in young people's cognitive skills, governmental leaders view PISA tables as a reliable indicator of the overall health of an economic system. They enter OECD education networks to learn about cutting-edge curricular practices and the latest ways to evaluate teachers, and engage in transnational communications with hopes of cross-national lesson drawing and policy borrowing. They join into partnership with governors, foundation heads, corporate executives, and academic experts, among others, to support their domestic reform agendas; and dismiss opponents of curricular standardization and mandated yearly testing as ill-informed or indifferent to the future of American schooling.

The Obama administration under Arne Duncan, the U.S. Secretary of Education, is one among many neoliberal elites who project an imaginary that OECD's PISA benchmarking is good for school children. Young people are assessed triennially via PISA (since the year 2000), which measures achievement in reading, mathematics, and science to a representative sample of 15-year-old students. In 2012, the two-hour test was administered to 34 OECD countries and another 30 nonmember affiliates.

THE PISA EFFECT

In 2010, Secretary Duncan commissioned the OECD to write a report on how the highest-performing nations on the PISA test, in 2009, incorporated rigorous academic standards into an instructional system aligned to quality teaching (OECD, 2011). Titled *Strong Performers and Successful Reformers in Education: Lessons from PISA for the United States*, the federal policy document informed the American public that "comparative international assessments can extend and enrich the national picture by providing a larger context within which to interpret national performance" (p. 18). By profiling high-achieving countries like Canada, China, Finland, Japan, and Singapore, the OECD (2011) authors argued, "The yardstick for judging public policy in education is no longer improvement against national educational standards, but also improvement against the most successful education systems worldwide" (p. 18). The report noted that by studying exemplary educational systems in OECD member nations, a reformist agenda "could address the current problem of widely discrepant state standards and cut scores that have led to non-comparable results" (p. 49) in our federated system. Secretary Duncan said upon release of the commissioned report: "I wanted to know what the U.S. could learn from the practices of those high-performing and rapidly improving countries. In a globally competitive economy, the value of benchmarking the practices of high-performing education systems seemed like a no-brainer" (U.S. Department of Education, 2011b, para. 3).

That same year the *Blueprint for Reform* (U.S. Department of Education, 2010a) was distributed by the administration delineating a proposed policy agenda for the reauthorization of the Elementary and Secondary Education Act. The document was "not only a plan to renovate a flawed law but also an outline for a re-envisioned federal role in education" (U.S. Department of Education, 2010a, p. 2). The White House desired improvements upon standardized testing for all grade levels under the No Child Left Behind Act, now termed *next generation assessments*, "to better capture higher-order skills, provide more accurate measures of student growth, and better inform classroom instruction to respond to academic needs" (U.S. Department of Education, 2010a, p. 4). The *Blueprint* sought a common core of national literacy and numeracy standards by providing states and local districts with baseline data to measure improvement or modifications towards reaching targeted goals, as scored on the PISA. Additionally, the states were incentivized to adopt common core standards with participation in the Race to the Top Fund (RTTF), a $4.4 billion competitive grants program for school reform. The carrot of federal awards provided state governors much needed revenue streams during recessionary times. The policy reforms conveyed in the *Blueprint* are deemed important for human capital development, economic growth, and business innovation—consistent with the OECD message of global competitive advantage.

The Obama administration is the first on record to draw inspiration from internationally benchmarked tests as in PISA, and also from the Trends in International Mathematics and Science Study (TIMSS) or the Progress in International Reading Literacy Study (PIRLS). However, Secretary Duncan has denied the government is mandating federal control over common core standards: "We have not and will not prescribe a national curriculum—and in fact we are barred by law from doing so" (U.S. Department of Education, 2011a, para. 24). Yet the U.S. Department of Education funded two large consortia of states working on the benchmarked assessments (Sawchuk, 2011). This is a strategic intervention by the government to shape educational reform through the OECD policy prism. PISA "serves as a political tool in the hands of experts and technocrats who directly influence its design and handing," according to Bulle (2011) who studied the international exams. PISA is supposed to measure learning outcomes of students at the end of their compulsory schooling, usually administered in the 10th grade before they move into further education or vocational training. At that point in many OECD countries, there is a clear demarcation between the lower and upper division of secondary schooling. The tests have become a gateway or key indicator for education ministers to judge whether young people have successfully navigated their national curriculums since the standards are written into a common core of academic subjects.

Dale (1999) claimed that international policy agendas emanating from the OECD promote a uniform ideology of responding to "the problems posed to rich countries by changing global economic circumstances" (p. 4). The member states have one allied agenda: They must rise to the challenges of attracting global business through competitive advantage. The OECD Secretariat publishes the results of PISA test scores triennially, disseminating the performance of educational systems while "promoting what amounts to a global ideology of educational management and change tied to broader public sector reform" (Henry, Lingard, Rizvi, & Taylor, 2001, p. 84). Germany felt a shock after PISA 2000 when they scored well below OECD averages on the assessment, and so they reformed their education system with the introduction of standards and gateway exams. Low PISA results usually scandalize a country's political leadership and engender public debates about quality and accountability "if a controversy over educational reforms in a particular country already exists" (Steiner-Khamsi, 2004, p. 208). The league tables become "a policy tool to certify the demands of reform proponents . . . attractive to politicians and policy makers only if they are, at that particular moment, in need of additional, external support for their reform agenda" (p. 208).

The Obama administration was so shaken by such a poor showing after PISA 2009 that Secretary Duncan (U.S. Department of Education, 2010b) immediately issued a short press release that read in part:

> Today's PISA results show that America needs to urgently accelerate student learning to remain competitive in the global economy of the 21st century. More parents, teachers, and leaders need to recognize the reality that other high-achieving nations are both out-educating and out-competing us. (para. 1)

PISA results serve as a proxy for competitive advantage. Governmental leaders claim the advancement of economic growth is predicated upon higher test scores. Below-average performance signals a nation's inability to ready the talent pool of college graduates needed to foster global business. Consequently, PISA data reinforce the ongoing initiatives governments have developed for the reform of their education and training systems. Taylor and Henry (2000) noted: "The key issue here is the strengthening of the OECD's normative role in policymaking and, more broadly, of the significance of the policy stances of international organizations in the framing of national policies" (p. 501).

Education ministers participate in OECD networks of expertise to buttress internal reform efforts. They are schooled in the so-called best practices of high-performing PISA nations for "domestic policy legitimation or as a means of defusing discussion by presenting policy as based on robust evidence" (Grek, 2009, p. 35). The term "best practice" comes from the language of corporate management to measure and evaluate strategic processes within organizations and firms, comparing those indicators across standards of efficiency and effectiveness—the purpose of which is to regulate uniformity and guarantee future outcomes (profits). The same holds true with PISA benchmarking practices. Their comparative metrics "are developed against a set of agreed criteria that constitute the reference points against which performance is measured and judged" (Henry et al., 2001, p. 92). Governmental leaders increasingly turn to the OECD for alignment of educational objectives, essentially nullifying the voices of citizens' groups desiring to weigh in on the affairs of state.

THE CONVERSATIONS OF MINISTERS

When Secretary Duncan went to OECD headquarters in November of 2010 for a two-day ministerial meeting, he entered a governance space that directs policy on a global scale. Grek (2009) claimed that the OECD brand is "indisputable"—"through its statistics, reports and studies, OECD's policy recommendations are accepted as valid by politicians and scholars alike" (p. 25). Prior to the meeting the attendees were provided background reading materials, including a white paper on the theme of human capital development and skills strategies, along with supporting statements by the Business and Industry Advisory Committee to the OECD. Grek (2012) noted: "Learning by meeting has emerged as by far the most significant instrument in their [OECD] efforts to create consensus around measurement goals" (p. 55). The keynote speakers, plenary sessions, and subsequent panel discussions in Paris provided an international forum in which to discuss comparative education and training systems while acknowledging the diversity of nations. This transnational reading of assessment data and best practices has resulted in policy convergence globally. In fact, the fetishizing of OECD benchmarks by the Obama administration "signals to an international audience, through PISA, the adherence of their nation to reform agendas" (Grek, 2009, p. 35).

High-performing Finland has become *the* exemplar of global education reform. That country regularly appears in top rankings on PISA and TIMSS indicators, and its rapid rise in the new millennia within the telecommunications industry (e.g., Nokia Corporation, makers of mobile phones) is an established fact. Finland has exceeded the OECD average for the number of research and development workers in the labor force and sits atop the World Economic Forum's global competitiveness index (OECD, 2011, p. 121). Corporate leaders "not only promoted the importance of mathematics, science and technology in the formal curriculum, but they also advocated for more attention to creativity, problem-solving, teamwork, and cross-curricular projects in schools" (OECD, 2011, p. 122). It could be argued that their national curriculum with common core standards for all elementary grade students was instrumental in transforming the formerly agrarian society into an innovative global economic powerhouse (although the thin national curriculum guidebook itself is merely a steering document that municipalities use to develop their own course objectives and local assessment criteria). Prospective Finnish teachers go through a rigorous selection and training process that is envied in international forums on the professional development of teachers. Unlike in the US, the ministry of education does not force teachers into delivering instruction for high-stakes tests or ask school leaders to impose market-based solutions when solving social problems (see Sahlberg, 2011). Darling-Hammond and Wentworth (2010) argued that among top-performing PISA nations, the Finnish schools "teach fewer topics more deeply each year, focus on applications of knowledge, rather than recall of facts, and have a more thoughtful sequence of expectations based on developmental learning progressions within and across domains" (p. 1).

PISA league tables "trigger convergence mechanisms," Bieber and Martens (2011, p. 112) explained, that alert national leaders to support the OECD paradigm of internationalization in education. Meetings and forums facilitate the study of best practices that leads to policy borrowing or lending. Knill (2005) clarified the mechanisms that hasten this process:

They include lesson-drawing (where countries deliberately seek to learn from successful problem-solving activities in other countries), joint problem-solving activities within transnational elite networks or epistemic communities, the promotion of policy models by international organizations with the objective of accelerating and facilitating cross-national policy transfer as well as the emulation of policy models. (p. 7)

The idea that governmental leaders would turn to a group of experts for lesson drawing is common practice in the field of public administration. Rose (1993) remarked: "If there is a positive consensus among experts about how a program will operate, this will reassure a policymaker who approves its goals. A consensus that a program will fail is a strong incentive to reject a proposal" (p. 15).

Secretary Duncan discovered at OECD headquarters just how transnational communication operated in the real world of policymaking, and to further his reform agenda hosted two, two-day forums in New York City on improvements to teacher quality. The yearly summits were cohosted by the U.S. Department of Education with support from the OECD and Education International, a nongovernmental organization based in Brussels representing teachers unions and education employees across the globe. The first summit was held in March of 2011 with a subsequent conference the following year. In 2013, a third teacher education forum was hosted in Amsterdam. More than 60 governmental leaders and teachers union representatives attended the first event—invitees from Belgium, Canada, Denmark, Finland, Hong Kong, Japan, Norway, and Singapore—and several nonmember affiliates were in attendance. Secretary Duncan expected the summits would highlight "the practices of top-performing countries" in order to "help America accelerate achievement and elevate the teaching profession" (U.S. Department of Education, 2011c, para. 3). "The lessons outlined in the International Summit on the Teaching Profession," he continued, "reinforce the understanding of education leaders around the world that a high-quality teaching profession is built on common principles and cornerstones in different education systems." The first summit was organized into four themes: teacher recruitment and preparation; development, support, and retention of teachers; teacher evaluation and compensation; and teacher engagement in education reform. The second summit dealt with the issues of preparing teachers to deliver 21st-century skills, matching the supply and demand for teachers, and training effective school leaders. The third summit dealt solely with the issue of evaluating teaching quality.

None of the summits endorsed a specific set of practices to adopt across the board, but various invitees talked about individual system enhancements to the profession and showcased best practices from their nations. After introductory welcomes by the host dignitaries, attendees were introduced to the conference themes by Andreas Schleicher, deputy director for education and skills and special advisor on education policy to the OECD's secretary-general, who highlighted findings from the background reports that framed each meeting. Then, several discussion starters from high-performing countries drew upon personal experiences to speak about the issues at hand. Additional conversation ensued "in which participants candidly explained the challenges their countries face; the strategies and innovations they are pursuing; and the areas in which there is consensus, controversy, or simply too little research" (Asia Society, 2012, p. 5). Daily question-and-answer sessions and a conference wrap-up identified potential take-away messages or next steps that attendees might consider implementing at home.

Given the diversity of nations, is policy borrowing a reality in the context of these education summits? Rose (1993) affirmed that lesson drawing "is driven by a desire to find a program that will deal with a pressing political problem" (p. 12). And "if there is a positive consensus among experts about how a program will operate, this will reassure a policymaker who approves its goals" (p. 15). Moreover, "the fungibility of programs is a matter of degree. Insofar as common problems make possible common responses," he continued, "national policymakers can learn something by looking abroad" (p. 118). For example, Japanese lesson study was named as an innovation in professional development at the first summit because "it works as a tool for continuous improvement" (Asia Society, 2011, p. 15). Lesson study involves collaboration between teams of school teachers and university researchers that disseminate public information useful on how to teach the national core standards. After a period of time in which the local teams have shared lesson information and obtained student feedback, the teaching method is opened to public review for parties interested in curricular implementation. Lewis (2010) judiciously studied this professional development technique abroad and indicated that "tens of thousands of educators, researchers, and policymakers who attended these public research lessons could see and discuss live instruction designed to enact the standards" (para. 4). Viewers might ask questions and tweak the lesson plans, if desired, but the impact of Japanese lesson study went beyond passive compliance with national curriculum guidelines. This method empowered teachers to inhabit the center of school improvement, Lewis (2010) wrote, with "many intertwined types of knowledge needed to implement standards well in the classroom—knowledge of instructional materials, teaching strategies, student thinking, and content at hand" (para. 7). Curiously, Japanese lesson study was proposed by several school districts in Florida in a winning U.S. Department of Education bid for teaching effectiveness under the RTTF (Cavanaugh, 2011). This may be a case of political elites in Washington valorizing one of the OECD's best-practices models due to Japan's eighth-place PISA 2009 ranking.

The common core standards movement is advanced by the Obama administration, a national curricular reform with benchmarked assessments in three subjects: English/language arts, mathematics, and science. The neoliberal elite demand more rigors and challenges in public schools by claiming young people are academically deficient and underprepared for high-skill employment. Yet growing public disapproval of the common core represents a wider spectrum of political viewpoints that threatens to derail the initiative.

THE COMMON CORE AGENDA

Young people are expected to learn college- and career-ready skills that best equip them for knowledge work. Perhaps this message of human capital development first resonated in the 1983 publication of *A Nation at Risk*, pointing out the failure of American schools to ensure global economic competitiveness. Additional reports on workforce readiness followed one after another demanding curricular reforms that would result in higher graduate rates and promises of labor market successes. One was the SCANS report, in 1991, named after the U.S. Department of Labor's Secretary's Commission on Achieving Necessary Skills that proposed a three-part foundation of basic skills (reading, writing, math, speaking, and listening), thinking skills (making decisions, solving problems, reasoning), and personal qualities (soft skills of individual responsibility, sociability, integrity). In addition, the foundational skills were coupled with a five-part component of workplace competencies, such as teamwork and leadership, understanding systems, using information and technologies, and organizing resources. About a decade later the accountability and standards movement gained traction through enactment of the federal No Child Left Behind Act that mandated annual high-stakes testing of students, with scores that could be used to reward or punish teachers and school districts alike (see Hursh, 2008). At the same time a powerful public–private partnership among state governors and corporate leaders named Achieve, Inc. (founded in the mid-1990s) launched an employability skills initiative in 2001 called the American Diploma Project, dedicated to aligning graduate requirements with college- and career-ready standards. Three years later the project staff worked closely with stakeholders to determine the core subjects needed for success in the new economy; and offered a set of standards in English and mathematics that aligned with symbolic tasks and class assignments "illustrating the intellectual demand that secondary-level students will encounter in high-performance workplaces or in credit-bearing first-year college courses" (Achieve, 2004, p. 21). In 2009, Achieve partnered with the National Governor's Association (NGA) and the Council of Chief State School Officers to align the standards with PISA benchmarks that were released at the end of that year. The science standards were cowritten in 2013 by Achieve.

Visible opposition to the common core first surfaced with a manifesto published in the national press in 2011 and signed by more than 100 think-tank researchers, current and former governmental officials, educational policymakers, and university academics. They penned: "We do not agree that a one-size-fits-all, centrally controlled curriculum for every K–12 subject makes sense for this country or for any other sizable country" (Gewertz, 2011, p. 9, para. 4). The signatories were conservatives, generally libertarians and/or Republican Party activists opposed to the Democratic Obama administration who argued that the federal government cannot force the states to innovate with a carrot-and-stick scenario of competitive grants, as it represents a direct violation of the U.S. Constitution on separation of powers. They charged that the U.S. Department of Education was prohibited by law from dictating the contents of a national curriculum. Subsequently, a handful of states led by Republican governors have opted out of the common core initiative claiming it an assault on state control of public education. And there is growing pressure to abandon the scheme at the local level as well. Recently, a metro-Atlanta county school board voted not to purchase new mathematics textbooks aligned with the common core. They were influenced by a grassroots group of Tea Party movement activists who have begun to call the policy reform *Obamacore*—a variation on the neologism coined by rightist opponents of the president's national health care legislation (Washington, 2013). Others complain that special interest groups like the liberal teachers unions have commandeered the entire process of dictating common core standards (McCluskey, 2010).

Certainly, the business community stands to reap large profits from upgrades to textbooks and assessments for the common core initiative. There are billions of dollars in revenue to be accumulated from selling and administering current educational products, and these firms are positioned to work in concert with federal, state, and local governments. At congressional committee hearings on the proposed common core standards, in 2009, the president and chief executive officer from the for-profit Pearson Assessment and Information group was invited to testify on producing the national benchmarking tests and related curricular materials. He offered that his global firm could deliver newer online evaluation technologies to capture annual data needed to measure high school students' college and career readiness (Kubach, 2009). The Bill & Melinda Gates Foundation in part funded Pearson's curricular efforts (Gates also endows Achieve, Inc.). They are shadow elites, Spring (2012) charged, instrumental "in promoting government policies related to online education and Common Core Standards" (p. 68). "Businesses and corporations not only collaborate intimately with state actors," Harvey (2007) clarified, "but even acquire a strong role in writing legislation, determining public policies, and setting regulatory frameworks (which are mainly advantageous to themselves)" (pp. 76–77). Democracy is corrupted when public funds are used for pecuniary gain with limited participation by an engaged citizenry (see Burch, 2009).

Interestingly, two camps of pedagogical progressives—liberal arts advocates and vocational educators—indict Obama's common core standards that valorize STEM readiness and a college-for-all mentality. (Obama's STEM advocacy began in 2009 with the *Educate to Innovate* campaign for raising student scores in science and mathematics, and highlighting school-based partnerships with business mentors and corporate sponsors.) The former group views this as a narrowing of the curriculum that squeezes out time during the day for the teaching of art, music, history, and foreign languages. In a recent survey of 1,000 public school teachers, about two-thirds of the respondents noted that non-common core subjects "get crowded out by extra attention being paid to math or language arts," and the vast majority believed it was driven by state-mandated testing (Common Core, 2012, p. 1). The language arts common core standards now emphasize reading nonfiction literature and informational texts. Other countries do not narrow their schooling to just the delivery and testing of basic literacy skills. A content-rich range of liberal arts subjects is evident in the curriculums of high-performing OECD member states "over and above the policies and systems of governance that shape how that content is delivered" (West, 2009, p. 14). The latter group desires multiple high school pathways that include experiential learning with vocational and technical education curriculums. An influential report written by three members of the Harvard Graduate School of Education entitled *Pathways to Prosperity: Meeting the Challenge of Preparing Young Americans for the 21st Century* indicated that non-college-bound students need access to training for middle-skill jobs. Authors Symonds, Schwartz, and Ferguson (2011) claimed "the lessons from Europe strongly suggest that well-developed, high quality vocational education programs provide excellent pathways for many young people to enter the adult work force" (p. 38). Hoffman (2011), too, noted how the highest-performing OECD nations with dual upper-secondary systems treat apprenticeships and work-based learning on par with university training for the professions. This camp believes the common core standards movement will fail those students already underserved by the system and push out others close to dropping out altogether.

Even so, the Obama administration steadfastly believes that OECD countries with common core standards have the highest rankings on international tests of academic competitiveness. Yet low-performing countries have national curriculums too. Researcher Mathis (2010) reported from a CATO Foundation study (a libertarian think tank) that eight of the top 10 highest-scoring nations on recent TIMSS tests had a centralized education curriculum; so did nine out of the top 10 lowest-scoring nations: "The presence or absence of national standards says nothing about equity, quality or the provision of necessary educational resources" (p. 7). Furthermore, of the 39 nations scoring below the US on that test, 33 of them had national standards. Given the heightened opposition to the common core, one could imagine the administration might want to modify its timetable for policy implementation. But they remain steadfast in adopting the reforms, insisting that the country is behind schedule in the making of a world-class education. Recently, Secretary Duncan (U.S. Department of Education, 2013) told an audience of news editors that the common core movement is under attack by "fringe groups" (p. 4) against state and local control or "from critics who conflate standards with curriculum, assessments and accountability" (p. 5).

CONCLUSION

When speaking to an assembly of American governors about world-class educational standards, OECD's Schleicher (NGA, 2008) proclaimed: "The world is indifferent to tradition and past reputations, unforgiving of frailty and ignorant of custom or practice. Success will go to those individuals and countries which are swift to adapt, slow to complain and open to change" (p. 19). OECD's PISA imaginary will guide the world to the promised land of postrecessionary progress. For example, the OECD (2010) report *The High Cost of Low Educational Performance* predicted that the rise of cognitive skills (as measured by PISA tests) resulted in long-term economic growth and found that a modest boost in scores will result in larger gains in a nation's gross domestic product (GDP) over time. In this sense PISA league tables are viewed as a barometer of economic health. The OECD report surmised that if all the member states could improve their scores by 25 points over the next 20 years (less than what Poland was able to accomplish in just six years), they would accrue an aggregate gain of GDP in the amount of $115 trillion over the lifetime of the generation born in 2010. If countries improved their PISA scores to the level of Finland's, the GDP would exceed $200 trillion. Economic modeling showed "the costs of inaction" (p. 10) on well-being and standards of living, but it could not predict what school reforms work best for raising test levels. Breakspear (2012) conducted an empirical study commissioned by OECD to verify the normative influence of PISA evaluations and found that the assessment "has the potential to 'define' the policy problems and set the agenda for policy debates at the national and state levels" (p. 27). Additionally, a "significant number" of member states had incorporated "PISA-like competencies" into their national standards and curriculum reforms (p. 27).

Business-driven intergovernmental organizations confirm an imagined future under global capitalism. The widespread referencing of the neoliberal imaginary materializes continuously in public speeches by political leaders, a vision of the knowledge economy already settled upon without vigorous public debate. For instance, in 2011 Secretary Duncan (U.S. Department of Education, 2011a) addressed members of the World Bank Human Development Network: "We share your commitment to results—to accelerating the acquisition of skills and knowledge. We share your commitment to cradle-to-career reform for students" (para. 11). Embedded in his reformist discourse are a number of assumptions that confirm a global policy agenda targeting human capital development and economic growth. *Results* represent accountability through international benchmarking practices; *skills and knowledge* the idea that competitive advantage will stimulate economic development; and *cradle-to-career reform* a curricular promise that educational systems will prepare all students as future knowledge workers. Then he articulated the administrative position on global capitalism:

> I want to make the case to you today that enhancing educational attainment and economic viability, both at home and abroad, is really more of a win-win game; it is an opportunity to grow the economic pie, instead of simply to carve it up. President Obama has said that improving education is vital to "win the future" for America. But accelerating learning can help all nations to win the future together. (para. 14)

This passage provides insight into the mindset that government leaders must facilitate business success by enabling the growth of new markets. That is, neoliberals believe education reforms and school improvements will drive innovation in the private sector. The government's role has become one of stimulating the conditions for capital accumulation through lessening regulatory control and simplifying bureaucratic channels, known as the new public management. Discourses about international education reform are repeated in policy circles worldwide, but particularly within the hegemony of OECD's PISA nations chiefly in the global North. Globalization has enriched a few at the expense of many by creating one hegemonic ruling class, according to Robinson (2004)—a transnational managerial elite "based in the centers of world capitalism" and "at the apex of the global economy" that "exercises authority over global institutions, and controls the levers of global policymaking" (p. 48). As a result, national education systems no longer are considered unique with long-standing historic, sociocultural, and political traditions. OECD treats all countries as "culturally indifferent" (p. 20) when comparing students on a number of school outputs related to academic achievement, such as reporting annual pass rates on subject-matter tests or the numbers of yearly school completers (Meyer & Benavot, 2013). The league tables do not drill down and compare the economic wealth of countries, states, cities or regions, and neighborhoods in an analysis of educational progress. The playing field has flattened as neoliberals contend, and national sovereignty is quickly dismissed as an obsolete and old-fashioned construct—except when other countries rich or poor alike are expected to emulate the best practices of a Finland or a Shanghai. This viewpoint now paves the way for what Kamens (2013) has called an international audit culture, with OECD's PISA the magnet that attracts nonmember states into the fold. "As benchmarking becomes the normative means for assessing national and world educational progress, adoption of like policies and approaches becomes more likely," Kamens (2013) offered; "copying and imitating 'leaders' is also likely to be taken as a positive sign internationally that a country takes very seriously its obligations to improve society by managing educational outcomes" (pp. 134–135). Such is the soft power of OECD's PISA.

REFERENCES

Achieve. (2004). *Ready or not: Creating a high school diploma that counts*. Washington, DC: Author.
Asia Society. (2011). *Improving teacher quality around the world: The International Summit on the Teaching Profession*. New York, NY: Author.
Asia Society. (2012). *Teaching and leadership for the twenty-first century: The 2012 International Summit on the Teaching Profession*. New York, NY: Author.
Bieber, T., & Martens, K. (2011). The OECD PISA study as a soft power in education? Lessons from Switzerland and the US. *European Journal of Education* (Part I), 46(1), 101–116.
Breakspear, S. (2012). The policy impact of PISA: An exploration of the normative effects of international benchmarking in school system performance. *OECD Education Working Papers*, No. 71. Paris: OECD.
Bulle, N. (2011). Comparing OECD educational models through the prism of PISA. *Comparative Education*, 47(4), 503–521.
Burch, P. (2009). *Hidden markets: The new education privatization*. New York, NY: Routledge.
Cavanaugh, S. (2011, April 19). Race to Top funds prompt district, school-level efforts: Districts using aid to experiment. *Education Week*. Retrieved September 28, 2013, from http://www.edweek.org/ew/articles/2011/04/20/28rtt_ep.h30.html
Common Core. (2012, March). *Learning less: Public school teachers describe a narrowing curriculum*. Retrieved February 7, 2013, from http://www.commoncore.org/_docs/cc-learning-less-mar12.pdf
Dale, R. (1999). Specifying globalization effects on national policy: A focus on the mechanisms. *Journal of Education Policy*, 14(1), 1–17.
Darling-Hammond, L., & Wentworth, L. (2010). *Benchmarking learning systems: Student performance assessment in international context*. Stanford, CA: Stanford University, Stanford Center for Opportunity Policy in Education.
Fairclough, N. (2010). *Critical discourse analysis: The critical study of language* (2nd ed.). Harlow, England: Pearson Education.
Gewertz, C. (2011, May 16). "Manifesto" proposing shared curriculum draws counterattack. *Education Week*, 31(33), 9.
Grek, S. (2009). Governing by numbers: The PISA "effect" in Europe. *Journal of Education Policy*, 24(1), 23–37.
Grek, S. (2012). Learning from meetings and comparison: A critical examination of the policy tools of transnational. In G. Steiner-Khamsi & F. Waldow (Eds.), *World yearbook of education 2012: Policy borrowing and lending in education* (pp. 41–61). London, England: Routledge.
Harvey, D. (2007). *A brief history of neoliberalism*. Oxford, England: Oxford University Press.
Henry, M., Lingard, B., Rizvi, F., & Taylor, S. (2001). *The OECD, globalisation and education policy*. Oxford, England: Elsevier Science.
Hoffman, N. (2011). *Schooling in the workplace: How six of the world's best vocational education systems prepare young people for jobs and life*. Cambridge, MA: Harvard Education Press.

Hursh, D. (2008). *High-stakes testing and the decline of teaching and learning: The real crisis in education.* Lanham, MD: Rowman & Littlefield.
Kamens, D. H. (2013). Globalization and the emergence of an audit culture: PISA and the search for "best practices" and magic bullets. In Hans-Dieter Meyer & Aaron Benavot (Eds.), *PISA, power and policy: The emergence of global educational governance* (pp. 117–139). Oxford, England: Symposium Books.
Knill, C. (2005). Introduction: Cross-national policy convergence: Concepts, approaches and explanatory factors. *Journal of European Public Policy, 12*(5), 1–11.
Kubach, D. (2009, December 8). Testimony of Douglas Kubach, Pearson Assessment & Information. U.S. House of Representatives, Committee on Education and Labor. Retrieved February 7, 2013, from http://archives.republicans.edlabor.house.gov/Media/file/111th/hearings/fc/120809/Kubach.pdf
Lewis, C. C. (2010, September 10). A public proving ground for standards-based practice: Why we need it, what it might look like. *Education Week.* Retrieved February 7, 2013, from http://www.edweek.org/ew/articles/2010/09/15/03lewis.h30.html?tkn=LLRFwPwaEDmY6b%2BaXu4NFGnY4c9QzBKs7U0n&cmp=clp-edweek
Mathis, W. J. (2010). *The "common core" standards initiative: An effective reform tool?* Boulder, CO: Education and the Public Interest Center & Education Policy Research Unit. Retrieved February 7, 2013, from http://greatlakescenter.org/docs/Policy_Briefs/Mathis_NationalStandards.pdf
McCluskey, N. (2010, February 17). Behind the curtain: Assessing the case for national curriculum standards. *Policy Analysis*, No. 661. Washington, DC: Cato Institute.
Meyer, H., & Benavot, A. (2013). PISA and the globalization of education governance: Some puzzles and problems. In Hans-Dieter Meyer & Aaron Benavot (Eds.), *PISA, power and policy: The emergence of global educational governance* (pp. 9–26). Oxford, England: Symposium Books.
Miller, P., & Rose, N. (2008). *Governing the present: Administering economic, social and personal life.* Cambridge, England: Polity Press.
National Governor's Association. (2008). *Benchmarking for success: Ensuring U.S. students receive a world-class education.* Washington, DC: Author.
OECD. (2010). *The high cost of low educational performance: The long-run economic impact of improving PISA outcomes.* Paris, France: Author.
OECD. (2011). *Strong performers and successful reformers in education: Lessons from PISA for the United States.* Paris, France: Author.
OECD. (2012). *Education at a Glance 2012: OECD Indicators.* Paris, France: Author.
Robinson, W.L. (2004). *A theory of global capitalism: Production, class, and state in a transnational world.* Baltimore, MD: Johns Hopkins University Press.
Rose, N. (1990). *Governing the soul: The shaping of the private self.* London, England: Routledge.
Rose, R. (1993). *Lesson-drawing in public policy: A guide to learning across time and space.* Chatham, NJ: Chatham House.
Sahlberg, P. (2011). *Finnish lessons: What can the world learn from educational change in Finland?* New York, NY: Teachers College Press.
Sawchuk, S. (2011, May 27). U.S. reforms out of sync with high-performing nations, report finds. *Education Week.* Retrieved February 7, 2013, from http://www.edweek.org/ew/articles/2011/05/27/33international.h30.html
Secretary's Commission on Achieving Necessary Skills. (1991). *What work requires of schools: A SCANS report for American 2000.* Washington, DC: U.S. Department of Labor.
Spring, J. (2012). *Education networks: Power, wealth, cyberspace, and the digital mind.* New York, NY: Routledge.

Steiner-Khamsi, G. (2004). Blazing a trail for policy theory and practice. In G. Steiner-Khamsi (Ed.), *The global politics of educational borrowing and lending* (pp. 201–220). New York, NY: Teachers College Press.

Symonds, W. C., Schwartz, R. B., & Ferguson, R. (2011, February). *Pathways to prosperity: Meeting the challenge of preparing young people for the 21st century*. Report issued by the Pathways to Prosperity Project. Cambridge, MA: Harvard Graduate School of Education.

Taylor, S., & Henry, M. (2000). Globalization and educational policymaking: A case study. *Educational Theory, 50*(4), 487–504.

U.S. Department of Education. (2010a). *A blueprint for reform: The reauthorization of the Elementary and Secondary Education Act*. Retrieved August 3, 2012, from http://www2.ed.gov/policy/elsec/leg/blueprint/blueprint.pdf

U.S. Department of Education. (2010b, December 7). *Education secretary Arne Duncan issues statement on the results of the Program for International Student Assessment*. Retrieved February 7, 2013, from http://www.ed.gov/news/press-releases/education-secretary-arne-duncan-issues-statement-results-program-international-s

U.S. Department of Education. (2011a, March 3). Improving human capital in a competitive world—education reform in the U.S. Retrieved September 28, 2013, from http://www.ed.gov/news/speeches/improving-human-capital-competitive-world-education-reform-us

U.S. Department of Education. (2011b, May 24). Lessons from high-performing countries. Secretary Duncan's remarks at National Center on Education and Economy national symposium. Retrieved September 28, 2013, from http://www.ed.gov/news/speeches/lessons-high-performing-countries

U.S. Department of Education. (2011c, June 6). U.S. Department of Education and Asia Society release report from International Summit on the Teaching Profession, showcase lessons from around the world. Retrieved September 28, 2013, from http://www.ed.gov/news/press-releases/us-department-education-and-asia-society-release-report-international-summit-tea

U.S. Department of Education. (2013, June 25). Duncan pushes back on attacks on the common core standards. Retrieved September 28, 2013, from http://www.ed.gov/news/speeches/duncan-pushes-back-attacks-common-core-standards

Washington, W. (2013, May 2). New national academic standards stoke new fears. *Atlanta Journal-Constitution*. Retrieved September 28, 2013, from http://www.myajc.com/news/news/local-education/new-national-academic-standards-stoke-new-fears/nXfQj/

West, M. (2009). High achieving countries don't narrow. In Common Core (Ed.), *Why we're behind: What top nations teach their student but we don't* (pp. 13–16). Washington, DC: Common Core.

8 Charter Schools
Appearance Versus Essence

Shawgi Tell

Since their inception 23 years ago, charter schools have been sold as a popular silver bullet for the ills ailing the public education system. Advocates claim that charter schools will raise student achievement, increase autonomy for teachers and administrators, expand choices for parents, enhance efficiency, eliminate bureaucracy, engender pedagogical innovation, and compel traditional public schools to improve through competitive pressures. The impression is created that charter schools will ultimately change the equation in society (Betts & Hill, 2010; Chubb & Moe, 1990; Lake, 2013).

From the beginning, however, charter schools have been plagued by problems, controversy, scandal, criticism, and resistance. Fisman (2013) points out that "on June 4, 1991 [less than five months after starting his term], Minnesota Gov. Arne Carlson signed into law a [charter school] bill that set in motion one of the most significant—and controversial—education reform movements in modern [American] history" (para. 1). Many have now exposed charter schools as little more than antipublic, union-busting, cost-cutting, pay-the-rich schemes cynically promoted under the banner of high ideals (Giroux, 2012; Karp, 2010; Lipman, 2011; Saltman, 2010; Weil, 2009).

By sorting through the disinformation on this topic, this chapter shows that charter schools, now in their third decade, are a direct product of the neoliberal agenda of corporate education reform and are not only not delivering on what they promise, but fundamentally represent a program that lowers the level of education, violates the public interest, and promotes capital-centered interests in the name of "improving schools," increasing "achievement," and serving the common good. The chapter concludes with an alternative to neoliberal arrangements in education and society by outlining a modern definition of rights. The violation of the right to education is the main source of problems in education.

CHARTER SCHOOL DEFINITION

State charter school laws typically define a charter school as a publicly funded, tuition-free, nonsectarian school open to all students. Charter schools are considered "schools of choice" that operate independently of existing public school districts. A charter is a contract between the charter school and a charter authorizer. Speaking properly, a charter school is a contract school.

The word "contract" is a market category, which is significant because it speaks to the political, economic, and legal philosophy behind charter schools. According to this philosophy, in the capitalist marketplace, people are self-interested actors who voluntarily enter into exchange relations with each other for their own personal gain. This commercial relationship is based on "perfect competition," "scarcity," private property, and possessive individualism. Those who "survive" are deemed the "fittest."

Most dictionaries define a contract as a legally binding agreement between two or more parties to perform, or refrain from performing, something within a specified period of time. Rewards and sanctions are usually part of such agreements. At the institutional level, contracting usually involves some form of privatization and restriction of public right.

Charter school contracts are typically five years long and stipulate how a school will operate, who it will educate and employ, where it will be located, how and when performance goals will be reached, and how funds will be obtained and used. Some charters can be as short as 3 years, while others may be as long as 10 or 15, such as in Alaska, Washington, DC, and Arizona. The school's contract is essentially an education and business plan outlining a broad range of curricular, financial, and administrative provisions, which tend to differ from school to school.

At the end of the term of the contract, the charter authorizer examines the charter school's performance to determine whether or not to renew, revoke, or restrict the charter. Scores on high-stakes standardized tests produced by a handful of for-profit companies are the main criteria of performance. This setup compels charter schools to heavily emphasize test drills because their fate rests on these scores. This intense preoccupation with test scores is also often linked to more authoritarian student discipline codes as well as selective enrollment patterns in charter schools. There is now a large body of literature that shows that charter schools intensify segregation due to selective student enrollment and attrition practices (Bifulco & Ladd, 2007; Frankenberg, Siegel-Hawley, & Wang, 2010; Rotberg, 2014; Scott, 2005).

It is essential to appreciate that today's high-stakes standardized tests not only are not the product of the public will, but are punitive, time consuming, curriculum narrowing, expensive, developmentally inappropriate, and based on pseudoscience (Au, 2009; FairTest, 2007; Garrison, 2009; Nichols & Berliner, 2007; Ravitch, 2010). They are philosophically, statistically, and methodologically flawed. This is why, as Berliner (2008) shows, improved test scores do not mean improved learning. The widely viewed film *Race to Nowhere* also proves this point. Even though students can frequently ace standardized tests, they still often need extensive remedial instruction when they get to college because good performance is not the same as good learning.

In most states charter school authorizers include local public school boards, the state board of education, universities, and not-for-profit agencies. Some states set up "independent" bodies and "commissions" to approve and authorize charter schools. Many believe these are unconstitutional and lower the bar for charter approval and expansion. They are seen as additional top-down arrangements that further circumvent publicly elected bodies.

Charter school proponents favor states with multiple authorizers as this allows them to "charter hop" until they find an authorizer that will approve them. Ohio, the so-called wild west of charter schools, has 67 authorizers (National Association of Charter School Authorizers [NACSA], 2013). Local school boards tend to be more reluctant than other bodies to grant charters because charter schools siphon millions of dollars from them (Hopper, 2011; Kight, 2008), usurp their authority, and frequently produce lower test scores. Various reports from NACSA and other sources show that charter school accountability generally remains weak. Importantly, many authorizers are only nominally public; they are not public in the modern sense of the word.

CHARTER SCHOOL FACTS

Charter schools have been expanding rapidly since the first charter school law was passed in Minnesota in 1991. Today, more than 2.3 million students are enrolled in over 6,000 charter schools across the country (NAPCS, 2013). Lake (2013) says charter schools are growing at a rate of 300–400 a year and that 547 new ones opened in 2011–2012.

During the last 20 years, however, well over 1,000 charter schools have been closed for poor academic performance, unethical practices, or mismanagement, according to the Center for Education Reform (2011, p. 7). Many are actually closed for financial fraud and embezzlement. Given that these closures have generally taken place under weak oversight, it is not unreasonable to assume that far more charter schools would have been closed had accountability been more serious and effective. Across the country, 143 charter schools closed in 2008–2009 and 152 closed in 2010–2011 (Lake & Gross, 2012). In addition, many charter schools are on some sort of probation list or close to landing on one. In Ohio alone, nearly 30% of charter schools have been closed since 1997. A record 17 charter schools in that state closed in 2013 alone (Richards & Bush, 2014).

Instability has long characterized the charter school sector. Oddly, though, many charter school advocates view the closing and opening of charter schools ("charter churn") as something of a virtue, as an affirmation of the "value" of the "free market." Turnover and instability are seen as good things. The "logic" here is that if charter schools are "successful," if parents like them, if test scores are high, then charter schools will remain open. If, on the other hand, parents are unsatisfied, test scores are low, or corruption and patronage are the norm, then the charter school may close. In other words, you live and die by the market, like a business. A November 4, 2013, article by Jeff Bryant of *Salon*, "The Charter-School Lie: Market-Based Education Gambles With Our Children," states that:

> This faith in churn rate is behind the movement for expanding charter schools. Writing at his blog at the education trade newspaper Education Week, teacher and edu-blogger Anthony Cody recently observed, "Charter supporters are now advocating that charter schools that are not producing results must be closed with the same ruthlessness as traditional public schools ... This is how markets function ... We don't need to wait long to find out if schools are 'good' or 'bad.' These judgments should be made fast, and acted upon immediately." Leading charter school advocates tell us, in fact, that closing charters down and interrupting more children's education is a really good thing. According to the National Association of Charter School Authorizers, the overall closure rate of charters has ballooned by over 255 percent. This is "a positive trend," said that association's president and CEO. (section Welcome to the Charter Churn, paras. 8–10)

However, a human-centered approach, with no ruthlessness, is what is actually needed in an enterprise created to nurture the educational, social, and emotional needs of youth who, by definition, are the future (Dewey, 1900).

In reality, school closings are disruptive and stressful for students, parents, teachers, and administrators. They leave people feeling demoralized and disillusioned. People may also start questioning the wisdom of marketized education arrangements. It is simply not possible to build community, collegiality, continuity, and stability—key ingredients of success—when teachers, students, parents, principals, and schools are continually subjected to the chaos, anarchy, and violence of the market. Learning can be optimized only under stable, secure, predictable, and supportive conditions. Parents, teachers, and students should not have to wake up one morning, as so often happens, and suddenly learn that their school is being closed abruptly.

Charter schools now make up almost 6% of all public schools (Lake, 2013) and about 5% of the entire K–12 student population (Resmovits, 2012). There are roughly 99,000 public schools (US Department of Education, 2013) and approximately 50 million public K–12 students in the US (US Department of Education, 2013).

The US Department of Education (2012) also points out that:

> In 2009–10, over half (54 percent) of charter schools were elementary schools. Secondary and combined schools accounted for 27 and 19 percent of charter schools, respectively. In that year, about 55 percent of charter schools were located in cities, 21 percent were in suburban areas, 8 percent were in towns, and 16 percent were in rural areas.

While more than half the students enrolled in charter schools are eligible for free lunch (Lake, 2013), many charter schools do not offer food services or facilities. Most charter schools, it should also be noted, are newly created; they are not conversion schools. In addition, most use lottery systems when applications exceed seats available.

Today, 42 states, Puerto Rico, and Washington, DC, have charter school laws. The 8 states without charter school laws include Alabama, Kentucky, Montana, Nebraska, North Dakota, South Dakota, Vermont, and West Virginia (Center for Education Reform, 2013). Given the relentless top-down drive for neoliberal arrangements in education, charter school laws are likely to be passed in one or more of these states in the foreseeable future.

Charter schools receive most of their funding from the public purse, mainly in the form of per-pupil funding. Typically, when a student leaves a traditional public school to enroll in a charter school, most of the public per-pupil funds linked to the student follow the student to the charter school. These are mostly state and federal funds, but in some instances can also include local taxes, which raises serious concerns over who decides the use and fate of local public funds (Miron & Urschel, 2010).

Charter schools on average receive 70–90% of the per-pupil funding that goes to traditional public schools. A main reason for this amount of funding is because charter schools tend to provide fewer programs, resources, and facilities than traditional public schools and usually rely on host public school districts for many services that do not usually show up in their budgets. Many, perhaps most, charter schools are simply not as well established, well developed, and well resourced as traditional public schools.

Besides this source of funding, venture philanthropists like Bill Gates, Sam Walton, and Eli Broad have poured billions of dollars into the charter school sector over the years. They have also spent many years and dollars demonizing public schools. For its part, the federal government uses the Public Charter Schools Program, authorized in 1994, to funnel hundreds of millions of public dollars to the charter school sector.

About 88% of charter schools are not unionized (NAPCS, 2010). For this and other reasons, the teacher and student turnover rate in charter schools exceeds that found in regular public schools (Miron & Applegate, 2007). Even the principal turnover rate in charter schools is very high. Cuban (2007) says, "Seventy-one percent of charter school principals expect to leave their posts within five years" (para. 1).

Teachers usually leave charter schools because they are dissatisfied with working conditions in charter schools (Miron & Applegate, 2007). In general, charter school teachers are younger, less experienced, and paid less than teachers in traditional public schools. They also tend to have fewer benefits and weaker retirement plans, if any. Many states actually allow uncertified teachers to teach in charter schools. Charter schools also tend to have longer school days and years than traditional public schools, even though there is no evidence that more seat time ensures more learning. Predictably, burnout is more common in charter schools (Stuit & Smith, 2009).

Charter schools are deregulated schools, which means that they do not have to follow many district, local, or state laws, rules, regulations, and contracts traditional public schools are legally required to uphold. This "autonomy" is said to be in exchange for "accountability," that is, better student performance on curriculum-narrowing high-stakes standardized tests. Because of their deregulated nature, charter schools have a much more private and corporate character to them than traditional public schools; they more closely resemble private schools than public schools.

Even though they are supposedly tuition-free, nonsectarian, "innovative" public schools open to all, charter schools tend to underenroll students with disabilities and English Language Learners, which violates both federal and state laws. They also underenroll other high-needs/high-cost students, such as pregnant students, homeless students, and students with "behavior problems." These groups are typically considered "poor test takers" and a "drag" on the school (Howe & Welner, 2002; Miron, Urschel, Mathis, & Tornquist, 2010; Rich, 2012; Zehr, 2011; Zollers & Ramanathan, 1998).

INFORMATION, MISINFORMATION, DISINFORMATION

To better understand charter schools it is helpful to briefly distinguish among information, misinformation, and disinformation. Information refers to the process of giving shape or form to something. To provide information is to shape or form knowledge. To distort information is to undermine its coherence, validity, and integrity. How information is communicated, shaped, and presented is thus very critical, especially in a society defined by antagonistic and irreconcilable interests.

Misinformation takes place when a person unintentionally communicates the wrong information to someone. This is accidental and not meant to harm anyone. It may take the form of an individual unwittingly communicating information from the wrong source, while mistaking it for the correct source. Misinformation is often easy to rectify and people are generally understanding of such human errors.

Disinformation, on the other hand, is the purposeful use of information in a way that hides the real context of things so as to ideologically and politically disarm people in order to confuse them and render them vulnerable to unwittingly adopting ideas, views, and agendas that are actually harmful to their interests. Disinformation relies on deception and promotes incoherence, usually in the service of a self-serving agenda. It often combines false information with correct information to achieve its goals and is more than mere propaganda. It is a form of what sociologists call false consciousness. The problem of disinformation is significant because "the public, even the attentive public, depends heavily on the media to keep informed and to sort through competing claims," observes charter school proponent Jeffrey Henig (2008, p. 4).

Disinformation also promotes individual and collective amnesia and relies heavily on undermining the ability of humans to cognize their experience and reality. It divides people into competing camps so as to pit them against each other and conquer them. Furthermore, it instills the belief that people have no capacity to oppose attacks on their rights and that their only role is to go along with decisions made by others. One example of this is the intense disinformation that always surrounds the worn-out discourse on "balancing the budget" at the state and federal levels. People are routinely presented with false choices like cutting social programs or raising taxes, as if these are the only ways to deal with budget concerns. Capital-centered discourse promotes the disinformation that there is "no money," therefore bad things must happen. Things will supposedly improve in some vague future that never arrives. Meanwhile, trillions of dollars continue to be used for war, repression, "security," interest payments to the banks, and Wall Street bailouts. Pay-the-rich schemes continue to multiply while millions of people grow more impoverished and insecure.

Disinformation also violates the right to free speech and undermines the public interest because deception, incoherence, and narrow agendas are incompatible with the common good. The public needs enlightened, accurate, coherent information and analysis at all times.

Importantly, disinformation has intensified as media ownership has become more concentrated in fewer hands. Today the entire media is controlled by a handful of major corporations, which is inconsistent with democracy. Fortunately, the internet is providing many individuals and groups with a space to share more accurate and prosocial information. There is a great need for information, analysis, and coherence that favors the public interest.

Most of the "information" surrounding charter schools may be called disinformation and often comes from "balanced" writers and proponents of charter schools. Charter school advocates often exclude negative information about charter schools, or, once a problem is exposed, they "spin" it in order to downplay it. This sometimes involves lowering the level of culture through gossip, innuendo, slander, or character assassination of people who expose problems—the politics of personal destruction. Only through disciplined and uninterrupted investigation can a person really learn things about charter schools that one cannot learn just by reading the most available sources. Anti-consciousness, the product of no inquiry, only perpetuates disinformation.

DEMYTHOLOGIZING CHARTER SCHOOLS

Charter School Performance

One of the most significant myths about charter schools is that they will raise student "achievement" as "measured" by curriculum-narrowing high-stakes standardized tests produced by a handful of for-profit corporations. Besides the fact that the majority of charter schools do not actually outscore traditional public schools (Buchheit, 2012; CREDO, 2009; Ravitch, 2011; US Department of Education, 2010), this diversionary focus makes it seem like the tests and the scores students attain on them are somehow legitimate, valid, meaningful, unassailable, and scientific.

Various scholars, however, have exposed the logical, philosophical, statistical, and methodological flaws with these tests and shown how they are political tools used to justify new arrangements in education and have little or nothing to do with "improving schools" (Au, 2009; Garrison, 2009; Nichols & Berliner, 2007). The tests are used mainly to justify the vertical classification of humans according to their "worth." They emphasize speed, competition, and memorization and fail to prepare young people for life. The widely viewed 90-minute documentary *Race to Nowhere* makes this point effectively. Yet charter school advocates are preoccupied with scores on curriculum-narrowing high-stakes standardized tests and use and manipulate such "information" to simultaneously advance their cause and demonize traditional public schools.

It is also not clear how creative, unique, or pedagogically independent charter schools can be when they, like traditional public schools, have to submit to the same top-down time-consuming tests mandated by the corporate-government sector. Teachers have long highlighted the loss of joy, creativity, and knowledge caused by high-stakes standardized tests.

To date there is little evidence that turning schools into performance-based contractual arrangements has raised the level of education, culture, and knowledge in society. However, there is extensive evidence that such arrangements in education generate considerable cheating, corruption, scandal, and failure. Websites such as *Schools Matter* (http://atthechalkface.com) and *Charter School Scandals* (http://charterschoolscandals.blogspot.com) keep the public regularly apprised of numerous charter school improprieties.

Selective Enrollment in Charter Schools

Although charter schools are ostensibly nonsectarian, tuition-free schools open to all, it is a well-established fact that they underenroll students with disabilities, English Language Learners, and other high-need/high-cost students (Fabricant & Fine, 2012). This (a) keeps costs down and profits up, and (b) ensures higher test scores so as to increase the likelihood of charter renewal. High-need/high-cost students tend to score more poorly on standardized tests than their less-needy/less-costly peers.

To claim that charter schools are public schools and that they are open to and admit all students, when in reality they do not, is straightforward disinformation. Scott (2005) and Lubienski and Weitzel (2010) show that charter schools frequently "counsel out" or "steer" away students with disabilities through a variety of explicit and implicit methods. Welner (2013) details many of these methods in an article titled "The Dirty Dozen: How Charter Schools Influence Student Enrollment." Bulkley and Fisler (2002) state that "charter schools can use targeted recruitment, mandatory parental involvement policies, and applicants' prior records (in some states) to avoid students they do not want to enroll" (p. 7). Those excluded from charter schools usually end up being "dumped" back into traditional public schools, which accept all students. This, in turn, sets up these public schools for even greater hardship, ensuring further "failure" and "reform."

Parent Empowerment and Choice

Charter school advocates routinely argue that charter schools empower parents. The entire charter school discourse is imbued with this idea. The impression is created that modern schools exist mainly to serve parents; they are supposedly the main beneficiaries of modern education in a complex mass industrial society.

However, modern public schools exist to serve more than just parents. First and foremost, modern public schools, the product of 150 years of struggle, exist to serve society, its members, and the economy. Parents are certainly an important part of the equation, but they are hardly the only or main so-called stakeholders. This narrow self-serving focus on parents is evident in top-down schemes such as "parent-trigger" initiatives being attempted in various states. These are essentially psuedo-populist strategies to transfer public assets and control to the private sector in the name of "turning around" "failing" schools and "helping kids." California approved the nation's first parent-trigger law in 2010.

"Choice" is perhaps one of the most misleading concepts in charter school discourse and is closely linked to the notion of "parent empowerment." Charter school advocates claim that they want to "empower parents" by giving them an opportunity to escape their "failing" zip code through "innovative choices." Never in this narrative, however, is there any mention of the role of the corporate-government sector in organizing and mandating failure in these zip codes for generations. The root cause of problems is casually ignored in favor of an alternative reality created for consumption.

In the neoliberal context, "choice" really means government abdicating responsibility for the provision of education and opening up the sphere of public education to the market and "education service providers," including EMOs (education management organizations). In plain language, it means pillaging the public sector and privatizing public schools. "Choice," in other words, has much more to do with serving capital-centered interests than it does with helping families and their children succeed. "Choice" actually negates human-centered educational arrangements in the name of "empowering parents" and "improving schools." It is significant that:

> In 2011–2012, 36% of all public charter schools in the U.S. were operated by private EMOs (this includes both for-profit and nonprofit EMOs), and these schools accounted for almost 44% of all students

enrolled in charter schools. The proportion of students in for-profit EMO-operated schools is slightly larger than the proportion of students enrolled in schools operated by nonprofit EMOs. (Miron & Gulosino, 2013, p. i)

Miron and Gulosino indicate that there are roughly 100 for-profit EMOs and 200 nonprofit EMOs operating in the US. It should be noted that nonprofit EMOs received large amounts of private funding and engage in extensive contracting with for-profit entities. These are essentially "backdoor" for-profit arrangements.

In the name of "empowering parents" and "giving them choices," school choice advocates seek to make public education, a monumental historic achievement, more rapidly and fully available to major owners of capital, thereby undermining the public good while further enriching a handful of wealthy individuals and organizations. With more than $600 billion at stake and nowhere else for owners of capital to invest "their" money in a continually failing economy, it is easy to see why K–12 public education is an attractive "market" for the rich. A quick Google search generates many examples of private investors pursuing charter school arrangements for the purpose of maximizing profits. Most do not know the first thing about running a school or educating young people. Even green cards are being offered to those who wish to start charter schools in the US and "make money" (Simon, 2012).

Of course, providing options in education does not have to coincide with creating charter schools. Choices can exist without charter schools. In fact, traditional public schools have been offering a broad range of programs, pedagogies, and learning experiences to students with diverse abilities, aspirations, and desires for generations—well before the "school choice" movement emerged (Corwin & Schneider, 2005).

Are Charter Schools Public Schools?

Does calling something public automatically make it public? The vast majority of charter school advocates insist that charter schools are public schools and that they should be treated and funded like public schools, but without adhering to many of the public rules, regulations, and agreements traditional public schools are required to follow.

In reality, charter schools are run by boards of trustees comprised of individuals who are not publicly elected. They frequently engage in selective student enrollment and attrition practices. Many require admissions exams. Some are sectarian. Many charge parents "voluntary fees" or compel them to sign contracts to perform free work at the charter school. Most have no unions. Thousands are operated by for-profit entities. Many also violate open-meeting laws and/or dodge state audit requirements. Very few are run by teachers. And many are authorized by bodies that are only nominally public. Charter schools more closely resemble private schools.

In some instances, charter school operators have gone out of their way to stress that they are private organizations so as to block union drives by teachers as well as any public scrutiny of their operations (Hood, 2011). It is also worth noting that charter schools operated by private entities do not have to uphold some of the constitutional rights of students and employees because such entities are not considered "state actors," a legal classification with significant implications (Baker, 2012).

Garrison (2009) asks, if charter schools are public schools, why does the word "charter" appear before the word "school"? It is helpful to keep in mind that a charter is a contract and that a contract is a market category. Charter schools are capital-centered arrangements.

Hoffman (2010) points out that while charter schools get most of their money from tax dollars, "that is not enough to render them public schools. There are many other organizations that pay for operations with public funds but are still private organizations" (para. 3). Ravitch (2012) agrees that charter schools "are public when it comes to collecting tax money, *but not in most other respects*" (para. 5, emphasis added). Besides these considerations, a recent poll shows that "the majority of American parents support public education and oppose reform mandates that favor the proliferation of corporate-backed charter schools" (McCauley, 2013, para. 1).

NEOLIBERALISM PRODUCES CHARTER SCHOOLS

Lipman (2011) writes that:

> When President Obama appointed Arne Duncan, former-CEO of Chicago Public Schools, to head the U.S. Department of Education in 2008, he signaled an intention to accelerate a neoliberal education program that has been unfolding over the past two decades. This agenda calls for expanding education markets and employing market principles across school systems. It features mayoral control of school districts, closing "failing" public schools or handing them over to corporate-style "turnaround" organizations, expanding school "choice" and privately run but publicly funded charter schools, weakening teacher unions, and enforcing top-down accountability and incentivized performance targets on schools, classrooms, and teachers. (section Neoliberal Restructuring of Public Education, para. 1)

Few have heard of the term "neoliberalism" before, but it is slowly catching on as more articles and books on the topic appear. Perhaps the best known of these books is David Harvey's *Brief History of Neoliberalism* (2007). "Neo" means new, while "liberalism" refers to the economic doctrine of laissez-faire capitalism, the so-called free market. Strung together, the words "neo" and "liberal" mean a rebirth of liberalism, or the new "free market."

The "free market" is based on the exchange of commodities produced by private competing producers who are part of a complex social division of labor. Private ownership of property, individualism, competition, the pursuit of self-interest, profit maximization, and anarchic social production are at the heart of the "free-market" economy. All these features stand in sharp contradiction to the large-scale, cooperative, and social character of modern-day production and distribution. Most problems are rooted firmly in this contradiction.

Due to its very nature, the "free market" prevents conscious overall human planning of the economy, ensuring continual disharmony between production and consumption. The so-called business cycle is but one expression of the chaos, anarchy, and violence of the "free market." In addition, the "free market" tolerates only that which is marketable, and its advocates vigorously oppose any political economy that differs from it, which belies the notion that "free-market" advocates defend freedom and choice.

Today's economy is of course far from "free." It is highly monopolized by a few banks and corporations; they dominate all aspects of the economy. Keeping in mind that economic domination means political domination, those without capital, the vast majority, have no say over the direction of the economy or politics; they remain broadly marginalized from the affairs of society.

Neoliberalism emerged around 1980 at home and abroad. Heavily promoted by President Ronald Reagan and Prime Minister Margaret Thatcher, neoliberalism marks a new set of political and economic arrangements to help the rich escape the law of the falling rate of profit. The main features of neoliberalism are privatization, deregulation, the abdication of government responsibility for the well-being of the people, the elimination of the public, greater repression at home, and more wars abroad. The dismantling of the welfare state created between 1935 and 1975 is a main object of neoliberal wrecking. To put it another way, neoliberalism essentially abolishes the equilibrium that existed for generations between capital and labor, and launches an all-out assault on the rights of the people and the claims of the working class. This naturally necessitates greater repression, militarization, spying, and other police-state arrangements.

Under neoliberalism, there are no citizens with political rights, only consumers, "innovators," and heroic entrepreneurs. Individuals "get ahead" by fending for themselves and competing with others for so-called scarce resources in a society that is actually drowning in overabundance. Saltman (2010) explains further that:

> [Neoliberal doctrine] aims to eradicate the distinction between the public and private spheres, treating all public goods and services as private ones. It individualizes responsibility for the well-being of the

individual and the society, treating persons as economic entities—consumers or entrepreneurs, and it has little place for the role of individuals as public citizens or the collective public responsibilities of democracy. (pp. 36–37)

Charter schools emerged only after neoliberalism took hold. They are a main form of "free-market" and deregulatory education "reform." In 1988, only five years after the call in *A Nation at Risk* (National Commission on Excellence in Education, 1983) for "restructuring" K–12 public schools, Ray Budde, an obscure New England educator, officially promoted the first blueprint for charter schools in the US in a 126-page publication titled *Education by Charter: Restructuring School Districts. Key to Long-Term Continuing Improvement in American Education.* He quickly received strong support for the idea of charter schools from Albert Shanker, president of the United Federation of Teachers from 1964 to 1984, as well as president of the American Federation of Teachers from 1974 to 1997.

It is strange that Shanker, a so-called tough labor leader and defender of teachers, supported an education arrangement so hostile to unions and public right. Nearly 90% of today's charter schools lack unions (NAPCS, 2010). Forces on the left have long believed and argued that Shanker did not support charter schools as they exist today. They claim that Shanker was against privatization and for-profit arrangements in education, and that he would never promote something hostile to teachers or the public interest. He certainly would not support union-free public schools.

But the following statement from Shanker that appeared in the *Wall Street Journal* in 1989 reveals his dedication to the neoliberal program in education:

> It's time to admit that public education operates like a planned economy, a bureaucratic system in which everybody's role is spelled out in advance and there are few incentives for innovation and productivity. It's no surprise that our school system doesn't improve: It more resembles the communist economy than our own market economy. ("Reding, wrighting & erithmatic," 1989, p. A14)

This was a clarion call for *perestroika* in American public education by a labor leader who "represented" thousands of teachers for decades. It appeared in a major organ of big business only one year after Budde's blueprint for charter schools was published and sounds like something a right-wing politician would say.

It is also significant that the first for-profit charter schools emerged in the mid-1990s, *very soon* after the first charter school was established in Minnesota in 1992. The fact that they appeared around the same time as the first charter school law was passed is revealing. Given these facts, and given Shanker's close collaboration with pro-charter school Minnesota legislators that got the nation's first charter school law passed in 1991, it is hard to argue that charter schools started out as a noble, progressive, grassroots vision that was hijacked much later by major owners of capital. Is it an accident that, among other things, so few charter schools, then and now, are started or operated by teachers?

It is important to recall once again that charter means contract, and that contract refers to a market category. Charter schools are, by definition, a way to marketize schools, and marketizing schools means eliminating propublic regulations, including those governing labor relations, for example, collective bargaining agreements. Perhaps Shanker and Budde were not thinking of matters in this way—perhaps they overlooked the capital-centered nature of contracts, which is hard to believe—but that does not change the fact that contracting is a form of privatization that places roles and responsibilities outside traditional public governance arrangements.

Whether Shanker or Budde predicted or could predict every development in the charter school sector is irrelevant in the sense that what both men consciously or unconsciously supported was consistent with neoliberal doctrine and arrangements. To be sure, both men put forward their views on the topic in the midst of the neoliberal period. Both, moreover, praised and drew on corporate-government education reports of the time like *A Nation at Risk* and similar reports.

Casting him in a light that most are unaware of or tend to forget, teacher union activists Swerdlow and Wainer (1997) state that:

> [Shanker] was deeply involved in the AFL-CIO's American Institute for Free Labor Development, which cooperated with the U.S. State Department, to undermine independent unions throughout the world. Shanker consistently supported U.S. foreign policy objectives, endorsing the Vietnam War in the 1960s and 1970s and the Nicaraguan contras in the 1980s. . . . In 1983 he shocked many union leaders when he endorsed the Reagan administration's National Commission on Excellence in Education's report on public schools. Entitled "A Nation at Risk," the document called for tougher graduation standards, longer school days and merit pay for teachers. (section Pro-imperialist Ideologue, paras. 2 & 4)

Shanker may have defended working-class interests at certain times, but he also betrayed them on many occasions. He was not a consistent principled defender of the working class.

Charter schools are part of arrangements in education to help the rich avoid the law of the falling rate of profit, which is inevitable under capitalism. They are a main means of transferring public wealth, assets, and control to the private sector. They are essentially pay-the-rich schemes cynically promoted under the banner of "putting kids first." They provide guaranteed profits with little risk—a businessman's dream.

Deregulation and contracting facilitate privatization. This is why charters schools are largely deunionized, do not uphold many public laws, rules, and regulations, and lack many of the other public features of public schools. Such arrangements enable cost cutting in order to increase profits. Deregulation, weak oversight, and contracting also permit charter schools to use tactics like real-estate manipulation to maximize profits.

The notion that charter schools nevertheless "do some good" or that "they are really not that bad" or that "the public and private sector can really work together for the common good" or that "blanket statements about charter schools cannot be made because they are all so unique and different from each other" are all forms of disinformation. Once the root of the problem is understood, its countless manifestations are secondary. From an education perspective, there is no justification for the existence, let alone expansion, of charter schools.

EDUCATION IS A RIGHT, NOT A "CHOICE"

Education cannot be reduced to an issue of choice. It is not a commodity. It is not meant to be bought and sold for private profit. It is not a business or commercial activity. Nor can it be treated as a privilege or opportunity. Education is a basic human right and social responsibility, essential to the survival and progress of society, its members, the public, and the socialized economy. It cannot be left to the anarchy, chaos, and violence of the "free market."

Education is a right that belongs to all by virtue of their being and for no other reason whatsoever. This right is inviolable and inalienable, and cannot be given or taken away by God, king, president, major owners of capital, or any other power. Rights can only be affirmed or suppressed, not extinguished. If something can be given or taken away, that makes it a privilege. A privilege presupposes a bestower and a bestowee—an unequal relationship. Rights, by contrast, belong to all equally and are the product of history. Most societies are based on privilege distribution systems, a hierarchy of rights; they are not truly humane.

Rights are not earned, deserved, or based on merit. They are not things you compete for or negotiate. They are not based on talent, ability, brotherhood, love, compassion, "good ideas," or the "right attitude." Nor are they based on wealth, skin color, nationality, religion, ability, political affiliation, or sexual orientation. Human rights go beyond choice, "scarcity," self-interest, and private property, and do not rest on agreements or contracts. Rights, moreover, cannot be reduced to policy objectives to be fulfilled in the vague "distant future." Rights are not ideals that are chased eternally; they exist objectively here and now and demand affirmation in the present.

The simple *act of being* is the source of rights. The act of being refers to the very reality of existence, and built into the meaning of existence is the understanding that one has a valid and legitimate claim to make on reality. For example, a baby has a claim to water, food, shelter, education, love, and support by virtue of its being, its very existence, regardless of what anyone thinks or believes, regardless of whether one agrees or not. Rights in this sense are objective, not subjective or arbitrary.

As the representative of society, it is the responsibility of government to provide rights with a guarantee. Lip service and rhetoric are not enough here; real mechanisms are required. Discrimination, oppression, and inequality will intensify so long as the existing authority refuses to come into harmony with the demands of the times. Conditions today are screaming for a government that serves the public interest, not corporations. The historic demand for a modern public authority that affirms the popular will directly contradict the existing authority and the powerful private interests it privileges.

"Choice" in the neoliberal context is a mechanism for removing government responsibility for education and placing it in the hands of the private sector. In this setup, families and individuals have to fend for themselves as they shop like consumers for the "best" school. They have no rights. "Buyer beware" is the only "defense" they have, a frank admission that they may be misled or cheated. To be sure, when charter schools fail and close, students, teachers, families, and communities are shocked, stressed, and disrupted. As mentioned earlier, well over 1,000 charter schools have closed in a single generation—and that is with poor oversight and accountability. Why does this situation prevail in the 21st century?

And what happens when traditional public schools are closed by government and people are forced to compete with others for a quality education? These 4,000 shuttered schools—"dropout factories" as US Secretary of Education Arne Duncan derogatorily calls them—tend to be in poor, segregated, urban settings where people lack the discretionary time and money needed to find and access a good school. How are they supposed to maneuver in this situation? Will charter school supporters target them with door-to-door canvassing, glossy literature, and inflated promises of success at a nearby newly created charter school? What happens when a charter school holds a lottery and many students are not able to enroll? As the pro-charter school film *Waiting for Superman* makes clear, all some parents have going for them in the 21st century is luck. Many feel demoralized and abandoned when their child fails to win a seat at the school. Will charter schools eagerly enroll—and keep enrolled—students with disabilities and English Language Learners? Homeless students? Pregnant students? The evidence does not support this. Nothing is guaranteed. In this way, people are to accept as normal a new level of insecurity, uncertainty, and stress in a society with more than enough wealth and resources to meet the needs of all.

REFERENCES

Au, W. (2009). *Unequal by design: High-stakes testing and the standardization of inequality.* New York, NY: Routledge.

Baker, B. (2012, May 4). Follow up on why publicness/privateness of charter schools matters. *School Finance 101.* Last Accessed June 4, 2014 from http://schoolfinance101.

wordpress.com/2012/05/04/follow-up-on-why-publicnessprivateness-of-charter-schools-matters/
Berliner, N. (2008, November 3). Why rising test scores may not equal increased student learning. *Dissent*. Last Accessed June 4, 2014 from http://www.dissentmagazine.org/online_articles/why-rising-test-scores-may-not-equal-increased-student-learning
Betts, J. R., & Hill, P.T. (Eds.). (2010). *Taking measure of charter schools: Better assessments, better policymaking, better schools.* Lanham, MD: Rowman & Littlefield Education.
Bifulco, R., & Ladd, H. F. (2007), School choice, racial segregation, and test-score gaps: Evidence from North Carolina's charter school program. *Journal of Policy Analysis and Management, 26,* 31–56.
Bryant, J. (2013, November 4). The charter-school lie: Market-based education gambles with our children. *Salon*. Last Accessed June 4, 2014 from http://www.salon.com/2013/11/04/the_charter_school_lie_market_based_education_gambles_with_our_children/
Buchheit, P. (2012, September 24). Greed at the top in education. Flunking charter schools. *Counterpunch*. Last Accessed June 4, 2014 from http://www.counterpunch.org/2012/09/24/flunking-charter-schools/
Budde, R. (1988). *Education by charter: Restructuring school districts. Key to long-term continuing improvement in American education.* Regional Laboratory for Educational Improvement of the Northeast & Islands, Andover, MA. Last Accessed June 4, 2014 from http://www.eric.ed.gov/ERICWebPortal/search/detailmini.jsp?_nfpb=true&_&ERICExtSearch_SearchValue_0=ED295298&ERICExtSearch_SearchType_0=no&accno=ED295298
Bulkley, K., & Fisler, J. (2002, April). A decade of charter schools: From theory to practice. CPRE Policy Briefs. Last Accessed June 4, 2014 from http://www.cpre.org/images/stories/cpre_pdfs/rb35.pdf
Center for Education Reform. (2011, December). *The state of charter schools: What we know—and what we do not—about performance-based accountability.* Last Accessed June 4, 2014 from http://www.edreform.com/wp-content/uploads/2011/12/StateOfCharterSchools_CER_Dec2011-Web-1.pdf
Center for Education Reform. (2013, January 15). The last eight states without charter school laws. Last Accessed June 4, 2014 from http://www.edreform.com/2013/01/the-last-eight-states-without-charter-school-laws/
Chubb, J., & Moe, T. (1990). *Politics, markets, and America's schools.* Washington, DC: Brookings Institution.
Corwin, R. G., & Schneider, J. E. (2005). *The school choice hoax: Fixing America's schools.* Westport, CT: Praeger.
CREDO. (2009, June). *Multiple choice: Charter school performance in 16 states.* Last Accessed June 4, 2014 from http://credo.stanford.edu/reports/MULTIPLE_CHOICE_CREDO.pdf
Cuban, L. (2007). "Burn and churn" among charter school principals. *Larry Cuban on School Reform and Classroom Practice.* Last Accessed June 4, 2014 from http://larrycuban.wordpress.com/2010/12/07/burn-and-churn-among-charter-school-principals/
Dewey, J. (1900). *The school and society.* Chicago, IL: University of Chicago Press.
Fabricant, M., & Fine, M. (2012). *Charter schools and the corporate makeover of public education: What's at stake?* New York, NY: Teachers College Press
Fair Test. (2007). *The dangerous consequences of high-stakes standardized testing.* Last Accessed June 4, 2014 from http://fairtest.org/dangerous-consequences-highstakes-standardized-tes
Fisman, R. (2013, May 22). Do charter schools work? Yes, but not always and not for everyone. *Slate*. Last Accessed June 4, 2014 from http://www.slate.com/

articles/news_and_politics/the_dismal_science/2013/05/do_charter_schools_work_a_new_study_of_boston_schools_says_yes.single.html

Frankenberg, E., Siegel-Hawley, G., & Wang, J. (2010, January). Choice without equity: Charter school segregation and the need for civil rights standards. *The Civil Rights Project*. Last Accessed June 4, 2014 from http://civilrightsproject.ucla.edu/research/k-12-education/integration-and-diversity/choice-without-equity-2009-report/frankenberg-choices-without-equity-2010.pdf

Garrison, M. (2009). *A measure of failure: The political origins of standardized testing*. Albany, NY: State University of New York Press.

Giroux, H. A. (2012). *Education and the crisis of public values: Challenging the assault on teachers, students, & public education*. New York, NY: Peter Lang.

Harvey, D. (2007). *Brief history of neoliberalism*. Oxford, England: Oxford University Press.

Henig, J. (2008). *Spin cycle: How research is used in policy debates: The case of charter schools*. New York, NY: Russell Sage Foundation Publications.

Hoffman, A. (2010, March 6). Are charter schools public schools? I'm afraid not. Chalkbeat. Last Accessed June 4, 2014 from http://ny.chalkbeat.org/2010/03/26/are-charter-school-public-schools-im-afraid-not/#.U49sxijyTh9

Hood, J. (2011, February 22). Charter school says it's private, though it gets millions in tax dollars. *Chicago Tribune*. Last Accessed June 4, 2014 from http://articles.chicagotribune.com/2011-02-22/news/ct-met-charter-school-fight-0222-20110221_1_charter-schools-timothy-knowles-urban-education-institute

Hopper, T. (2011, February 24). Charter schools mean less money for public schools. *The Duncan Banner*. Last Accessed June 4, 2014 from http://duncanbanner.com/local/x962029876/Charter-schools-mean-less-money-for-public-schools

Howe, K. R., & Welner, K. G. (2002, July/August). School choice and the pressure to perform: Deja vu for children with disabilities? *Remedial and Special Education, 23*(4), 212–221.

Karp, S. (2010, April 5). School reform we can't believe in. *Rethinking Schools*. Last Accessed June 4, 2014 from http://www.zcommunications.org/school-reform-we-cant-believe-in-by-stan-karp

Kight, J. (2008, February 2). Charter schools siphon public funds. *Voices of Central Pennsylvania*. Last Accessed June 4, 2014 from http://voicesweb.org/node/1256

Lake, R. J. (Ed.). (2013, April). Hopes, fears, & reality: A balanced look at American charter schools in 2012. Center on Reinventing Public Education. Last Accessed June 4, 2014 from http://www.crpe.org/sites/default/files/pub_hfr12_may13.pdf

Lake, R. J., & Gross, B. (Eds.). (2012, January). Hopes, fears, & reality: A balanced look at American charter schools in 2011. Center on Reinventing Public Education. Last Accessed June 4, 2014 from http://crpe.org/sites/default/files/pub_crpe_HFR11_Jan12_0.pdf

Lipman, P. (2011, July–August). Neoliberal education restructuring. *Monthly Review, 63*(3). Last Accessed June 12, 2014 from http://monthlyreview.org/2011/07/01/neoliberal-education-restructuring

Lubienski, C., & Weitzel, P. (Eds.). (2010). *The charter school experiment: Expectations, evidence, and implications*. Cambridge, MA: Harvard Education Press.

McCauley, L. (2013, July 22). Poll: American parents want public schools, not charter schools. *Common Dreams*. Last Accessed June 12, 2014 from https://www.commondreams.org/headline/2013/07/22-4

Miron, G., & Applegate, B. (2007, May). Teacher attrition in charter schools. *Education Public Interest Center*. Last Accessed June 12, 2014 from http://nepc.colorado.edu/files/EPSL-0705-234-EPRU.pdf

Miron, G., & Gulosino, C. (2013). *Profiles of for-profit and nonprofit education management organizations: Fourteenth edition—2011–2012*. Boulder, CO: National Education Policy Center. Last Accessed June 12, 2014 from http://nepc.colorado.edu/files/emo-profiles-11–12.pdf

Miron, G., & Urschel, J. L. (2010). *Equal or fair? A study of revenues and expenditure in American charter schools*. Boulder, CO: Education and the Public Interest Center & Education Policy Research Unit. Last Accessed June 12, 2014 from http://epicpolicy.org/publication/charter-school-finance

Miron, G., Urschel, J. L., Mathis, W. J., & Tornquist, E. (2010, February). Schools without diversity: Education management organizations, charter schools, and the demographic stratification of the American school system. Last Accessed June 12, 2014 from http://nepc.colorado.edu/publication/schools-without-diversity

National Alliance for Public Charter Schools. (2010). *Unionized schools*. Last Accessed June 12, 2014 from http://dashboard.publiccharters.org/dashboard/schools/page/union/year/2010

National Alliance for Public Charter Schools. (2013, January 15). Public charter schools reach new milestone: Record 6,000 schools are serving 2.3 million students. *NAPCS Press Releases*. Last Accessed June 14, 2014 from http://www.publiccharters.org/press/public-charter-schools-reach-milestone-record-6000-schools-serving-2–3-million-students/

National Association of Charter School Authorizers. (2013, March 5). Ohio charter authorizers. Last Accessed June 14, 2014 from http://www.qualitycharters.org/authorizer-comparison/state-by-state-overviews-ohio.html

National Commission on Excellence in Education. (1983). *A nation at risk: The imperative for educational reform*. Washington, DC: US Department of Education.

Nichols, S. L., & Berliner, D. C. (2007). *Collateral damage: How high-stakes testing corrupts America's schools*. Cambridge, MA: Harvard Education Press.

Ravitch, D. (2010). *The death and life of the great American school system: How testing and choice are undermining education*. New York, NY: Basic Books.

Ravitch, D. (2011, April). Dictating to the schools: A look at the effects of the Bush and Obama administrations on schools. *Virginia Journal of Education*. Last Accessed June 14, 2014 from http://www.veanea.org/home/907.htm

Ravitch, D. (2012, May 29). Are charter schools public schools? *Education Week*. Last Accessed June 11, 2014 from http://blogs.edweek.org/edweek/Bridging-Differences/2012/05/are_charter_schools_public_sch.html

Reding, wrighting & erithmatic. (1989, October 2). *Wall Street Journal*.

Resmovits, J. (2012, November 14). Charter schools grow rapidly, adding 200,000 students: Report. *Huffington Post*. Last Accessed June 11, 2014 from http://www.huffingtonpost.com/2012/11/14/charter-schools-growth_n_2125286.html

Rich, M. (2012, June 19). Charter schools still enroll fewer disabled students. *The New York Times*. Last Accessed June 11, 2014 from http://www.nytimes.com/2012/06/20/education/in-charter-schools-fewer-with-disabilities.html?hpw

Richards, J. S., & Bush, B. (2014, January 12). Columbus has 17 charter school failures in one year. Schools closing at alarming rate, costing taxpayers and disrupting the lives of hundreds of students. *The Columbus Dispatch*. Last Accessed June 11, 2014 from http://www.dispatch.com/content/stories/local/2014/01/12/charter-failure.html

Rotberg, I. (2014, February). Charter schools and the risk of increased segregation. *Phi Delta Kappan, 95*(5), 26–30.

Saltman, K. (2010). *The gift of education: Public education and venture philanthropy*. New York, NY: Palgrave Macmillan.

Scott, J. T. (Ed.). (2005). *School choice and diversity: What the evidence says*. New York, NY: Teachers College Press.

Simon, S. (2012, October 12). New US visa rush: Build charter school, get green card. *Reuters*. Last Accessed June 11, 2014 from http://www.reuters.com/article/2012/10/12/us-usa-education-charter-visas-idUSBRE89B07K20121012

Stuit, D., & Smith, T. M. (2009). Teacher turnover in charter schools. National Center on School Choice. Last Accessed June 5, 2014 from http://www.ncspe.org/publications_files/OP183.pdf

Swerdlow, M., & Wainer, K. A. (1997, July–August). Albert Shanker, image and reality. *ATC*, 69. Last Accessed June 5, 2014 from http://www.solidarity-us.org/site/print/819

US Department of Education. (2010, June). *The evaluation of charter school impacts*. Last Accessed June 5, 2014 from http://ies.ed.gov/ncee/pubs/20104029/pdf/20104029.pdf

U.S. Department of Education, National Center for Education Statistics. (2013). Digest of Education Statistics, 2012 (NCES 2014–015), Chapter 2. Last Accessed June 14, 2014 from http://nces.ed.gov/fastfacts/display.asp?id=84

U.S. Department of Education, National Center for Education Statistics. (2013). Digest of Education Statistics, 2012 (NCES 2014–015), Chapter 1. Last Accessed June 14, 2014 from http://nces.ed.gov/fastfacts/display.asp?id=65

US Department of Education, National Center for Education Statistics. (2012b). The condition of education 2012 (NCES 2012–045), indicator 4. Last Accessed June 14, 2014 from http://nces.ed.gov/pubs2012/2012045.pdf

Weil, D. (2009). *Charter school movement: History, politics, policies, economics and effectiveness* (2nd ed.). Amenia, NY: Grey House.

Welner, K. G. (2013, April 22). The dirty dozen: How charter schools influence student enrollment. *Teachers College Record*. Last Accessed June 5, 2014 from http://www.tcrecord.org

Zehr, M. (2011, April 1). KIPP schools enroll fewer ELLs and special ed. students. *Education Week*. Last Accessed June 5, 2014 from http://blogs.edweek.org/edweek/learning-the-language/2011/04/kipp_schools_enroll_fewer_ells.html

Zollers, N. J., & Ramanathan, A. K. (1998, December). For-profit charter schools and students with disabilities: The sordid side of the business of schooling. *Phi Delta Kappan*, 80(4), 297–304.

9 The Myth of Preparation and the Futility of Teacher Education Programs

Eric C. Sheffield

> Now "preparation" is a treacherous idea. In a certain sense every experience should do something to prepare a person for later experiences of a deeper and more expansive quality. That is the very meaning of growth, continuity, reconstruction of experience. But it is a mistake to suppose that the mere acquisition of a certain amount of arithmetic, geography, history, etc., which is taught and studied because it may be useful at some time in the future, has this effect, and it is a mistake to suppose that acquisition of skills in reading and figuring will automatically constitute preparation for their right and effective use under conditions very unlike those in which they were acquired.
>
> —Dewey (1936/1997, p. 47)

> We are the Borg. Your biological and technological distinctiveness will be added to our own. Resistance is futile.
>
> —*Star Trek: First Contact* (1996)

INTRODUCTION

The essential question addressed in this chapter goes something like this: "Have teacher education programs been complicit in the corporate takeover of public schooling in the US?" And, the answer: "Well . . . yes." In fact, I was tempted to pose the question, answer it, and then see if I had broken the *Guinness Book of World Records* for the shortest chapter ever penned for a scholarly collection. On the other hand, I'm fairly sure that when the editors of this collection invited me to participate in this project they had something else in mind and that the readers of this volume might be looking for at least a small bit of explanation. And, the explanation itself can, I think, help untangle both new and old mythical matters within programs that claim to "prepare" teachers for working with their future students.

The explanation that follows begins with the assumption that corporate America is, at the very least, moving quickly, and in Borg-like fashion, to take over public schooling in this country and has been unapologetically doing so for more than a generation now; at most, they have already succeeded in this takeover. I say "unapologetically" because historically speaking corporations have—at least since the early days of the Industrial Revolution—had an eye on, and a hand in, directing public education policy and practice: Industrial age business moguls, as an example, benefited greatly from a poor, docile, and punctual workforce produced in factory-like schools of that (and this) era. And, I say "Borg-like" because I find the hive-mind Borg of the Star Trek saga to be an apt metaphor for the manner in which postmodern corporations are moving to appropriate public schools and teacher education programs, en masse: without input from those who know teaching and learning best; with little to no critical variety of perspective or context; and, with absolutely no concern about the existing schools and the human beings who daily inhabit them. These corporations operate with a single-mindedness not seen before and, just as the Borg believe, the corporate assimilation process is an a priori "good" for all concerned.

The Borg in the Star Trek saga travel between and betwixt galaxies, assimilating whole planets and their inhabitants' "biological and technological distinctiveness" into their own and in so doing destroy everything in sight in their insatiable hunger to possess and control. This, I believe, is precisely how contemporary postmodern corporations are approaching their takeover of public education and teacher preparation programs—and the planet that legislative policy makers once inhabited as a unique space was, it seems, assimilated some time ago. However, these Borg-like postmodern/contemporary corporations no longer need remain part and parcel of the covert "hidden curriculum" of years gone by. They are now free to operate overtly under a variety of mythical understandings about human beings, schools, technology, and control, to name just a few. I provide a tip-of-the-proverbial-iceberg snapshot of the increasing influence corporations wield over public school policy and practice (with particular attention to teacher education) to flesh this assumption out.

I then suggest that teacher education programs sit in a very important place and space in the public school endeavor—a space that once was a potential site of resistance to the increasingly overt Corporate Borg-like intrusions into public schooling. However, that space has since the early part of the 20th century increasingly accepted the prevailing myth that "preservice teacher candidates" can be "prepared" to "teach." Given that teaching is currently viewed as a technical scientific endeavor of "best practices," I suppose we should not be surprised to hear such claims. In the early days of this mother of all myths, complete preparation of teachers was seen as an important ideal-to-strive-for . . . a hope-to-hold . . . an unattainable-goal-towards-which-to-aim. However, as the years have passed, the myth of preparation has become increasingly rationalized and is now unquestioned common sense; and in its rationalization, the myth has become a goal that is absolutely to be achieved rather than a hope for which to strive.

The Myth of Preparation 155

As the mother of all teacher education myths, and much like Cronus's birthing of his long-ingested children, the myth of preparation has been spewing a whole new postmodern generation of mythical educational understandings of late. I take up the following of Preparation's teacher education progeny below: the myth of control, the myth of measurement, the myth of technology, and the myth of teacher educator resistance. Finally, and in light of these myths, I suggest three courses of action for the future of teacher education programs: (a) Revitalize social foundations studies in teacher education programs as they currently stand—studies that directly confront and challenge these mythological understandings; (b) completely restructure teacher education programs, eliminating the practices undergirded by these mythical understandings; or, (c) get rid of teacher education programs altogether.

As the reader will see below, I begin most sections with stories from my teaching career—a career that has now grown long in the tooth and a career that has completely convinced me that teaching has precious little to do with adjectives, mathematical formulas, dates in history, or plot structure. Teaching is an ethical endeavor concerned with young, whole, flesh-and-blood, human beings and how they might come to see themselves in the world. And so, a bit of introduction about that: I found my way into a teacher education master's program at a major university ("Down South") in 1987 and graduated from that program in 1989 with a degree and certification in secondary English education. As I finished up that degree, I began diligently applying for teaching jobs and took the first one offered without really examining the school's context—I needed a job and this high school was only a 30-minute drive away. I remember quite vividly the day I excitedly drove out to the school to see my room. I walked in to find eight buckets scattered around on the floor catching the rainwater that was seeping through the roof. I was certainly not in Kansas anymore, Dorothy.

I remember the per capita annual stats for the district: top three in the state every year in poverty rates, teen pregnancy, cases of reported incest, and alcohol-related automobile deaths among teens; I remember calling the homes of my students the first few days of school to find that 70% of them were not living with their biological parents; I remember realizing with white, male, middle-class dismay, as one of my students delivered a demonstration speech on "weaves," that some African-American women supplement their hair with both human and synthetic hair (!); I remember the racial strife caused by adults (not the students) when our Latino/a population began exploding; I remember a student not getting her homework done because the car battery her family used to power their lights finally died; I remember when in my first year I was called a racist by one of my students and what one of the few African-American teachers at the school said when I approached her about it: "Eric, given our history, you have to prove yourself to them before they will ever trust you." And, I remember the bitter sweetness I felt when, after 14 years, I left for my new life teaching future and practicing teachers at a public university in the heart of the Midwest. I learned more from my young students in that poverty-stricken high school community about life and living than I could ever have imagined—I was *their* student—and nothing had, nor ever could have, prepared me for my work there.

THE CURRENT STATE OF CORPORATE INTRUSION: THE NEWS

When I walked into my classroom to get ready for my third year of teaching, I saw it immediately: High in the corner, bolted onto a swiveling stand, was a television. Interesting, I thought; what had I done to deserve such largesse? I wandered next door to my colleague's room to find that she too had a television bolted to a swiveling stand high up in the corner of her room. In fact, they were in every room! My dismay may seem a bit out of place now in our brave new world circa 2014—well, of course every room should have a television, or at least a screen of some kind. But this was 1991 and this was one of the most impoverished schools in one of the most impoverished areas in one of the most impoverished states in the country.

I discovered at our faculty meeting later in the day that each room was provided a television by a media corporation; and in exchange for all the televisions, we had agreed to broadcast their news program every morning at precisely 7:47 a.m. The news broadcast was hosted by three or four perfectly groomed, perfectly diverse, and perfectly beautiful teenagers (several of whom are now well-known cable news personalities—Lisa Ling and Anderson Cooper being two). It was quite magical. There was no need to watch the clock, grab the remote, turn on the TV, and tune in to the broadcast. At precisely 7:47 every morning, every media corporation-provided television in the school mysteriously turned on and flooded the school with their news. And, in between the news reports? Commercials (of course). Not just any commercials, but commercials for everything the typical teenager "needed" to be socially acceptable (acne medicine, toothpaste, gum, shoes, clothes, etc.).

It was not long before the novelty of these broadcasts wore off and I became increasingly bothered by this spectacle. Not only were the images being beamed down at my eager and captured students potentially damaging to their identity (particularly images of young women), but the news itself was terribly soft, patriotic, and pedestrian. I also suspected that the news portion of the broadcast was, over time, becoming shorter and the commercial portion was becoming longer. I began timing them. Sure enough, slowly but surely, commercial time crept up and news time crept down. Thankfully, this early and naïve corporate intrusion into classrooms was resistible: The corporate installers had not hard-wired the televisions—they could be unplugged ... and, like a 21st century-Jean-Luc Piccard, I did so.

As I mentioned at the outset and as I'm sure the other chapters in this collection attest to, the Corporate Borg is succeeding magnificently in its takeover of every level of educational practice. The media corporation intrusion of the early 1990s signaled the beginning of the unapologetic overt version of this corporate infestation—even Bill Gates was still at that time only covertly tapping into the potential lifelong consumers and revenue streams that captured audiences in schools provided for his burgeoning corporate empire: When you took "computer" classes at this time (and still) they should have been titled Microsoft I, Microsoft II, and so forth. And, granted, we were a Coke school (later having a Coke scoreboard in our gym), and over time our football stadium became littered with local business advertisements; on the other hand, this corporate media intrusion marked a shift. This intrusion was expansive, generated huge commercial revenues, and, most crucially, was "sold" to us as an innovative teaching tool—it was "educational." This is the hive-mind, Borg-like approach still in practice today: Package technology as "educational" and it will be swallowed hook, line, and sinker.

The overt Corporate Borg-like assimilation of the educational narrative that began in the early 1990s is almost complete; and, as the Borg warning above promises, corporations have had great success in completely destroying the technological and biological distinctiveness of the American schooling context. Gone is the language of education and in its place is the language of corporations: Human development has become human production; responsibility has become accountability; growth has become measurement; teacher creativity has been replaced with scripted universal curriculum; democracy has become consumption; and school superintendents have become CEOs (Noddings, 2007). This assimilation is no longer limited to producing educational tools such as Channel One to be used in classrooms. Corporate leaders are now focused on creating and running entire school districts and, in a stroke of Borg-like genius, on directing teacher preparation programs as well. In fact, as I sit here writing, I have received two emails inviting me to workshops on Missouri's version of the Pearson edTPA teacher candidate assessment program, MoTPA—workshops that go completely unquestioned these days.

The evidence that corporations, by way of their wealthiest shareholders, are (and already have in many places) moving to create and run schools is unabashedly clear. This evidence can be found with little effort because corporate school reformers are no longer shy about advertising their invasion of what once was the public spaces of American schools. The film *Waiting for Superman* is one such example of how overt the Corporate Borg has become. And, as the old saying goes, follow the money and you will see how close the Borg is to completing its takeover (Barkin, 2011; Day, 2010; Schneider, 2013). The Corporate Borg has assimilated much strategic knowledge over time and it has clearly realized of late that to complete its takeover of American schools it must focus on that space so crucial to the entire endeavor: teacher education programs.

THE QUEEN BORG: PEARSON PUBLISHING

Targeting teacher preparation programs for assimilation into the Corporate Borg is nothing short of genius. I remember when I started my current life as a teacher educator thinking that if I could just convince a couple preservice teachers a year that education is about guiding young people in such a way that they become compassionate, loving, open-minded democratic citizens and those teachers convinced their students of that . . . well, my influence would be geometrically more expansive. That thinking has certainly not been lost on the Borg; particularly on the part of what I now think of as the Borg queen known as Pearson Publishing and its national coup in convincing state boards of education to adopt its teacher evaluation system, edTPA.

Yes, edTPA, already fully implemented or at various stages of implementation in all but 17 states, is steamrolling across teacher preparation programs nationwide. Developed in conjunction with the Stanford Center for Assessment, Learning, and Equity, edTPA claims its process can evaluate "teacher dispositions" (more on that below) and is

> a preservice assessment process designed by educators to answer the essential question: "Is a new teacher ready for the job?" edTPA includes a review of a teacher candidate's authentic teaching materials as the culmination of a teaching and learning process that documents and demonstrates each candidate's ability to effectively teach his/her subject matter to all students. (American Association of Colleges for Teacher Education, 2013b)

And Pearson's "fair take":

> The $300 fee (estimated) that will be charged to teacher candidates for edTPA is fair. That cost covers all edTPA assessment services, including a professional, qualified evaluator who has been trained to edTPA rubrics, expectations of performance, and standardized scoring procedures, and who will be monitored during scoring activities to maintain high quality. (American Association of Colleges for Teacher Education, 2013a)[1]

Admittedly, it has been a while since I've done much high-level math, but $300 times the number of teacher candidates in 33 states and the District of Columbia (and more no doubt soon joining in) is no small chunk of change. And, it puts the Pearson Publishing Corporation in charge of determining when a teacher is "ready for the job."

I was recently told by the dean of the college that "prepares" more teacher candidates than any college in the country and that has been legislatively mandated to use edTPA that their strategy has been to "flood Pearson with our own reviewers." This is an admirable strategy; the problem is there are very few Jean-Luc Picards in the world—those who can and do successfully infiltrate the Borg and substantially resist it particularly given the money reviewers will receive for their work and the technological critical restrictions that bind the reviewers' work. I don't know much, but I do know that it doesn't matter how much corporate production and accountability language you use or how many quality assurance systems you devise, no one is ever prepared to teach: One learns to teach by teaching.

THE MYTH OF PREPARATION: TRAGEDY

Tina

I had "Tina" (I use pseudonyms throughout) in class my second year of teaching. She was not the model student—but she did come to school regularly and worked somewhat diligently at her studies—a rarity at this school given that many or most only hoped there would be a meal for them when they got home. She was a sophomore and I believe she had just turned 16. One day after class, Tina stopped me saying she needed to talk about something. She proceeded to inform me that she had a feeling that her stepfather was "making the moves" on her. He had "bumped up" against her several times of late and had made some comments that might be construed as sexual in nature. I advised Tina to go home, make an appointment with her mom when they could talk this over, and, I said, "Do it immediately." A couple days later Tina said she had talked to her mom about the matter and that although her mom seemed a bit strange about it, she thought it was taken care of.

Six or eight weeks later, Tina missed several days of class and when she returned she once again wanted to talk. I said, "Sure," and we ducked out into the hallway for a moment. She said, "Four nights ago, my stepfather came into my bedroom, put his hand over my mouth, dragged me out to the living room, and raped me. I don't know what to do." I didn't know what to do either.

Sally

Sally was a student of mine in 1997—a sophomore in English II as it is so cleverly named; Sally's half sister, "Julie," was also a sophomore in my class that year—English II Honors—an equally clever name. Sally had just moved to this little piece of heaven the previous summer to live with Julie, their father, and Julie's mother. Julie was an incredible young lady—an

"A" student—and not just because she knew how to play the schooling game; a favorite among teachers and students alike—a sharp mind, a heart of gold, a state-ranked cross-country runner and, at the end of her high school career, a deserving salutatorian for what was the most impressive class that high school ever had walk its halls.

Sally, equally incredible, though differently so (an artist, a lover of music, not a great student, but certainly an insightful soul), seemed to see the world differently—rather than the eternal, somewhat naïve optimism manifested in Julie, Sally sensed the world as it is: emotional, troubling, and inhabited by social, political, and personal demons at nearly every turn. I will never forget that phone call from Charlotte Smith—longtime school counselor—nor the numerous excruciating conversations with Julie that followed over the next years: Charlotte called me to report that Julie had walked into the room that she shared with Sally earlier that evening to find Sally lying in bed having blown her head off with one of her father's shotguns.

Joan

I was just leaving town on a Friday evening when I heard the news: Joan Johnson, a recent graduate of ours, had been in a car wreck; it was 1996 or '97. I had Joan in class both her sophomore and junior year and we had a bit of a love–hate relationship . . . though in the end the love part of it won out. I had seen Joan early in the summer after her graduation at a lake I frequented in an attempt to swim off the inevitability of age and she had proudly, and with something of a spirited "I told you so" tone, informed me that she had been accepted to the University of Florida the following fall term. Because I had already departed and because I was headed to a "no way out" family event, I would not be able to do what I certainly would have done—immediately head to the hospital—that would have to wait until the following Monday.

Upon arriving at the regional medical center early that following Monday morning, I went through what had become an all too regular ritual when it came to my students: Get the room number; find the family; chat quietly; go in to see the student patient; give encouragement; and head home. However, after securing Joan's room number and heading towards the hall/waiting room area, I discovered that the family members had gone down to the hospital cafeteria and I followed suit. Just as I sat down to have the traditional quiet chat with family and friends, a man who looked to be a doctor motioned from the top of the stairs leading down to the cafeteria; en masse, with me swept along in what I remember now as a strange familial wave of sorts, we retreated back up the stairs—the family to a room where they, I realized in hindsight, were meeting with doctors, leaving me to sit in the hallway waiting for permission to see Joan . . . several minutes passed when the family reappeared, Joan's mother coming straight to me saying, "Mr. Sheffield, we would like you come in with us."

Great, I thought, finally I can visit with Joan, give her some encouragement, listen again to her college plans, and get back home to spend a day with my own two sons. The next several minutes were by far the most surreal of my life: Upon entering the room it was clear that Joan was not in the best of shape—unconscious, tubes running in and out of her like some kind of Borg-like creature, her head heavily wrapped. Without speaking a word, Jeff, Joan's brother, and Cecily, Joan's closest friend, grasped my hands . . . Jeff to my right, Cecily to my left, and Joan's father pushed the play button on one of those old-school cassette players—the music of Bjork filling the room. My confusion ended quickly as I watched in horror Joan's mom and dad going through the process of taking Joan off life support. It didn't take long . . . and when it was over I walked out of that room, down the elevator, and literally sprinted through the hallway to the hospital exit where I had the most severe sobbing explosion I have ever experienced. Several weeks later when the new school year began, Jeff came walking into my class—he was enrolled in my English III Honors class . . . I had not seen him except at the funeral since letting go of his left hand and bolting out of that hospital room.

I began this chapter with one of my favorite John Dewey quotes—the one about "preparation" and, as he says it, its "treacherous" nature. He certainly could not have known that this myth of preparation would open the door to the corporate treachery we now see. He certainly *did* know that no amount of preparation could prepare any teacher for the tragedy manifested in these three stories from my public school teaching career—and these are only three among many. I am often asked by my preservice teachers about my experiences in the classroom, and though those years provided the greatest of joys as well as the greatest of sorrows, these are the kind of stories that come to mind . . . and these stories should remind us all that teaching is much more about young whole human beings than about plot structure, the Pythagorean theorem, or the history of the American Revolution.

The myth of preparation was the key that unlocked the public spaces of schooling in this country, allowing for the flood of corporate intrusion. The myth, once rationalized, once made into unquestioned common sense, convinced policy makers of the following: If students in teacher education programs can, in fact, be made "ready for the job" (similarly to the myth that students-as-data-points can be measured for "career and college readiness"), then that readiness is a product that can be tested and measured for its relative worth—much like a widget is product-tested before it is placed on the shelf for sale. And, if it can be measured as a product for consumption, then those with such product testing know-how can and should take the reins of developing the technologies required to judge the product's market value. Those with such know-how are found in corporations who are skilled at product measurement and testing. And, given that the myth of preparation naturally births the myths of control, measurement, and technology, it also naturally entails that corporations are the best positioned to make such judgments. This data-driven product judgment of "readiness" is precisely what Pearson's edTPA is meant to achieve. And, state boards of education, accreditation bodies, and even professors in teacher education programs have fallen prey to the lure of the myth of preparation and its progeny.

THE MYTH OF CONTROL: MARBLES

A few days before I was to start my new life as a high school English teacher, I attended several mandated "beginning teacher" meetings. One of the mandated meetings was a half-day professional development workshop on "Assertive Discipline."[2] *I was already scared to death, and as the assertive discipline guru (who, no doubt, had been paid a ridiculous amount of money for his presentation) continued talking, I became literally paralyzed with fear. How was I possibly going to "manage" six classes of 30 ninth and tenth graders, coming in continual waves, every 50 minutes of every day? I had up to that point somehow convinced myself that I would know what to do when the time came. Fortunately (I thought at the time), there was the Assertive Discipline program. When I left the workshop, I drove straight to the nearest store where I could buy marbles and mason jars.*

Though there are numerous suggestions that the Canters make about incorporating assertive discipline behaviorist management techniques into the classroom, it was the marbles that caught my attention. It works like this: Reward individual students with a public plunking of a marble into a jar—yep, their name publically announced and a marble dropped into a jar. I initially had my doubts, but good God it was the most manipulatively magical thing I could have ever imagined. The first day of class I explained to my students the game: "When you follow my directions, you get a marble in your name. When your mason jar is full, we will take two days off and watch a movie." I also asked them to get a notebook that would be a journal; "and, tomorrow when you come to class, be in your seat with your journal ready to write."

When the second day came, only four or five students in each class had their journals out—and each one of them received a marble into the jar with their name on it. On the second day, half the class got marbles. By the third day, every student received a marble. And, as time went on, I discovered I could get these young human beings to do most anything for those damn marbles . . . anything.

Certainly, behaviorist mechanisms of manipulation and control have been around for a long, long time. On the other hand, until recently—in fact, since the rationalization of the myth of preparation—this kind of control was reserved for school-aged children who many (still) believe need some behaviorist shaping in order to "motivate" them to learn. However, the myth of preparation has allowed this thinking to become part and parcel of teacher preparation in the form of growing, corporate-produced systems of classroom management. The Canters were way ahead of their time on this. One way to ensure that preservice teachers are "ready for the job," the myth of preparation explains, is to provide them with these prepackaged, scripted, management programs so they can control their students into learning—and then we won't have to depend on teachers being imaginative, creative, or even interesting.

Over the past decade and a bit more that I have been "preparing" preservice teachers for their future classrooms, the number of these programs has grown in staggering ways. I increasingly hear my students discussing "Love and Logic," "Positive Discipline Interventions," "Classroom Dojo," "Netsupport School," "NETOP Classroom Management," and yes, even still, "Assertive Discipline," all available for purchase from corporations increasingly interested in school-based profits. This should not be surprising as the myth of preparation naturally births the myth of control: For teachers to be totally prepared, they must be made ready to "manage" a class, and that can be accomplished via corporate-produced systems akin to product quality control. As to my own mythical marbles, I realized in my third year of teaching that my students were learning that the value of literature and writing was to be found in the number of marbles one received. I stopped the manipulation and found a way to "manage" their "behavior": Creatively engage them with what they were interested in . . . who knew?

THE MYTH OF MEASUREMENT: JAMES

James was in my class his sophomore year and we hit it off immediately. Partly that was because I had several of his brothers, sisters, cousins, and even an aunt in class before him. James was very hardworking, but when it came to language, it just never clicked for James. James's plans were to graduate from high school and work or join the military. He was one of those kids people would describe as "salt of the Earth." James was also a tenth grader the first year that high-stakes testing appeared on the scene: Take the test your sophomore year; if you don't score "proficient" in language arts and math, try again early your junior year. If a student still did not perform proficiently, he or she got one more chance later that year.

James took the test and passed the math portion; however, he had missed the cutoff score on the language arts section by two points. So, we started prepping. James met me after school two days a week and we went over everything: reading comprehension, grammar, sentence structure, setting, plot, and back to reading comprehension. Drill, drill, drill. James took the test again, missing the cutoff score by one point. Back to it: Drill, practice, memorize, drill, practice, memorize. This time he would certainly make it. On his third and final try, James missed the cutoff score by two points. He passed all his classes and received a Certificate of Completion, which did not even qualify him to enlist.

Another of the preparation myth's progeny is the myth of measurement. As I noted above, if one believes that teachers can be "prepared," can be made "ready for the job," then that readiness can be measured. It is the same kind of logic to which James fell victim: If an "educated" human being is one who "knows" information, then that can certainly be measured. And that measurement can be accomplished by a standardized test. When it comes to testing, and even testing in relation to teacher preparation, we have been doing so for a long time, and testing corporations, particularly since the requirements of No Child Left Behind, have been making a killing.

Evaluative tests such as the praxis exam (a common national test that measures teacher "readiness to teach" published and sold by another Borg-like corporation, ETS) were and are meant to evaluate general pedagogical understandings and content knowledge. However, this "accountability" step is no longer enough to sate the Borg hunger. Corporations have now convinced us—and state legislatures and boards of education have mandated—that "teaching dispositions" themselves can be measured; that is, human personality traits that lend themselves to teacher preparedness can be evaluated and "taught." Based on this mythological belief, one grown out of the myth of preparation, the Pearson edTPA system requires the uploading of student teaching video to Pearson where it is utilized to judge whether or not the candidate is dispositionally "ready for the job." James, my student, was "ready for the job," but wasn't allowed to prove that because he did not "measure up" to the corporate-produced standardized test. And I don't know about my readers, but some of my best teachers possessed dispositions that were . . . different, sometimes strange, and very often quirky. Those very human teacher qualities, if the Borg has its way, will, I'm afraid, very soon be assimilated out of existence.

THE MYTH OF TECHNOLOGY: THE INTERCOM

For the last four years of my public school teaching life, I taught all the seniors and only seniors. This was a result of one of those typical educational strokes of logic: Give the experienced teachers the older, more mature, successful students and the tougher ones to the new inexperienced teachers—gotta love seniority! A good number of my "successful" seniors teetered on the edge of not graduating. And, I had learned early on to save the public speaking requirement for the last grading period. There were pedagogical/community reasons for this. By the last grading period, they trusted me and their classmates enough to get up and speak publically. There was also a personal reason . . . no papers to grade! They spoke, I evaluated. They spoke, I evaluated. They spoke . . . well, you get the point.

However, every year I had several students teetering on that cliff of graduation who had to do well on the public speaking unit in order to "make it." And, these were often the same ones who were scared to death of delivering speeches. To get those students ready to perform, we worked diligently together, as speakers and audience members, supporting one another in both roles. This particular year, the administration had also begun an annoying practice: interrupting class with announcements that had been left out of our regular morning school announcements. I went to the principal with a simple request: Delay those announcements until the final 30 seconds of the school day.

One minute into Adam's two- to four-minute speech to persuade—a speech that had to be done well in order for him to graduate—it happened: "Please excuse the interruption, we have several late announcements to inform you of . . ." I was livid; so livid that I grabbed the nearest desk, slammed it against the wall underneath the fucking intercom (excuse my French), climbed onto the desk, reached up, and ripped all the wires out of the intercom, my students in varying degrees of dismay, shock, and laughter.

Now, for those readers who have not yet taught or those who teach in smoothly running bureaucracies, I will give you a bit of advice I learned early on at my particular school: If I needed something fixed in my room, I knew better than to go through the mandated process because if I did that I could depend on it not happening for months. After crippling the intercom system, I knew I could safely make it through the last few weeks with no interruptions because it would never be fixed by the end of the year. However, and much to my dismay, the very next morning as I walked through the main office Ms. Little, one of our secretaries, stopped me: "Mr. Sheffield, I noticed yesterday that your intercom was not working, so I've had it fixed for you!" I mumbled a quiet "thank you" and headed to my room.

Sure enough, that very same day, in a different class period and as one of my teetering seniors stumbled her way through a speech, the intercom once again interrupted: "Excuse the interruption . . ." Before the voice could make it to the actual announcement, I had once again climbed the wall and ripped out the wires of the intercom. This time, however, I had a plan: Ben was in my class—yes, Ben—the student who went on to start his own car audio business after graduation. I looked at Ben and said, "Hey Ben, you can fix this right?" "Sure, Mr. Sheffield, a piece of cake." From that day on until the year ended, Ben came to my class first period and after the morning announcements carefully crippled the intercom. He then returned at the end of the day and rewired it. The teetering seniors all made it.

The youngest of preparation's progeny, technology, is, I believe, also the final nail in the corporate takeover coffin. As the child of Preparation and the sibling of measurement and control, technology is the prized myth of the Corporate Borg: The myth of preparation as a matter of being "ready for the job" implies and then entails control and then measurement . . . and both can be accomplished via "objective" technology. Those televisions that appeared in my classroom circa 1991 have certainly come a long way. They are now the screens upon which video uploaded into the Pearson cloud can be viewed, measured, and utilized as a source of controlling teachers into a very narrow instrumental/technocratic/scientific pedagogy of a limited number of best practices.

Of course, the story of technology is not new. However, the last 20 years or so have seen it evolve into what Neil Postman has termed an educational god. That is, it has become god-like because technology goes unquestioned: If it is technology, it is a good, and as an a priori good, it is rarely or ever critically examined in any way. I remember when the first surveillance cameras were installed in that high school: There was never any question that as an "objective" technology of surveillance for protection, it was good. Recently, I watched a TED talk by the author of *You Are Not a Gadget*, Jaron Lanier. Jaron is one of the young trailblazers of contemporary technological advances. He had some interesting advice. He suggested that "you must first hate technology" before you can trust it . . . "you must first hate your computer before you use it." I agree and certainly hated that intercom. But his point is important: Treat new technological advances with skepticism, else we find ourselves in a place we don't much like. The Corporate Borg will advance ever more quickly without this skepticism. And if you don't believe me, do an online search for the newest and greatest technological educational advancement: teaching robots.

THE MYTH OF TEACHER RESISTANCE: THE DEATH OF FOUNDATIONS

Dear Foundations Scholar:

We write today to invite your participation in a special theme issue of the Academy for Educational Studies' online journal, Critical Questions in Education (CQIE). CQIE is a fledgling journal, having published five issues to date, and one envisioned as a refuge for important foundationally oriented manuscripts. CQIE submissions go through a double-blind peer review process by way of a cadre of more than fifty reviewers nationwide.

As you certainly know, foundational studies in colleges of education have been weathering a rather vehement and continual attack of late brought about by an unfortunate corporate conception of teaching and learning as technocratic, statistical, narrow, and "data-driven." Recently an assistant commissioner in Missouri's Department of Elementary and Secondary Education was anecdotally reported as saying, "there is no evidence to support that foundations courses make anyone a better teacher"; the University of Georgia is dropping its foundations program at the end of this academic year; and, colleges of education nationwide are rapidly replacing foundations courses with those reflective of this corporate mentality.

With that in mind, and because of your scholarship and leadership in educational foundations, we invite you to contribute a manuscript in defense of foundations to this special issue. Our hope is that it can be one of a growing number of "places" to which we can point policy makers who want to eliminate foundations courses based on the misguided perception that such courses do not make for more enlightened teaching and learning.

The above invitation was used to solicit, as the letter explains, submissions for a special theme issue meant to "protect" foundations of education courses and scholars. I include this as an opening to the myth that teacher education programs have any way to resist the corporate takeover because I don't believe the withering of foundations just as corporations are taking over educational practice at all levels to be mere coincidence. I'm not necessarily a conspiracy theory nut; on the other hand, critical social foundations study is the only place where a resistance to the Corporate Borg can be mounted and sustained. I was recently told by my very own department chair that "within 16 or 17 months, there will be no foundations courses left in our college."

Let's face it, the Corporate Borg will never present "data" showing that foundations of education courses are valuable—we are the one and only threat to their complete assimilation of educational policy, practice, and profit. Teacher education programs were in a bad enough place before the erosion of foundations: Trapped by federal, state, and local government and beholden to accrediting bodies for our very lives, we have relatively few ways to fight back, to resist . . . increasingly we are trapped by legislative mandate . . . it feels exceedingly futile. As foundations courses are increasingly removed from programs of study meant to "prepare" teachers to be "ready for the job," the outlook is quite bleak.

On the other hand, I know history well enough to know that the weakening and withering of philosophical, sociological, critical, etc., understandings found in social foundations of education has gone through such downward cycles before, only to at least partially rebound. There is some evidence that this rebound may once again come: Increasingly, we hear stories of resistance from around the country, particularly on the parts of students and parents—those most severely impacted by the ongoing assimilation. Those of us who work in the foundations world must remain diligent in fanning the fires of this resistance lest we ourselves have our "technological and biological distinctness" assimilated under the myth of preparation and her progeny. George Counts (1932/1978) suggested nearly a century ago that students, teachers, administrators, and supportive parents—those human beings within the institution of schooling—might find a way to "build a new social order." We better get to it.

CONCLUDING THOUGHTS

And so, we come full circle: Are teacher education programs complicit in the corporate takeover of education? Yes, but not necessarily by choice but by trap ... and, as foundational studies wither, by ignorance. Is there anything we can do to resist that takeover? I see only three possibilities for such resistance. The first of these is for us foundations folks to get out of our ivory towers and become not only active in our scholarship but active in our politics. The fight is not totally lost and we are the last hope for pointing out the critical problems in the continuing corporate takeover of education.

The second is to completely reconstruct teacher education programs along the lines of the suggestions made by John Goodlad (1990, 1991) some 20 years ago: Preservice teachers earn a liberal arts degree that includes a strong social foundations load of course work. They then apprentice with an experienced "master" teacher for at least three years; then, and only then, should they be allowed their own classroom. In Goodlad's plan, I believe, lies a measure of hope. In his thinking, the school becomes the center for better understanding how best to run public schools while simultaneously making teacher preparation programs more critically strong. This, it seems, is exactly what is needed to battle the Borg: strong, critically oriented teachers and administrators willing to stand up to corporations, accrediting bodies, and legislators who understand that, as Dewey suggested, preparation happens when we take as much as we can from present experience to the next. This, I believe, is the only "disposition" worth considering and it is one that simply cannot be quantifiably "measured" or directly "taught." As I said early on, one prepares to teach by teaching.

The final option may, given the situation, be the best option: Let's just stop fooling ourselves into believing that we can teach people to teach and get rid of teacher education programs altogether. I have not yet completely given up the hope that sensible and sane human understandings of teaching and learning can, in fact, once again win the day. And, it is from the deepest of tragedies that hope lives—maybe the depth of this particular institutional tragedy has yet to be seen, and maybe when we do see it, hope will again be rekindled and we can reverse what the myth of preparation has wrought. Only time filled with critical effort on the parts of everyone, particularly foundations scholars, will tell. In the meantime, the Corporate Borg is closing in on completely "assimilating" our "biological and technological distinctiveness" via the taken-for-granted mythical structure outlined in this discussion. It may, in fact, already be too late to save ourselves . . . where is Jean-Luc Picard when you need him/her?

NOTES

1. An interesting note to this citation: I accessed this originally in January 2014. When I went back to it today, February 27, 2014, it is no longer there.
2. The Assertive Discipline program was created by Lee and Marlene Canter. It is a prepackaged classroom management system based on behaviorism. For more information see: http://www.canter.net/about-canter/mission-and-values.aspx. The Canters are clearly cashing in on the myth of preparation.

REFERENCES

American Association of Colleges for Teacher Education. (2013a). Retrieved January 4, 2014, from http://edtpa.aacte.org/faq#17
American Association of Colleges for Teacher Education. (2013b). Retrieved February 27, 2014, from http://edtpa.aacte.org/faq#19
Barkin, J. (2011). Got dough? How billionaires rule our schools. *Dissent* (Winter). Retrieved February 13, 2014, from http://www.dissentmagazine.org/article/got-dough-how-billionaires-rule-our-schools
Counts, G. S. (1978). *Dare the school build a new social order?* Carbondale: Southern Illinois University Press. (Original work published 1932)
Day, R. E. (2010). Venture Philanthropy Money Map. Retrieved November 21, 2013, from http://2.bp.blogspot.com/_SJpQvXL0IzI/S9n33yt_NnI/AAAAAAAAFSs/oHWSqSz2wyU/s1600/Bill+and+Melinda+Gates+Foundation+-+affiliations+%26+supported+groups.jpg
Dewey, J. (1997). *Experience and education.* Washington, DC: The Free Press. (Original work published 1936)
Goodlad, J. I. (1990). *Teachers for our nation's schools.* Hoboken, NJ: Jossey-Bass.
Goodlad, J. I. (1991, November). We need a complete redesign of teacher education. *Educational Leadership*, 49(3), 4–10.
Hornstein, M., Lauritson, P., Berman, R. (Producers), & Frakes, J. (Director). (1996). *Star trek: First contact* [Motion picture]. Hollywood, CA: Paramount Pictures.
Noddings, N. (2007). *When school reform goes wrong.* New York, NY: Teachers College Press.
Schneider, M. (2013, October 7). Gates money and common core: Part vi. *Huffington Post.* Retrieved March 2, 2014, from http://www.huffingtonpost.com/mercedes-schneider/gates-money-and-common-co_4_b_4050075.html

10 From K to EdD
Understanding the Cycle of Compliance and Teacher Education's Complicity in Neoliberal School Reform

David Gabbard

In this chapter, I will present an argument to explain why teacher educators and teacher education programs comply with neoliberal school reforms. Much of this hinges on our understanding of neoliberalism, its origins, and its demands. In an earlier writing, I argued that there is nothing "neo" (new) about neoliberalism (Gabbard, 2007). Upon further reflection, I should amend this statement to say that neoliberalism does more than merely *reflect* the principles of economic liberalism; it has reasserted those principles with a vengeance. I am not being hyperbolic here. I literally mean a vendetta!

SYMBOLIC ORDERS OF THE STATE AND THE MARKET REGIME

In Western Europe, and even more dramatically in what would become the US—a former colonial possession of European powers—the modern state originated as a consequence of marketization of society. The financial power of the new merchant class translated into political power, allowing this class to rival and, ultimately, triumph over the feudal aristocracy. In the US, the successful revolution and consequent independence of the former colonies meant that merchants, bankers, and other men "of property," unlike their European contemporaries, would no longer be impeded in their economic pursuits by monarchial authority as vested in the remnants of the feudal state. In effect, independence meant that they could create their own state that would "serve and protect" their liberty to pursue their economic interests—the essence of economic liberalism. In their ascendancy, they forged a state apparatus to serve two fundamental purposes. First, at an individual level, the state would play an active role in advancing their freedom to pursue profit. Second, at a more communal level, the state would also assist in the enforcement and expansion of the market regime as a whole and for the benefit of "all." This, for them, was democracy.

Organizing the state as a nation-state was critical to the success of the market regime. On the one hand, it defined the territorial boundaries of the market regime's reach in relation to that of other emergent market regimes in other nations, though all of them sought to expand their respective reach and the size of their territory to gain access to more resources. This led, of course, to inevitable conflicts, necessitating the creation and maintenance of a military force large enough and powerful enough to secure the interests of the market regime. The military requirements themselves created a market need for weaponry, transport, and other accoutrements of war. Those requirements also intensified the need to mobilize the population behind the interests of the market regime. Not only were their energies needed to fuel the productive capacities of the market; they were also needed to fuel the military capacities of the state to expand and enforce the market regime across greater territory. The formation of the nation-state would play a tremendous role in this as well.

Not only did the idea of the nation define the territorial limits of the market regime; it tied its identity and the identity of the state to that territory. Mobilizing the population to serve the interests of the regime, lending their energies to the pursuit of profit, meant working to attach their own identity to that territory, state, and regime as well. From this came the need to formulate two separate but interrelated symbolic orders. Or, to be more precise, it created a need for a symbolic order that would contribute to the individual's docility to overlay the already existing symbolic order of the market regime that demanded her or his utility. The idea of nationhood provided a partial basis for this symbolic order, cultivating people's sense of loyalty and commitment to *their* country, for they had to be made to feel part of something larger than themselves. But this symbolic order required something more concrete against which they could measure their loyalty and commitment. Their loyalty and commitment to "their" country had to measure up against the loyalty and commitment of the state and their "public servants." Thus this symbolic order included the conception of a benevolent state, dedicated to serving and leading the country and its people to ever-greater glory and abundance. The state inscribed itself, then, with what Michel Foucault referred to as pastoral power.

Particularly in the US, much of the contents of this pastoral symbolic order that sought to ensure the docility of the population in order to better secure its utility expressed itself through the language of democracy. After all, elites of the market regime had, in fact, established a democratic state for themselves that would enhance their individual autonomy as well as their collective interests. Such democratic values found little substantive expression in the lives of the majority of the population. Initially, we must remember, the property-owning elite who designed the state granted the franchise to vote solely to themselves. For the rest of the population, those democratic values served an almost exclusively symbolic function, designed to increase their docility by reducing any potential resistance they might mount against the imperatives of the state/market regime, including the imperative to increase their utility through the cultivation and channeling of the population's energies in the service of the market regime more directly.

In this sense, the symbolic order of the political sphere was authentically meaningful only for the elites of the market regime who served as the architects and directors of the state. For the majority of the population, it was an illusion created only to make them feel part of something in which they had never been fully enfranchised. On the other hand, they experienced the symbolic order of the market regime that sought to increase their utility as something far more real. While the pastoral imagery of the state emphasized the values of autonomy and community, the disciplinary language of the market regime privileged the values of heteronomy—submitting one's will to external authority—and individualism. In other words, one advances one's own economic self-interest by doing what one is told and doing it to maximal efficiency.

Problems arose, of course, when the population began taking democracy seriously, giving rise to what the market regime recognized as dangerous demands of collectivism being placed upon the state. In fact, the population had made some significant inroads towards making the state functionally more democratic. Over the course of the 19th century and into the mid-20th century, minorities, women, and workers had all struggled for and won important concessions from the state that increased their franchise. Nevertheless, the idea of the state responding to populist demands was anathema to the orthodoxy of the market regime. The principles of economic liberalism demanded that the state function only to enforce, expand, and increase the efficiency of the market regime. So, neoliberalism can be read only as an effort to restore market domination and the hegemony of market values.

SCHOOLING AND SYMBOLIC ORDERS

Perhaps because the US Constitution grants no direct authority to the federal government to either establish or operate schools, most Americans have learned somehow to disassociate schools from the state. At the same time, however, the pastoral symbolic order of the state conditions many of us to view schools as inherently benevolent institutions dedicated to the education and welfare of our children. In presuming this benevolent purpose of serving the value of education, we do more than simply lose sight of the compulsory nature of schooling. We come to view schooling as a right to which we are entitled. When we hear or use the phrase "public school," we presume that schools were created to serve the public. It never dawns on us that perhaps schools were created to target the public. In order to detect the presence of the symbolic order of the market regime as it operates in schools, however, we need to recognize schools as inseparable from the state and, therefore, the dangers of compulsory schooling.

Credited with developing the first comprehensive anarchist critique of government schools in his *Enquiry Concerning Political Justice* in 1793 (Godwin, n.d.), William Godwin viewed freedom of thought as fundamental to political liberty. As Joel Spring explains, Godwin believed that "since people constantly improve their reasoning power and their understanding of nature, their understanding of the best form of government is constantly changing" (Spring, 1994, p. 42). While he recognized that education was crucial towards the development of individuals' powers of rational thought that would guide them in self-government, Godwin also, Spring notes, "considered national systems of education one of the foremost dangers to freedom and liberty" (Spring, 1983, p. 68). "'Before we put so powerful a machine [education] under the direction of so ambiguous an agent [government],'" Godwin warned, "'it behooves us to consider well what it is we do. Government will not fail to employ it, to strengthen its hands, and perpetuate its institutions'" (Spring, 1994, p. 73).

Echoing Godwin's concerns and armed with 200 years of historical hindsight, contemporary anarchist theorist Noam Chomsky describes "the basic institutional role and function of the schools" as providing "an ideological service: there's a real selection for obedience and conformity" (Chomsky, 2003, pp. 27–28). In Chomsky's analysis, compulsory, government schooling brings children at a very early age into an indoctrination system "that works against independent thought in favor of obedience" with the goal of keeping people "from asking questions that matter about important issues that directly affect them and others" (Chomsky, 2000, p. 24).

Emma Goldman made similar observations early in the 20th century. "What, then, is the school of today?" she asked. "It is for the child what the prison is for the convict and the barracks for the soldier—a place where everything is being used to break the will of the child, and then to pound, knead, and shape it into a being utterly foreign to itself. . . . It is but part of a system which can maintain itself only through absolute discipline and uniformity" (Goldman, n.d.).

Goldman's description of schools receives considerable support in the more heavily analytic writings of Michel Foucault. In books such as *Madness and Civilization* and *Discipline and Punish* (Foucault, 1988, 1995, respectively), Foucault points out for us a very peculiar historical oddity. Systems of government-sponsored compulsory schooling did, in fact, begin to emerge at the same point in history as the modern prison, and each was modeled on the army barracks. Compulsory schooling of the masses has always had less to do with education and more to do with discipline. By "discipline," Foucault refers to a form of treatment that

> increases the forces of the body (in economic terms of utility) and diminishes those same forces (in terms of political obedience). In short, it disassociates powers from the body; on the one hand it turns it into an "aptitude," a "capacity," which it seeks to increase; on the other

hand, it reverses the course of the energy, the power that might result from it, and turns it into a relation of strict subjugation. If economic exploitation separates the force of and the product of labor, let us say that disciplinary coercion establishes in the body the constricting link between an increased aptitude and an increased domination. (Foucault, 1995, p. 138)

In keeping with the imperatives of state power as conceived by the market regime, compulsory schooling functions to discipline individuals in a manner that increases the productive power that their bodies offer to the economic system while simultaneously diminishing their power to resist economic exploitation and the political system that initiates that exploitation by compelling students to attend school in the first place.

The writings of Benjamin Rush, a signer of the Declaration of Independence and recognized "father of American psychiatry," are particularly illuminative of how the early advocates of compulsory schooling viewed the importance of diminishing individuals' powers of resistance by building up their emotional attachments to the state. Rush wrote his "Thoughts Upon the Mode of Education Proper in a Republic" in 1786, just seven years before Godwin wrote his *Enquiry Concerning Political Justice*. Rush declared, "The principle of patriotism stands in need of the reinforcement of *prejudice*, and it is well known that our strongest prejudices in favor of our country are formed in the first one and twenty years of our lives.... Our schools of learning," he argued, "by producing one general and uniform system of education, will render the mass of the people more homogeneous and thereby fit them more easily for uniform and peaceable government" (Rush, 1786). The quotes below come from the same document:

> In order more effectually to secure to our youth the advantages of a religious education, it is necessary to impose upon them the doctrines and discipline of a particular church. Man is naturally an ungovernable animal, and observations on particular societies and countries will teach us that when we add the restraints of ecclesiastical to those of domestic and civil government, we produce in him the highest degrees of order and virtue... Let our pupil be taught that he does not belong to himself, but that he is public property. Let him be taught to love his family, but let him be taught at the same time that he must forsake and even forget them when the welfare of his country requires it... In the education of youth, let the authority of our masters be as *absolute* as possible. The government of schools like the government of private families should be *arbitrary*, that it may not be *severe*. By this mode of education, we prepare our youth for the subordination of laws and thereby qualify them for becoming good citizens of the republic. I am satisfied that the most useful citizens have been formed from those youth who have never known or felt their own wills till they were one

and twenty years of age, and I have often thought that society owes a great deal of its order and happiness to the deficiencies of parental government being supplied by those habits of obedience and subordination which are contracted at schools. . . .

From the observations that have been made it is plain that I consider it as possible to convert men into republican machines. This must be done if we expect them to perform their parts properly in the great machine of the government of the state. (Rush, 1786)

Noah Webster, known as "the schoolmaster of America," could not have agreed more. "Good republicans," Webster wrote, "are formed by a singular machinery in the body politic, which takes the child as soon as he can speak, checks his natural independence and passions, makes him subordinate to superior age, to the laws of the state, to town and parochial institutions" (Spring, 2005, pp. 48–49). Webster's real significance as a force in shaping the direction of American education and culture rests with his creation of a series of books that were the major school texts in 19th-century America, selling more than a million and a half copies by 1801 and 75 million copies by 1875. As Webster's biographer, Harry Warfel, characterized them, "'This series of unified textbooks effectually shaped the destiny of American education for a century. Imitators sprang up by the dozens, and each echoed the Websterian nationalism. The word "American" became indispensable in all textbook titles; all vied in patriotic eloquence'" (Spring, 2005, p. 48).

"Our schools," wrote a veteran schoolteacher in 1910, "have failed because they rest on compulsion and constraint . . . It is deemed possible and important that all should be interested in the same things, in the same sequence, and at the same time . . . Under the circumstances [of 1910] teachers are mere tools, automatons who perpetuate a machine that turns out automatons" (Goldman, n.d.).

THE CYCLE OF COMPLIANCE BEGINS IN KINDERGARTEN

While we should hesitate before going so far as to label teachers and teacher educators as "automatons," the preceding macroanalysis of how the disciplinary symbolic order of the market regime shaped the purposes and effects of state-sponsored compulsory schooling forces us to consider how that symbolic order impacts the attitudes and practices of teachers at a microlevel of analysis. I will approach this through an examination of the available research of teachers' attitudes towards students who demonstrate creative personalities compared to their attitudes towards students who demonstrate more compliant personalities.

Frequently, when those of us in teacher education ask our students—would-be teachers—why they want to teach, they tell us that they want to teach because they love children. What if we pursued our line of inquiry by asking them what kinds of children they like and what kinds they dislike? According to Westby and Dawson, "One of the most consistent findings in educational studies of creativity has been that teachers dislike personality traits associated with creativity" (Westby & Dawson, 1995, p. 1). Instead, "teachers prefer traits that seem to run counter to creativity, such as conformity and unquestioning acceptance of authority (Westby & Dawson, 1995). Westby and Dawson help us recognize that there is a rich tradition of research supporting their conclusion. Among the studies they cite, we find works dating back as far as 1961 (see Meyers & Torrance, 1961).

In addition to citing Westby and Dawson, Kyung Hee Kim draws upon an equally impressive body of literature to support her conclusion that "research has shown that teachers are apt to prefer students who are achievers and teacher pleasers rather than disruptive or unconventional creative students" (Kim, 2008, p. 236). As she elaborates:

> Scott reported that teachers see creative children as a source of interference and disruption. Westby and Dawson found that teachers' judgment of their favorite students was negatively correlated with creativity. Teachers prefer students to exhibit traits such as unquestioning acceptance of authority, conformity, logical thinking, and responsibility that make students easy to manage in the classroom. Teachers' images of the ideal student emphasize traits that were conformist and socially acceptable. (Kim, 2008, p. 236)

Drawing upon the work of Everett E. Hagen (Hagen, 1962), as well as that of Meyers and Torrance (Meyers & Torrance, 1961), Ronald Urick and Jack R. Frymier help us extend beyond recognizing how teachers' attitudes have historically contributed to the creation of classroom norms that are hostile towards creativity (Urick & Frymier, 1963). Their work helps us understand why those same attitudes work to ensure that the learning environments in our nation's system of compulsory schooling will likely never change. The majority of teachers deplore and resist change as much as they deplore and punish creativity.

With regard to people's attitudes towards change, Hagen distinguishes between two different personality types: innovational and authoritarian. He describes the innovational personality as demonstrating "an openness to experience, a confidence in one's own evaluations, a satisfaction in facing and resolving confusion or ambiguity, and a feeling that the world is orderly, and that the phenomenon of life can be understood and explained" (Urick & Frymier, 1963, p. 109). Conversely, Urick and Frymier explain, Hagen views the authoritarian personality as "characterized by a fear of using his initiative, an uncertainty concerning the quality of his own judgment, and tendency to avoid frustration and anxiety, an uneasiness in facing unresolved situations, and a tendency to see the world as arbitrary and capricious" (and therefore in dire need of management) (Urick & Frymier, 1963, p. 109).

Studies by Myers and Torrance reveal that teachers who resist change demonstrated the characteristics of "authoritarianism, defensiveness, insensitivity to pupil needs, preoccupation with information-giving functions, intellectual inertness, disinterest in promoting initiative in pupils, and preoccupation with discipline" (Urick & Frymier, 1963, p. 109). This latter authoritarian preoccupation with discipline reveals itself in the feedback received by teacher education programs on surveys of their graduates in response to the question, "If you could have had more instruction in one area during your years spent in teacher training, what would that area have been?" Invariably, in my more than 20 years of experience in teacher education, across four different institutions in four different states, the most frequent response to that question has always been "classroom management."

This tells me, in light of all the research revealing their authoritarian personality, that most teachers must view the work they demand of students as being a kind of necessary drudgery. They also view it as immutable. In keeping with the market value of heteronomy—submission to external authority—the nature of the work is not up for questioning or challenge. It's a given. It's not going to change, but why should it? The program worked for them when they were students in school. They went along with it, and their teachers rewarded them with gold stars and praise and, ultimately, high grades. How could there be anything wrong with the program? The problem must be with the students, particularly their motivation. Perhaps the gold stars don't work to motivate these students. We need to increase the extrinsic rewards to get them to work harder at completing their assigned tasks. Unfortunately, as Amabile and Kramer's research demonstrates, people tend not to be motivated by extrinsic rewards:

> Ask leaders what they think makes employees enthusiastic about work, and they'll tell you in no uncertain terms. In a recent survey we invited more than 600 managers from dozens of companies to rank the impact on employee motivation and emotions of five workplace factors commonly considered significant: recognition, incentives, interpersonal support, support for making progress, and clear goals. "Recognition for good work (either public or private)" came out number one. . . . Unfortunately, those managers are wrong. (Amabile & Kramer, 2010)

Likewise, most teachers also believe that motivational issues need to be managed by external stimuli, rather than addressed through the intrinsic qualities of the work they ask students to undertake. They, too, are wrong, and the learning and working environments they create in their classrooms frequently reflect many of the same traits Amabile associates with creativity-killing environments (Amabile, 1998).

In Melissa Engleman's study of 213 graduate students in education with a median of four years of classroom teaching experience, for example, she found that more than half of her respondents fell into either the ISFJ (25%) or ESFJ (28%) personality type on the Humanetrics "Jung Typology" Test (2007). Another 6% fell into the ESTJ type and 10% fell into the ISTJ type, making a total of 69% of the teachers that fit the SJ temperament profile (Engleman, 2007).

In his *Learning Patterns and Temperament Styles*, Keith Golay characterized SJs as "Actual Routine Learners" (ARLs). These people feel a need to establish and preserve social units, which fits with their demand for clear expectations and specific, clearly defined procedures for accomplishing a task. These traits align with their tendency to be meticulous as well as highly industrious. As students, ARLs also display a very strong need to please and receive approval from authority figures, including and especially their teachers. In turn, they hold authority figures in reverence, deferring to that authority through obedience and conformity (Golay, 1982).

If we can accept Engleman's numbers as fairly representative of the broader population of those people who chose to enter teaching as a career, we can hypothesize that 70% of the classroom learning environments in America's system of compulsory schooling are created and maintained by *Actual Routine Teachers*. We can further hypothesize that those environments most heavily reward children who learn to revere the authority of teachers and who work diligently at their assigned tasks to win their approval through their obedience to and their conformity with the teacher's values and expectations. Because they experience these rewards from their teachers in these environments, ARLs/SJs might be more disposed towards choosing teaching as a career, but the *cycle of compliance* does not end here.

The vast majority of teacher educators have spent the majority of their lives in and around schools. Based on the preceding data, the majority of them likely grew up as Actual Routine Learners, became Actual Routine Teachers, and now function as Actual Routine Teacher Educators. While I worked in the teacher education program at East Carolina University, a faculty member there teamed with a colleague of his at UNC–Chapel Hill to formulate the idea of holding teacher education programs accountable by ranking them on the basis of how well the students of their graduates performed on their end-of-grade tests.

One of the assumptions here, of course, is that teachers actually teach in accordance with what they learn during their teacher education programs—that the professional culture of their schools actually supports that mode of teaching. Yet we frequently hear from our students that their mentor teachers tell them during their internships and student teaching to "forget everything they teach you in college; this is how we really do things in schools." Nevertheless, very few of my colleagues ever questioned the validity of the measure. Furthermore, when Secretary of Education Arne Duncan happened to mention the names of our colleague and his collaborator who originated this idea in one of his speeches, people sent a plethora of public emails, effusive with praise, celebrating the attention his achievement had brought to our College of Education. They were happy that one of their own had won accolades from the external authority of the state.

CONCLUSION

People's attitudes stem from their beliefs and values. We arrive at birth, however, with none of these things already intact. None of them are natural. They are social—created and evolved by other members of our species who preceded our arrival and who took part in some portion of our society's history. The majority of those people died long before we came upon the scene. Before they did, they generated ideas, beliefs, and values that evolved as they were transmitted across numerous generations until, finally, they reach us. To become members of the society into which we are born, we must undergo a process of socialization through which we learn those beliefs and values that comprise the shared social stock of knowledge (Berger & Luckmann, 1966). Which beliefs and values we make contact with most regularly is not a matter of caprice. As social animals, humans create and reproduce far more than just beliefs and values. We also produce institutions to provide a set of prefabricated patterns for guiding our behavior. For those who inherit a set of institutions from previous generations, the origins and meanings of those institutions do not appear as transparent. They require legitimations, a set of beliefs to explain the necessity of a given institution, the values it was created to serve, and how a particular institution fits within the larger network of institutions. The legitimations created for public dissemination, however, do not necessarily align with the real reasons why an institution was created and the values the institution actually serves. The case of compulsory schooling provides a powerful example of this. It also points to the second reason why the learning environments found in the vast majority of compulsory school classrooms have never and, probably, will never nurture creativity.

Our system of compulsory schooling was never intended to serve the value of education, though we seem incapable of recognizing or admitting this to ourselves. The origins and meanings of our institutions are not transparent to us, and very few people actually study the history of compulsory schooling. This leaves the vast majority of people vulnerable to being propagandized into blind acceptance of the illusions created to manufacture their consent. They are taught to believe, for example, that schools are inherently benevolent institutions. In fact, to speak legitimately about education in this country, one must present the school as a messianic institution capable of delivering the individual and/or society into some condition of secular salvation. Pastoral images of kind, loving, virtuous, and motherly female teachers serve to mask the more authoritarian reality.

Though a full accounting of its history lies beyond the scope of this chapter, compulsory schooling has always functioned as a social technology designed to discipline the population into compliance with the beliefs, ideas, and values requisite to reproducing society's dominant institutions. To gain some appreciation for the origins of schools, we simply need to consider the fact that they emerged alongside the system of workhouses and poorhouses throughout Europe to cope with the massive levels of homelessness and unemployment created by the Enclosure Movement that privatized land into property and the Industrial Revolution that transformed people into labor. The emerging factory system could not absorb the entirety of the population displaced by the agrarian reforms of the Enclosure Movement, but learning to labor within factories did not come naturally to people. A whole series of Poor Laws were created that criminalized charity—even charity from churches. The merchants and manufacturers of the 17th, 18th, and even 19th centuries used many of the same arguments used by their modern-day equivalents against welfare today, contending that charity undermined people's incentive to work, that is, your incentive to rent yourself to another person in exchange for a wage. Those same Poor Laws also criminalized unemployment and homelessness. If apprehended for being jobless, you were sent to a workhouse or a poorhouse to be reformed so as to learn to appreciate the value of work (see Foucault, 1995: Polanyi, 1944).

Schools served a more preemptive role, seeking to discipline children into proper work habits and render them "useful" or "productive" members of society before they could become vagrant delinquents. Yes, they were taught to read and write, but only to make them more useful and more productive. This new disciplinary regime also gave birth to the modern prison. Note how we sometimes refer to prisons as "correction facilities." The modern prison, it turns out, took its design from schools, not—as I'd always expected from the time I was a student in elementary school—the other way around.

Schools, workhouses, poorhouses, and prisons, then, share common origins as disciplinary institutions created to serve the market institutions that were rising to dominance in the 17th and 18th centuries. The dominance of market institutions, initially through the patterns of colonialism and imperialism, has now grown global. Very little has changed, however, with regard to the beliefs and values required to reproduce those institutions and maintain their dominance. If anything, the propaganda system required to insulate them from greater public awareness and dissent has grown stronger. People, for example, no longer view schools in terms of their compulsory nature and how they are tied to society's dominant institutions. They have learned to conflate schooling with education and to confuse that which is compulsory with a fundamental human right.

This is why we cannot view the teaching of creativity in our schools as a social justice issue and why we should never expect those institutions to promote creativity. The latter would require a fundamental shift in the values served by schools, a shift in what Takis Fotopoulos defines as our "dominant social paradigm" (Fotopoulos, 2003). In his analysis, the values of our present system stem from "its basic principles of organization: the principle of heteronomy and the principle of individualism which are built-into the institutions of the market economy and representative 'democracy'. Such values," he says, "involve the values of inequity and effective oligarchy (even if the system calls itself a democracy), competition and aggressiveness" (Fotopoulos, 2003, para. 2).

When viewed in these terms, we can recognize how the values and beliefs of the majority of teachers and teacher educators align with the values and beliefs of our society's dominant institutions. Those authoritarian traits of Actual Routine Teachers described earlier are not simply the expression of their individual personalities. Originally, women were recruited into teaching precisely because the dehumanizing forces of sexism could demand obedience from them. This partially explains why the teaching profession remains so deeply disrespected by our political and economic elites through the verbal assaults they launch against schools—berating them for not producing a sufficient number of the right kinds of workers to satisfy their demand for properly disciplined and trained labor. Those Actual Routine Teachers of both genders have internalized the values and beliefs of our dominant institutions. Through their routinization of those values in the authoritarian learning environments of their classrooms, they obviate the dangers of creativity and change, rewarding obedience and conformity while punishing any threat to the established order.

In Freirean terms, students in authoritarian classrooms stand in relation to their Actual Routine Teachers as the oppressed stand in relation to their oppressors. "The very structure of their thought has been conditioned by the contradictions of the concrete, existential situation by which they were shaped. Their ideal is to be human; but for them, to be human is to be oppressors. This is their model of humanity" (Freire, 1971, p. 30). Actual Routine Teacher Educators beget Actual Routine Teachers, who beget Actual Routine Learners who become Actual Routine Teachers who become Actual Routine Teacher Educators. And so the cycle continues.

REFERENCES

Amabile, T. M. (1998, September). How to kill creativity. *Harvard Business Review*. Retrieved from http://hbr.org/1998/09/how-to-kill-creativity/ar/1

Amabile, T. M., & Kramer, S. J. (2010, January). What really motivates workers? *Harvard Business Review*. Retrieved March 15, 2014, from http://hbr.org/2010/01/the-hbr-list-breakthrough-ideas-for-2010/ar/1

Bachtold, L. M. (1974). The creative personality and the ideal pupil revisited. *Journal of Creative Behavior, 8*, 47–54.

Berger, P., & Luckmann, T. *The social construction of reality: A treatise in the sociology of knowledge.* New York, NY: Anchor.

Chomsky, N. (2000). Beyond a domesticating education: A dialogue. In D. Macedo (Ed.), *Chomsky on miseducation*. Lanham, MD: Rowman & Litttlefield, 15–36.
Chomsky, N. (2003). *The function of schools: Subtler and cruder methods of control*. In D. A. Saltman & D. Gabbard (Eds.), *Education as enforcement: The militarization and corporatization of schools*. New York, NY: Routledge, 25–36.
Engleman, M. (2007). Applying learning styles and personality preference information to online teaching pedagogy. *Journal of Interactive Instruction Development, 19*(3), 3–10.
Fotopoulos, T. (2003, March). From (mis)education to paideia. *Democracy in Nature, 9*(1). Retrieved June 30, 2014, from http://inclusivedemocracy.org/dn/vol9/takis_paideia.htm
Foucault, M. (1988). *Madness and civilization: A history of insanity in the age of reason*. New York, NY: Vintage.
Foucault, M. (1995). *Discipline and punish: The birth of the prison* (Alan Sheridan, Trans.). New York, NY: Vintage.
Freire, P. (1971). *Pedagogy of the oppressed*. New York, NY: Herder and Herder.
Gabbard, D. (2007). Militarizing class warfare: The historical foundations of the neoliberal/neoconservative nexus. *Education Policy Futures, 5*(2), 119–136.
Godwin, W. (n.d.). *An enquiry concerning political justice*. Charlottesville, VA: Electronic Text Center, University of Virginia Library, n.d. Retrieved March 15, 2014, from http://etext.virginia.edu/toc/modeng/public/GodJust.html
Golay, K. (1982). *Learning patterns and temperament styles*. Newport Beach, CA: Manas Systems.
Goldman, E. (n.d.). The social importance of the modern school. Emma Goldman Papers, Manuscripts and Archives Division, New York Public Library, Astor, Lenox and Tilden Foundations. Retrieved March 15, 2014, from http://dwardmac.pitzer.edu/anarchist_archives/goldman/socimportms.html
Hagen, E. E. (1962). *On the theory of social change: How economic growth begins*. Belmont, CA: Dorsey Press.
Kim, K. H. (2008). Underachievement and creativity: Are gifted underachievers highly creative? *Creativity Research Journal, 20*(2), 235–242.
Meyers, R. E., & Torrance, E. P. (1961). Can teachers encourage creative thinking? *Educational Leadership, 19*, 156–159.
Polanyi, K. (1944). *The great transformation: The political and economic origins of our time*. New York, NY: Rinehart.
Rush, B. (1786). Thoughts upon the mode of education proper in a republic. In *A Plan for the establishment of public schools and the diffusion of knowledge in Pennsylvania; to which are added, thoughts upon the mode of education proper in a republic*. Retrieved March 15, 2014, from http://www.schoolchoices.org/roo/rush.htm
Spring, J. (1983). The public school movement vs. the libertarian tradition. *The Journal of Libertarian Studies, 7*(1). Retrieved March 15, 2014, from http://www.mises.org/journals/jls/7_1/7_1_3.pdf
Spring, J. (1994). *Wheels in the head: Educational philosophies of authority, freedom, and culture from Socrates to Paulo Freire*. New York, NY: McGraw-Hill.
Spring, J. (2005). *The American school 1642–2004*. New York, NY: McGraw-Hill.
Urick, R., & Frymier, J. R. (1963, November). Personalities, teachers and curriculum change. *Educational Leadership, 21*(2), 107–111. Retrieved June 30, 2014, from http://www.ascd.org/ASCD/pdf/journals/ed_lead/el_196311_urick.pdf
Westby, E. L., & Dawson, V. L. (1995). Creativity: Asset of burden in the classroom. *Creativity Research Journal, 8*(1), 1–10.

Afterword
Implications and Discussion

Leslee Grey

As the contributors to this book demonstrate, schooling is a strategic space for engineering and maintaining neoliberal myths. As such, schools are vital to the production and circulations of discourses about sociopolitical allegiances and identities. The knowledges and dispositions fostered in public schools point to larger narratives, or systems of beliefs, about what it means to be a responsible citizen, a moral agent, and a free and happy individual. As Apple reminds us, behind all educational proposals are particular visions of which practices and policies best contribute to the making of a good society (Apple, 2001, p. 71). These narratives and visions are neither politically neutral nor value free. Conversations about education initiatives are rife with values that are unarticulated, ideologies that are taken for granted, and rationalities that rely heavily on moralized assumptions rather than evidence. Similarly, Popkewitz describes reform movements as embodying "salvation narratives," motivations, and sensibilities that enable individuals "to act as the democratic citizen-of-the-future" (Popkewitz, 2002, p. 122). Because the space of an Afterword is not sufficient for an in-depth analysis of the ways in which myths are worked and worked upon for the purposes of governing individuals, I refer the reader to scholarship on neoliberal governance for such an analysis (Foucault, 1982/1983; Barry, Osborne & Rose, 1996; Rose, 1990). Nonetheless, it is crucial to at least mention that education reforms govern, or define and act on, the identities and subjectivities of individuals by drawing boundaries around possibilities for the ways in which citizenship, personhood, and the self can be envisioned and enacted. Through the circulation of discourses, which include myths that place parameters around what can be taught, learned, or known in educational contexts, citizens are essentially "constructed" in specific ways to serve specific interests.

As evidenced in the previous chapters of this volume, conversations, policies, and practices that surround schooling are built on a precarious foundation of unspoken values and meanings that a mythical community of corporate stakeholders, policy makers, educators, parents, and students are assumed to share. Goals of public education are constructed and circulated in ways that allow them to be understood as having been arrived at through consensus, debate, or common sense. The contributors to this book examine the origins and effects of a number of educational myths that are responsible for the ways in which so-called corporate elites and other powerful entities currently define the purposes, and assess the successes and failures, of public schools. The authors of this book deconstruct and decode the mythology of education reform movements, exposing the assumptions and ideologies that undergird beliefs guiding public policies and practices.

The purpose of this Afterword is to synthesize many of the ideas conceptualized in this volume, providing the reader with a summary of the major themes the authors address. I hope that this synthesis will encourage readers of this collection to reflect on how the ideas presented here affect their daily lives as educators and learners, both inside and outside of the classroom.

GUIDED BY "BIG LIES"

An earlier and widely read book addressing education reform myths, Berliner and Biddle's *The Manufactured Crisis* (Berliner & Biddle, 1995), provided data showing that although the commonsense notion that public schools are failing has been taken for granted, education in the US has in fact been improving, albeit in modest ways (see also Ravitch, 2013). For example, students today are "at least as well informed as students were in previous generations" (p. 13). Berliner and Biddle famously criticized the ideas behind *A Nation at Risk* as a "Big Lie" (p. 127) meant to "confuse and derail efforts that are badly needed to help the neediest schools" (p. 144), as the problems that schools do face are mostly due to a lack of resources and a high prevalence of social problems related to low-income neighborhoods (Anyon, 2005).

How is it that one of our most significant public institutions continues to be guided by such Big Lies? In Chapter 2, Metcalfe examines how neoliberal myths are able to gain the "ideological force" that allows them to normalize and "dominate much of educational discourse" by appealing to the *homo economicus*, the rational choice maximizer who potentially resides inside every person. Sharing much in common with Foucault's notion of the entrepreneurial self, Hamann describes the *homo economicus* as a "free and autonomous 'atom' of self-interest who is fully responsible for . . . using rational choice and cost-benefit calculation *to the express exclusion* of all other values and interests" (Hamann, 2009, p. 36, emphasis in original). Metcalfe explains that sociopolitical myths can help humans make sense of a complex and often irrational world. For both Costigan and Metcalfe, myths function as a kind of technology that not only governs identities and actions but also helps individuals understand and interpret the social and political spaces in which they live, albeit in ways that have already been defined for them. As Costigan puts it, myths are efficient ways of constructing and circulating narratives because they "eliminate the need for . . . time-consuming critical analysis." Similarly, Metcalfe contends that because neoliberalism situates education as "an instrument of economic growth," when members of educational communities take up, or internalize, the neoliberal myth, critical engagement with social and political issues is quashed. Metcalfe calls on educators to challenge the *homo economicus* archetype and to see schools as more than just sites of "economic development." Rather, schools should also be spaces where "democratic practices, values, and beliefs . . . are developed."

Critical scholars of education remind us that public schools have historically served various purposes, both explicit and implicit, and that these purposes have benefited some individuals and groups while marginalizing others. Explicitly, public schooling is responsible for expanding literacy and knowledge, producing citizens, and preparing young people for the world of work. Implicitly, the hidden curriculum (Anyon, 1980; Best & Kellner, 2003) represents ideological assumptions routinely passed on from administrators to teachers and from teachers to students as a form of hegemonic control. As Hill's Marxist analysis (Chapter 3) makes clear, schools also serve to assimilate and enculturate young people from diverse backgrounds to continue existing power relations, lessen cultural distinctions, and reproduce a division of labor. Likewise, McLaren's (1989) scholarship foregrounds the ways in which schools have always functioned in ways that rationalize the knowledge industry into class-divided tiers that reproduce inequality and fragment democratic social relations through an emphasis on competition and cultural ethnocentrism (McLaren, 1989, p. 161). The general public, including parents as well as school leaders, accepts the myth that accomplished business leaders know how to make schools successful. Modeling schools after corporations *must* produce a more efficient workforce, this line of thinking goes, and will help the US gain a larger purchase on the global marketplace. This approach holds that private enterprises are more effective catalysts for engineering social change than are public, that is, tax-funded, programs such as traditional public education.

WHAT OR WHO IS REALLY AT RISK?

As indicated by the allusion to *A Nation at Risk* in the subtitle Chapter 1, contributors to this volume trace the history of the mythologies of standards, measurement, and accountability in school reform to the interest in education fostered by the 1983 report *A Nation at Risk*, which famously links mediocre student performance on standardized national tests to mediocre economic performance in the global marketplace (National Commission on Education, 1983). In Chapter 4, Root provides a case study of a particular educational myth: that standardization promotes "equity and rigor." Root contextualizes her study within neoliberal education policies, including the perennially mythologized "Texas Miracle" manufactured in the 1980s in the wake of *A Nation at Risk*. It is in this chapter that the reader will see specific connections between the famous and oft-cited report and current neoliberal education policies and practices. For Root, standardization deprofessionalizes teachers, morphing their roles as "curriculum creators [to] implementers of prescribed, irrelevant activities and lessons." In line with Freire's (2000) "banking" concept of education, in which students are viewed as empty vessels to be deposited with bits of information and skills to be withdrawn later, standardization, not unfamiliar to many if not most readers of this volume, stands in sharp contrast to Root's vision of curriculum: "thoughtful, intellectual, and ethical . . . [creating] a bond between the learner and knowledge." In fact, today's standardized, scripted classroom materials and assessments begin with the myth that the teacher possesses no knowledge to deposit. As Root's case study demonstrates, students labeled "at risk" were more likely to be "spoon-fed" standardized curricula that focused on minimal standards, a far cry from the values of equity and rigor that supporters of standardization tend to mythologize. Such educational inequities are based on a separate but related myth that low-income children are, in Lesko's words, "worrisome yet passive recipients of knowledge and values" (Lesko, 2001, p. 105).

In Chapter 9, Sheffield points out that an additional aspect of education could also be resituated as "at risk": the critical strength of teacher education programs, especially given the rate at which courses on the social, cultural, and philosophical foundations of education seem to be vanishing from teacher certification requirements. Mythologized corporate education ideology, for Sheffield, creates a "Borg-like" hive-mind focused on assimilating individuals into a system of control concerned with narrow views of teacher preparation and technocratic best practices rather than seeing teaching as an "ethical endeavor concerned with young, whole, flesh-and-blood, human beings and how they might come to see themselves in the world." Indeed, as many of these scholars and others have argued, schools today neglect an important purpose of tax-funded public education: to transform children into civic-minded independent thinkers and socially responsible adults committed to democratic principles (Boyles, 2000; Giroux, 1989; Molnar, 1996). Economic imperatives have overshadowed democratic practices; the bottom line is the achievement of higher and higher test scores. As evidenced in this collection, although educational myths are not backed by substantiated data or research, they seem stronger than ever today, influencing policies and practices from teacher certification to testing, tenure, retention, and retirement. In Chapter 8, Tell's work on charter schools exposes the myths, or "disinformation," surrounding these schools, situating them as a "direct product of the neoliberal agenda of corporate reform." Using data from various research studies, Tell provides evidence that charter schools are not living up to their own mythology. Rather, because they tend to utilize standardized curricular materials and tests that narrow the curriculum and provide profits for the companies that publish them, Tell concludes that charters deliver lower levels of education as well as oppose the interests of the public. Charter schools, he argues, "are not public in the modern sense of the word."

Corporate stakeholders continue to imagine themselves as benevolent partners in educating the young people of the world. Giroux writes, "One of the most important legacies of American public education has been providing students with the critical capacities, knowledge, and values that enable them to become active citizens striving to build a stronger democracy" (Giroux 2000, p. 83). However, as Spring (2002) puts it, the preparation of students for the ever-changing workplace has emerged as public education's single most important goal. Spring explains that neoliberalism "calls for government intervention to promote and protect free markets" and for education to be evaluated as an "economic investment." As a result, public schools have become what Cuban (1984, p. 6) refers to as an "arm of the national economy."

Although considered a fairly radical, revisionist industry in the US in the 1970s and 1980s, exposing hidden assumptions, beliefs, and ideologies behind pubic policies such as how schools reproduce inequalities is no longer a radical endeavor among scholars of education. Ravitch's more recent work (Ravitch 2011, 2013) has brought the once-leftist critique of education reforms into the mainstream. Ravitch refers to neoliberal educational reform as a "hoax" (Ravitch, 2013). Even so, educators such as Barbara Madeloni of the University of Massachusetts risk their jobs for speaking out against corporate involvement in education (Winerip, 2012). Still, on a near-weekly basis, one can find newspaper articles and blog postings reflecting parents' and teachers' dissatisfaction with the current reforms and policies characterized as corporate reform models.

The neoliberalism paradigm governs public policy as the "dominant metanarrative" (Peters, 2011, p. 6), wherein "students are now 'customers' or 'clients' and teachers are 'providers'" (p. 157). "The teaching/learning relation," Peters posits, "has been reduced to an implicit contract between buyer and seller" (p. 157). Education is mythologized as an investment in the development of "human capital" (Lipman, 2011, p. 14); students are data points (Baez & Boyles, 2009); and learning is measured in inputs and outputs and standardized test scores so that each school, teacher, and student—and in some cases, even parents—can be ranked. A myth driving these initiatives is that the market functions in a way that is "morally superior" to the public sphere (Peters, 2011, p. 172). It is no longer considered cynical to see education as a political and cultural enterprise. Far from a neutral process, education is a form of cultural politics supporting forms of knowledge that embrace a particular vision of the past, present, and future that legitimizes only the experiences and knowledges of a dominant group.

Accepting the power of those on top is taken as common sense (Lewis, 1992) and leads one to accept a subordinate position in society. Burbules and Berk (1999) state, "Systems of education are among the institutions that foster and reinforce such beliefs, through the rhetoric of meritocracy, through testing, through tracking, through vocational training or college preparatory curricula, and so forth" (pp. 50–51). The end goals include greater accountability to taxpayers who foot the bill for public schools, better public images for politicians who are accountable to their constituencies, and with the proliferation of charter schools, increased accountability to stakeholders.

While all education initiatives govern citizenry, in the sense that they aim to direct the conduct of individuals, neoliberal educational initiatives construct the citizen/subject as "an individual who is morally responsible for navigating the social realm using rational choice and cost-benefit calculations grounded on market-based principles to the exclusion of all other ethical values and social interests" (Hamann, 2009, p. 40). Equality has been redefined as the right to enter into free competition. These governing technologies work not through force but by encouraging the individual to align her or his personal and educational goals with those of the nation. As these techniques become understood as commonsense, "individuals volunteer themselves to them" (Baez & Talburt, 2008, p. 35).

The contributors to this volume raise questions about naturalized inequalities, myths of opportunity, and other internalized beliefs. They argue that education for self- and social empowerment should precede "mastering" the skills of the marketplace and that youth should be encouraged to examine their surroundings, interpret them, and define for themselves the things that hold significance in their lives. In Chapter 5, Heybach sheds light on the myth that the classroom is a value-free space and that the teacher is a "neutral" individual. Her research examines the ways in which teachers and teacher candidates adopt antidemocratic practices that "obscure" lived experiences and thus prevent "civic connections from taking root." Heybach concludes that the "neutral teacher" is a mythologized "identity [that] supports only the curricular demands of corporate-owned textbook publishers." That the participants in Heybach's study refused to even consider the US's role in Abu Ghraib prison abuses because doing so might place America on the wrong side of "current global events" provides evidence that teachers and future teachers are not learning earlier in their educational careers to develop a sociopolitical consciousness that allows them to critique the cultural norms, values, mores, and institutions that produce and maintain social inequalities, as critical educators have recommended (Ladson-Billings, 1995). To paraphrase Ladson-Billings, if education is about preparing students for global citizenship, what better tool exists than the ability to critically analyze one's own society?

As Lakes points out in Chapter 7, neoliberalism offers a mythologized sense of agency to young people. "Adolescents," he writes, "are asked to think of themselves as do-it-yourself projects, fully engaged in . . . planning a life course in knowledge work" and armed with a "world-class education." Yet in Chapter 5, Heybach's ethnographic research shows that schools are not preparing graduates with such critical abilities. The teachers in her study lacked the resources to recognize the contradiction between their desires to teach students to become critical thinkers or to "spark genius" and their *own* refusal to examine the conditions of their own consciousness.

In line with education initiatives supported by Bill Gates, the Walton and Broad families, and other masters of industry (Boyles, 2005; Kovacs, 2011), neoliberal education reforms are not backed by substantiated research although their claims and ideology and practices—their mythologies—continue to influence public policies. Thus the general public, including parents as well as school leaders, accept the mythically constructed links between education and the economy as fact, so much so that proof of such a crisis has not been necessary because it has become a normalized way of thinking. There is little questioning of these ideas by mainstream news media, national leaders, or a significant portion of the public. Therefore reformers continue to link education to successful nation building. Failing at internalizing the mythology of education reform is a bad choice for the *homo economicus*. Making the wrong choices results in failing oneself, one's children, and one's country. The shame of failing is a significant motivating technique of neoliberal myths, as the US's success or failure in the global marketplace is shifted onto the individual citizen. Because the nation-state can no longer "generate real economic activity," as Torres points out, it is up to the "individual consumer" to become entrepreneurial and self-reliant to "drive the expansion and operation of the global economy" (Torres, 2002, p. 367). Business rhetoric redefines citizenship and freedom as the widening of opportunity to enter into global economic competition. Neoliberal reformers present their initiatives in a mythical and commonsensical fashion, as simply meeting the challenges of a contemporary, precarious, high-tech, and risky world.

As discussed previously, the mapping of neoliberal myths onto educational discourse is hardly a new discursive practice. Furthermore, neoliberal principles are no longer the sole property of the Republican Party. Many Democrats also see public funding as "contrary to corporate interests" (Hursh, Chapter 6). However, education reformers seem to have less need in recent years to attempt to hide the ideological underpinnings of their own mythology. For example, during the 2004 presidential debates, George W. Bush was surprisingly honest when admitting, "No Child Left Behind is really a jobs act, when you think about it" (Commission on Presidential Debates, 2004). In similar fashion, then-Secretary of Education Rod Paige stated, "If we can improve the educational system, we can improve the corporate bottom line" (US Department of Education, 2004). President Obama's educational mythology mirrors Reagan's and Bush's: "After graduating high school, all Americans should be prepared to attend at least one year of job training or higher education to better equip our workforce for the 21st century economy" (Obama, 2009). It seems as though the case is closed: The official purpose of education is to train young citizens with the skills necessary to join the marketplace (Grey, 2010). Lakes (Chapter 7) describes US Secretary of Education Arne Duncan as a "neoliberal elite" who projects neoliberal myths, or "imaginaries," that reinforce the idea that current reforms are common sense. In fact, Duncan refers to normative benchmarking practices as a "no-brainer." The myths guiding President Obama's Race to the Top competition could not be more clear: "Adopting standards and assessments that prepare students to succeed in college and the workplace and to compete in the global economy" and "Building data systems that measure student growth and success, and inform teachers and principals about how they can improve instruction" are this administration's top priorities. Unemployment, goes the myth, is really just a problem with the individual. If individuals would just make better decisions, then the economy would work itself out. However, most individuals—teachers, students, parents, and other citizens—are not often invited to engage in discussions where policy decisions are made, either inside or outside of schools. Competition, individualism, and isolation result in few opportunities for individuals to affect the conditions in which they live.

Some scholars hold that reforms based on market ideology support an agenda to end all government participation in education. Regardless of the agenda, the effects are clear, as Hursh contends: "Much of what was public about public education has disappeared over the last several decades" (Hursh, Chapter 6). Corporate stakeholders and their supporters have long adopted education reform and applied market-influenced solutions such as standards and accountability initiatives to improve public schools. The preparation of students for the ever-changing workplace has emerged as the most important goal (Spring, 2002). Education is evaluated purely as an economic investment. These ideas coincide with the free market's self-promotional campaign to "establish itself as the true provider of equity and opportunity in the 'objective' realm of capital, and to provide so-called objective 'proof' of public sector failure" (Shaker, 1998, p. i). Schools exist for market purposes.

Using the lens of mythology, we explore the narratives through which power is exercised, question the foundations on which neoliberal policies are based, and understand the ways in which citizens are made governable by these myths. The contributors to this volume explore the ways in which governing forces work on teachers, students, and parents through myths that constitute not only what is considered normal desirable behavior but also what are considered reasonable choices, good citizenship, and rational, responsible citizens. Because they are devised and implemented by so-called elites, experts, and wealthy businesspeople, such educational initiatives embody structures that define and order what counts as "normal" and "good." Myths shape the identities and actions of individuals and groups by allowing particular behaviors in forbidding others. In other words, certain people, those who are normatively rational and reasonable, are able to participate, while others are excluded. In this way good global citizenship is established. Looking at educational reforms, policies, and practices as myths illuminates the power of language and demonstrates the ways in which certain forces control the conversation to construct, package, and sell commonsense understandings of education and citizenship. Neoliberal education reform initiatives presuppose certain truths; thus myths structure reality.

THINKING THINGS THROUGH

The following questions are based on the book's chapters. We invite you to consider answering them—perhaps answering them with your own questions.

1. What are your own personal and professional myths? What values do they represent? How do you implement these myths in your own teaching and learning?
2. Do you agree that myths are "neither good nor bad, but rather useful or not"?
3. Can you identify beneficial myths in your own teaching or in your own school? What about harmful myths?
4. Can you identify policies and pedagogical practices that might be informed by neoliberal myths? How do these policies reinforce the idea that education is purely an instrument of economic growth or reinforce *homo economicus* as an ideal archetype?
5. Some defenders of neoliberal political policy have argued that neoliberalism is compatible with democracy. Do you think the neoliberal myth is compatible with democracy? In what ways is it compatible? In what ways is it antithetical to democratic aspirations?
6. Reflect on your own experience as a student. Have neoliberal myths informed your moral and ethical perspective as you progressed through the education system? How and in what ways?
7. Interview three to five students about the possible influence of myths on their ethical and moral perspectives. How do they understand the purposes and/or aims of education? How do they understand and determine what it means to be a high- and low-quality student? How will they determine whether schooling has contributed to their success or failure after they leave school?
8. How might teachers balance the demands of standardized education with a goal of providing a vigorous and equitable curriculum?
9. Who should determine what should be taught in the classroom?
10. What evidence of webs of interaction do you notice in modern schools?
11. If the educational reform movement is top-down, how can we teachers, parents, communities, and students develop a bottom-up, grassroots, or democratic approach to educational reform?

12. What possible responses to the standardization of education may affect change?
13. Do schools in areas of wealth experience the same standardized educational experience as those labeled "at risk"? How might they differ?
14. What does it mean when so much of what is happening in education is a result of agendas imposed by corporations and their political representatives? Why isn't education being defined, directed, and governed mainly by students, parents, educators, and the broader public?
15. Many teachers consciously and unconsciously reject the No Child Left Behind Act, high-stakes standardized tests, "performance pay," annual professional performance reviews, and the common core standards. These are arrangements that teachers and students would never support if they had real decision-making power; they are not grassroots products. What are possible politicized responses to this situation?
16. The fact that the vast majority have no effective say in the direction of education and society merely reflects their continued broad marginalization from the decision-making process. The problem at hand is therefore a *political* one. Who decides? Who should set the agenda and direction for education? A tiny ruling elite or the majority? If education was controlled by democratic processes, what would those processes look like?
17. Politics and power may not be what teachers and others want to think about and deal with. After all, they already have enough on their plate. However, this critical issue of power is being forcefully put on the agenda by history, and there is no way around it if education is to serve the public interest. What is your stance on this?

REFERENCES

Anyon, J. (1980). Social class and the hidden curriculum of work. *Journal of Education, 162,* 67–92.

Anyon, J. (2005). What "counts" as educational policy? Notes toward a new paradigm. *Harvard Educational Review, 75*(1), 65–88.

Apple, M. W. (2001). Comparing neo-liberal projects and inequality in education. *Comparative Education, 37,* 409–423.

Benjamin, B. & Talburt, S. (2008). Governing for responsibility and with love: parents and children between home and school. *Educational Theory, 58* (1), 25–43.

Barry, A., Osborne, T., & Rose, N. (1996). *Foucault and political reason: Liberalism, neo-liberalism, and rationalities of government.* Chicago, IL: University of Chicago Press.

Berliner, D. C., & Biddle, B. J. (1995). *The manufactured crisis: Myths, fraud and the attack on America's public schools.* New York, NY: Basic Books.

Best, S., & Kellner, D. (2003). Contemporary youth and the postmodern adventure [web page]. Retrieved January 1, 2006, from http://www.gseis.ucla.edu/faculty/kellner/papers/youth.htm

Boyles, D. (2000). *American education and corporations: The free market goes to school* (Vol. 1). New York, NY: Falmer.
Boyles, D. R. (2005). *Schools or markets? Commercialism, privatization, and school-business partnerships*. Mahwah, NJ: Erlbaum.
Burbules, N. C., & Berk, R. (1999). Critical thinking and critical pedagogy: Relations, differences, and limits. In T. Popkewitz & L. Fendler (Eds.), *Critical theories in education: Changing terrains of knowledge and politics* (pp. 45–65). New York, NY: Routledge.
Cuban, L. (2003). *Why is it so hard to get good schools?*. New York, NY: Teachers College Press.
Freire, P. (2000). *Pedagogy of the oppressed* (M. B. Ramos, Trans.). New York, NY: Continuum.
Giroux, H. (1989). *Schooling for democracy: Critical pedagogy in the modern age*. London, England: Routledge.
Grey, L. (2010). Governing Identity Through Neoliberal Education Initiatives: "Get[ting] Schooled" in the Marketplace. In P. E. Kovacs (Ed.), *The Gates Foundation and the Future of US "Public" Schools*. New York: Routledge.
Hamann, T. H. (2009). Neoliberalism, governmentality, and ethics. *Foucault Studies, 6*, 37–59.
Kovacs, P. E. (2011). *The Gates Foundation and the future of US "public" schools*. New York, NY: Routledge.
Ladson-Billings, G. (1995). But that's just good teaching! The case for culturally relevant pedagogy. *Theory Into Practice, 34*(3), 159–165. doi:10.1080/00405849509543675
Lesko, N. (2001). *Act your age!: A cultural construction of adolescence*. New York, NY: RoutledgeFalmer.
Lewis, M. (1992). Interrupting patriarchy: Politics, resistance and transformation in the feminist classroom. In C. Luke & J. Gore (Eds.), *Feminisms and critical pedagogy* (pp. 167–191). New York, NY: Routledge.
Lipman, P. (2011). *The new political economy of urban education: Neoliberalism, race, and the right to the city*. New York, NY: Routledge.
McLaren, P. (1989). *Life in Schools: An Introduction to Critical Pedagogy in the Foundations of Education*. New York and London: Longman.
Molnar, A. (1996). *Giving kids the business*. Boulder, CO: Westview Press.
National Commission on Excellence in Education. (1983). *A nation at risk: The full account*. Portland, OR: USA Research.
Obama, B. http://www.barackobama.com/issues/education/index.php. Accessed December 26, 2009.
Peters, M. A. (2011). *Neoliberalism and after?: Education, social policy, and the crisis of Western capitalism*. New York, NY: Peter Lang.
Popkewitz, T. S. (2002). Pacts/partnerships and governing the parent and child. *Current Issues in Comparative Education, 3*, 122–130.
Presidential Debate Transcript October 13, 2004 http://www.debates.org/index.php?page=october-13-2004-debate-transcript. Accessed June 13, 2014.
Pykett, J. (2007). Making citizens governable? The Crick Report as governmental technology. *Journal of Education Policy, 22*, 301–319.
Ravitch, D. (2011). *The death and life of the great American school system: How testing and choice are undermining education*. New York, NY: Basic Books.
Ravitch, D. (2013). *Reign of error: The hoax of the privatization movement and the danger to America's public schools*. New York, NY: Knopf.
Rose, N. (1990). *Governing the soul: The shaping of the private self*. London: Routledge.
Shaker, E. (1998). Privatizing Schools: Democratic Choice or Market Demand. *Education, Limited, 1*(3).

Spring, J. (2002). *American education* (15th ed.). New York, NY: McGraw-Hill.
Torres, C. A. (2002). Globalization, education, and citizenship: Solidarity versus markets? *American Educational Research Journal, 39*, 363–378.
US Commission on Excellence in Education. (1983). *A nation at risk*. Washington, DC: Author.
Winerip, M. (2012, October 1). Older, wiser and not giving in to fear. *The New York Times*. Retrieved from http://www.nytimes.com/2012/10/01/booming/01winerip-booming.html. Accessed April 25, 2014.

Contributors

Arthur T. Costigan is assistant professor of education and is a codirector of English Education Programs at Queens College, the City University of New York. He received a PhD in English education from New York University (2000), and his original research interest was in the experiences and understandings of beginning teachers, including the New York City Teaching Fellows, as they encounter the landscape, environment, or ecology of diverse urban schools. Since NCLB, these new teachers have been overwhelmed by educational reforms, including testing, mandated and scripted lessons, and high levels of accountability. His most recent project is designing and editing a special issue of *Teacher Education Quarterly*, "Ecological Perspectives of Learning to Teach" (Winter 2014). This issue explores ways to reinvigorate narrative inquiry into the autobiographical and situational experiences of new teachers, particularly as a response to the hegemony of a neoliberal, corporatized discourse of schooling.

David Gabbard associate professor in the Department of Curriculum, Instruction, and Foundational Studies at Boise State. Most noted for his work as a critical educational theorist and policy analyst, Gabbard's research has reflected his quest to understand the phenomenon of compulsory schooling as an instrument of statecraft created, in part, to enforce the conditions of a market society. Hopeful that public schools might one day come to serve more genuinely democratic values, Gabbard's scholarship, teaching, and service focus on nurturing critically reflective and democratic dispositions in teachers. His research interests are in cultural studies, curriculum and instruction, new literacies, and anarchist pedagogy.

Leslee Grey is an assistant professor of foundations of education at Queens College, the City University of New York. Her scholarship offers several interrelated strands including privatization and education, gender studies and education, adolescent and youth culture, and teaching for social change. Grey's publications include: critical investigation of school-business partnerships and corporate-sponsored educational reform movements; exploration of young adult literature relating to the schooling experiences of young people; and ethnographic study of the ways in which young people learn and negotiate multiple identities. She is currently researching parental involvement in public school reform in New York City.

Jessica A. Heybach is an assistant professor of education at Aurora University. Her scholarly interests lie at the intersection of curriculum theory, visual culture, and philosophy of education. She has published journal articles in *Education and Culture, Critical Questions in Education,* and *Philosophical Studies in Education.* She recently coedited the book *Dystopia and Education: Insights Into Theory, Praxis, and Policy in an Age of Utopia-Gone-Wrong* with Eric C. Sheffield.

Dave Hill teaches at Middlesex University, London, England, and is visiting professor of education at the University of Athens, Greece, and visiting professor of critical education policy and equality studies at University of Limerick, Ireland. He founded and is chief editor of the *Journal for Critical Education Policy Studies.* He recently edited/coedited four books in the *Neoliberalism and Marxism* Routledge series (all 2009); *Teaching Class: Knowledge, Pedagogy, Subjectivity* (edited with Deb Kelsh and Sheila Macrine); and the 2010 Palgrave Macmillan book (edited with Sheila Macrine and Peter McLaren) *Revolutionizing Pedagogy: Education for Social Justice Within and Beyond Global Neo-Liberalism.* Other, shorter items appear in the wider socialist press, such as his recent *Socialist Manifesto for Education.*

David Hursh is a professor in the Warner Graduate School of Education at the University of Rochester. His recent research focuses on the politics of high-stakes testing in neoliberal times and education for sustainability. His most recent book is *High-Stakes Testing and the Decline of Public Education: The Real Crisis in Education.* In 2011–2012, Hursh was a visiting scholar at the Earth Institute and the School for International and Public Affairs at Columbia University. In 2004 he was a visiting fellow at Bristol University, and in 2014 at Victoria University and University of New South Wales in Australia, and Waikato University in Hamilton, New Zealand.

Richard D. Lakes is a professor of educational policy studies at Georgia State University–Atlanta. He teaches graduate courses in the social foundations of education, and researches the impact of globalization on education for work. Lakes has written *Critical Education for Work: Multidisciplinary Approaches* (1994, edited); *Youth Development and Critical Education: The Promise of Democratic Action* (1997); *Globalizing Education for Work: Comparative Perspectives on Gender and the*

New Economy (2004, coedited); and numerous book chapters. His refereed articles have appeared in *Career and Technical Education Research*; *Community College Journal of Research and Practice*; *Globalisation, Societies and Education*; *Pedagogies: An International Journal*; *Policy Futures in Education*; and *Urban Review*, among others.

Bryan Metcalfe is a secondary school teacher and has been teaching both English and the social sciences in Ontario, Canada, since 2006. He received his PhD in philosophy of education from OISE/University of Toronto in 2013. His dissertation entitled "Pedagogy of Mythos" (2013) is a philosophical examination of function of sociopolitical myths within North American schools from a critical democratic pedagogical framework. His main research interests include philosophy of education, educational policy and governance, and democratic education.

Debra A. Root is the head of St. Thomas Episcopal School of San Antonio as well as a special graduate faculty for the University of Texas at San Antonio. Root earned her doctorate in interdisciplinary learning and teaching; her area of specialty is curriculum design and theory. She has worked in the field of education for 30 years having taught preschool through sixth grades; additionally she has taught graduate and undergraduate courses at the University of Texas at San Antonio. In her years of teaching, she has taught at public and private schools with an emphasis on working with Title I English Language Learners in Southern California. Her master's in education is from the University of California–San Diego.

Eric C. Sheffield is a professor in the Reading, Foundations, and Technology Department (College of Education) at Missouri State University (MSU) in Springfield. Prior to coming to MSU in 2003, Eric taught high school English for 14 years in Putnam County, Florida. Eric's most recent book, coedited with Jessica A. Heybach, is *Dystopia and Education: Insights Into Theory, Praxis, and Policy in an Age of Utopia-Gone-Wrong*.

Shawgi Tell is an associate professor of education in the Department of Social and Psychological Foundations of Education in the School of Education at Nazareth College. He has been teaching in-service and preservice teachers for the last 16 years. He received his PhD in social foundations of education from the University at Buffalo in 1997. His main research interests include education reform, educational governance, and the political economy of schooling. His forthcoming book on charter schools, titled *Charter School Report Card*, will be released in 2015.

Index

A
aims, in education, 21–27, 52, 104, 111
A Nation at Risk, v, 1, 3–4, 18, 69, 115, 125, 145–146, 151, 184–186, 193–194
Abu Ghraib, 89, 91–97, 100, 102, 188
academy, 46–47, 63, 67, 166
accountability, viii, 16, 18, 53–54, 68–71, 73, 78, 84–87, 115, 120, 125, 128–129, 135, 138, 143, 157, 185, 188, 190, 195
actual routine
  learners, 178, 181
  teacher educators, 178, 181
  teachers, 181
Amabile, Teresa, 177, 181
Annual Professional Performance Review, 110
Anti-American, 96–97, 100
Assertive Discipline, 162–163, 169
at risk (schools, students), 71, 73, 192
Atlanta, 104, 116, 126, 132, 196

B
Ball, Stephen, 44–45, 50, 52, 58, 63–64, 105, 110–111, 113–114
Barthes, Roland, 88, 102
Belgium, 42, 123
benchmarking, 118–119, 121, 126, 129–131, 190
Berliner, David, 4, 16, 104, 112–115, 134, 140, 149, 151, 184, 192
best practices, 70, 76, 122–123, 129, 131, 166, 186
Bloomberg, Michael, 14–15, 106–107, 109, 112, 115
Blumenberg, Hans, 20–22, 32
Borg, 16, 153–154, 157–159, 161, 164, 166–168, 186

Bottici, Chiara, 20–22, 32
Britzman, Deborah, 99, 102
Bronx High School of Science, 6
Budde, Ray, 145–146, 149
Bush, George H.W., 5
Bush, George W., 13, 71, 106, 112, 135, 151, 189

C
Canada, 22, 29–30, 33, 119, 123
capitalism, 32, 34, 36–38, 42–43, 49–51, 56–57, 59–67, 118, 128–129, 131, 144, 193
capitalist, v, 23–24, 34–38, 40, 42–44, 48–51, 55, 59–62, 65, 134
charter schools, i, vi, 1, 46–48, 63, 104, 109–110, 112, 133–143, 145–152, 186–188, 197
China, 1, 119
Chomsky, Noam, 173, 182
class, v, 6, 8, 13, 17–18, 26, 28, 32, 34–41, 43, 45–51, 53–63, 65–67, 79–80, 82, 102, 107–108, 111, 118, 125, 127–129, 131, 144, 146, 155, 159–163, 165, 170, 182, 185, 189, 192, 196
closure rate, 136
Coleman, James, 8, 16
Common Core, vi, 104–105, 109, 114, 117, 119–132, 169, 192
  standards, vi, 114, 117, 119–127, 129, 131–132
  State Standards (CCSS), 109
communism, 37, 65
communist, 34, 37–38, 55, 57, 59, 145
competition, i, 11–12, 15, 27, 35, 39, 43–45, 87, 105, 134, 140, 144, 181, 185, 188–190

Index

competitiveness, 122, 127
compulsory schooling, 172–176, 178–180, 195
corporate, ii–v, vii, 2, 9, 11, 13, 15, 46, 52, 59, 68–70, 75, 78, 83, 87–88, 100, 104–105, 109, 111–112, 115, 118, 121–122, 127, 133, 138, 141, 143, 146, 149, 153–154, 156–157, 159, 161, 163–168, 183–184, 186–190, 195
Counts, George, 167, 169
critical
  education, 56–57, 63–67, 196
  educators, 49, 56–58, 188
Cuomo, Andrew, 107, 110, 115
curriculum, v, 4, 9, 17–18, 33, 42–43, 47–50, 53, 57–58, 64, 68–88, 96, 100–102, 105–106, 111, 113–114, 117, 120, 122, 124, 126–128, 130–131, 134, 138–140, 154, 157, 185–187, 191–192, 195–197
cycle of compliance, vi, 170, 175, 178

D

data, iv–v, 18, 29–30, 53, 65, 68–69, 74–76, 78, 80, 104–107, 109, 111–113, 115, 117–119, 121–122, 126, 161–162, 166–167, 178, 184, 186–187, 190
democracy, 20, 31–33, 35, 61, 64–66, 83–86, 88, 96, 107, 126, 139, 145, 157, 170–172, 181–182, 191, 193
democratic, v, 20–21, 28, 30–31, 35–37, 43, 50–51, 56, 58–59, 62, 66, 78, 101–102, 111, 126, 171–172, 183, 185–186, 191–193, 195–197
Denmark, 123
Dewey, John, 2, 7, 11, 17, 26, 32, 72, 84, 136, 149, 153, 161, 168–169
difficult knowledge, 88, 99
discourse, i, viii, 3, 20, 23–24, 26–27, 29–30, 39, 58, 86–88, 93, 110, 128, 130, 139, 141, 184, 189, 195
Duncan, Arne, 5, 7, 17, 118–121, 123, 128, 132, 143, 148, 178, 190

E

economic liberalism, 170
economically challenged, 69, 71, 78
economy, i, 1, 5–6, 17, 23, 27–28, 31, 34, 37–38, 42, 50, 67, 117–119, 121, 125, 128–129, 132, 141–142, 144–145, 147, 181, 187, 189–190, 193, 197
edTPA, 157–159, 162, 164, 169
education, i–iii, v–2, 4–5, 10, 12–13, 15–21, 23, 26–37, 39–45, 47–53, 55–59, 61, 63–75, 77–89, 101–102, 104–124, 126–137, 140–143, 145–155, 157–158, 161–162, 164, 166–170, 172–175, 177–180, 182–197
  ministers, 118, 120–121
Engleman, Melissa, 178, 182
equality, 16, 64, 112, 188, 196
equity, ii, v, 64–65, 68–69, 71, 73, 75–79, 81, 83, 85–86, 127, 150, 158, 186, 190

F

Finland, 1, 6–7, 18, 36, 58, 119, 122–123, 128–129, 131
Florida, 11, 104, 124, 160, 197
Fotopoulos, Takis, 181–182
Foucault, Michel, 114, 171, 173–174, 180, 182–184, 192–193
free-market, 22–23, 27, 118, 144–145
Freidman, Thomas, 5
funding, 12, 44, 46, 48, 70–71, 109, 112, 137, 142, 189

G

Gates, Bill, 13, 15, 24–25, 106, 112–113, 115, 126, 137, 157, 169, 189, 193
Godwin, William, 173–174, 182
Golay, Keith, 178, 182
Goldman, Emma, 173, 175, 182
Goodlad, John, 168–169
Gove, Michael, 42, 63
government, 8, 23, 26, 38, 42, 44–50, 55, 59, 93, 98, 105, 111–112, 114, 118, 120, 126, 129, 137, 140–141, 146, 148, 167, 172–175, 187, 190, 192
governmental leaders, government leaders, 118, 121, 123
governor(s) (state), 43, 47, 49, 113, 118, 120, 125–126, 128

H

homo economicus, 5, 15–16, 23–27, 184–185, 191

Hong Kong, 123
human
　capital, 26, 39, 118, 125, 129, 132, 187
　rights, 37, 88, 91, 95, 147

I

ideology, 23, 35–36, 39–40, 49–50, 57, 60, 63–64, 87, 120, 186, 189–190
image, 81, 97, 152
immiseration, 35, 56, 62–66
inequality, 35, 41, 46, 50, 59, 63, 66, 109, 113–114, 148, 185, 192
inequities, viii, 15–16, 28, 186
innovation, 117, 120, 124, 129, 133, 145

J

Japan, 1, 36, 119, 123–124
Jobs, Steve, 14–15

K

King, John, Commissioner, 110
King, Dr. Martin Luther, Jr., 107
Klein, Joel 110, 112

L

league tables, 44–46, 118, 120, 122, 128–129
lesson drawing, 118, 123
liberalism, 55, 64, 85, 111, 114, 143–144, 170, 172, 191–192
literacy, 119–120, 127, 185
Lowrey, Annie, 113, 115

M

managerialism, 39, 44, 51–52, 60, 63
Manufactured Crisis, The, 16, 112, 114, 184, 192
market regime, 170–172, 175
Marx, Karl, 34, 37–38, 57, 59, 61
Marxism, 37, 62, 66, 196
Marxist, v, 34, 36–38, 42, 49, 55–60, 62, 65–66, 185
moral, 23, 25–26, 28, 30–31, 92, 100, 183, 191
morality, 39–41, 49
myth(s)
　of control, 162–163
　definition of, 2
　as governing technology, 188
　of measurement, 163–164
　neoliberal, 20, 22, 24, 26, 28, 30, 32
　of preparation, 159–62
　purpose of, 12
　of teacher resistance, 166–168
　of technology, 164–166
　sociopolitical, 20–25
mythical community, 183

N

National Commission on Excellence in Education, 18, 112, 115, 151, 193
national curriculum, 48, 53, 120, 122, 124, 126, 131
National Governors Association, 113
No Child Left Behind Act, The, (NCLB) 1, 5, 13, 71, 78, 75, 84, 87, 105–108, 112, 116, 125, 164, 189, 195
neoconservative, 17, 40–43, 182
neoliberal elites, 117–118
neoliberalism, neoliberal, i, v, vii, 18, 20–25, 29–34, 38–43, 45, 48, 50–51, 55–56, 64–66, 106, 111, 113, 130, 143–145, 150, 170, 172, 185, 187–188, 193, 196
neutrality, v, 26, 87–89, 91, 93, 95, 97, 99–101, 103
New York City, 6, 14, 16, 108–109, 112, 123, 195
New York State Department of Education, 105–106, 108

O

Obama, Barack 3, 5, 13, 41, 66, 118, 120–122, 124, 126–127, 129, 143, 151, 189–190, 193

P

Paige, Ron, 106–107, 115, 189
panopticon, 13
Pearson, 63, 126, 130–131, 157–158, 162, 164
Picard, Jean-Luc, 169
Poland, 128
policy borrowing, 118, 122, 124, 130
policymakers, 117, 124, 126
private, 8, 14–15, 26, 34, 39, 44–48, 50, 58–59, 67, 88, 112, 114, 125, 129, 131, 134, 138, 141–144, 146–148, 150, 174, 177, 185, 193, 197
property, 134, 147
schools, 8, 14–15, 39, 45, 47–48, 50, 58–59, 138, 143, 197
sector, 39, 46, 114, 129, 141, 146–147

privatization, viii, 2, 12, 18, 38–39, 44, 46, 50, 55, 60, 64–65, 103, 110, 112–113, 115, 130, 134, 144–146, 193, 195
public
  education, v, vii, 16, 34, 50, 63, 65, 70–71, 114, 118, 126, 133, 141–143, 145, 149–151, 154, 183, 185–187, 190, 196
  interest, 131, 133, 139, 148, 150, 192

R

Race to the Top, 12, 105, 119, 190
Ravitch, Diane, vii-viii, 2, 5, 7–8, 12, 18, 68, 85, 87, 104, 108, 112–113, 115, 134, 140, 143, 151, 184, 187, 193
reform, i–ii, v-5, 8–9, 11–13, 15–17, 43, 48, 52, 62, 64, 68–76, 78, 83–85, 87, 104, 107, 112, 114–115, 118–124, 126, 128–129, 131–133, 135, 137, 141, 143, 145, 149–151, 169–170, 183–187, 189–191, 195–197
resistance, v, 20, 31, 42, 55–58, 62–66, 112, 133, 153–155, 166–168, 171, 174, 193
Rhee, Michelle, 14–15, 116
Rice, Condoleezza, 112
rights, iv, vii, 12, 35–37, 39, 41, 43, 48, 51, 59, 61, 65, 85, 88–91, 95, 106, 111, 115, 133, 139, 143–144, 147–148, 150
rigor, v, 68–69, 71, 73, 75–79, 81, 83, 85, 186
Rochester, New York, 104, 109–110, 196
  City School District, 109
  Teachers Association, 110
Rush, Benjamin, 174–175, 182

S

SAT, 10–11, 16, 54, 71, 160
Schleicher, Andreas, 123, 128
schooling, i, 2, 8–10, 12, 26, 30, 39, 42–43, 45–46, 64, 84, 87, 100–101, 105–106, 111, 113–114, 118, 120, 127, 130, 152–154, 157, 160–161, 168, 172–176, 178–180, 183, 185, 193, 195, 197
  and competition, i, 11–12, 15, 27, 35, 39, 44–45, 87, 105, 140, 185, 188, 190
  and disciplinary power, 174
  and formation of compliant personalities, 175
  and symbolic order, 170–172, 175
Schwab, Joseph, 72–73, 84–86
selective enrollment, 134, 140
Shanker, Albert, 145–146, 152
Singapore, 119, 123
Snow, David, 68–69, 75–76, 78–79, 81, 83, 86
Social Studies, 69–70, 72, 78–80, 82–86, 95, 102
Socialism, 37, 61, 66
Society, i, 3, 5, 7, 14–15, 17–18, 22–24, 28–29, 34–35, 37–39, 42–43, 49–51, 59, 61–62, 64, 69–70, 72, 75, 78, 80, 83, 88, 90, 100, 102, 112–114, 122, 124, 130, 132–133, 140–141, 144–145, 147–149, 170, 175, 179–181, 183, 188, 192, 195
Spring, Joel, 17, 126, 131, 173, 175, 182, 187, 190, 194
standardization, 29, 68, 71, 73, 75, 78–80, 87, 118, 148, 186, 192
standardized tests, v, 68, 72, 77, 82, 104, 106, 108–109, 113, 134, 139–140, 192
state, the
  and the market regime, 170
  and militarism, 59, 91, 93, 97, 144, 171
  and symbolic order, 170–172, 175
  and territory, 118, 171
STEM, 117, 127, 179, 181
students as customers, 39
Symbolic Interactionalism, 79
symbolic order, 171–172, 175

T

Teach for America (TFA), 7, 15–16
teacher
  education, i–ii, vi, viii, 17, 40, 84, 86–89, 102, 123, 153–155, 158, 161–162, 167–170, 175, 177–178, 195
  neutrality, 87–88, 100
teachers, i, vii, 1–4, 6–12, 15–20, 28–32, 39–41, 47–49, 51–54, 56–57, 60, 63, 65–70, 72–79, 81–85, 87–88, 99–102, 104–107, 109–111, 114–115, 118, 121–127, 130–133, 136–137, 140, 142–143, 145–146, 148–156, 158, 160–161, 163–164, 166–169, 175–179, 181–182, 185–193, 195, 197
  and creativity, 140, 157, 176, 177, 180–181

defective, deficient, 7–9
and the market regime, 171–172, 175
and resistance, 55–8, 154–155, 166–168, 171
shaping compliance of, 34, 175, 178, 180
tests, testing
high stakes vii,8–9, 44–45, 84, 85, 104,107, 109, 111, 115, 122, 125, 131, 134, 138, 140, 148–149, 151, 163, 192, 196
scores, 1, 7–8, 45, 68, 77–78, 80, 83–84, 104–105, 109–111, 113–114, 120–121, 134–135, 140, 149, 186–187
standardized, v, 9, 19, 30, 68–69, 71–73, 75–83, 85, 101, 104–109, 113, 117, 119, 134, 138–140, 149–150, 158, 164, 185–187, 191–192
performance-based, 71, 73, 140, 149
Texas, 11, 68–71, 73–74, 79–80, 84–86, 104, 186, 197
Texas Miracle, 71, 84, 186
Thatcher, Margaret, 35, 40, 43–45, 48, 144
Tisch, Merryl, 109
torture, 89, 91–94, 97–99, 101–103
tragedy, 98, 159, 161, 168
Trotsky, Leon, 61–62, 67
Turkey, 35, 40–42, 49–51, 56, 60, 64–66
turnover rate, 137

U

university, i, 16–18, 32, 39, 41, 44, 57, 63–64, 66–68, 74, 84–85, 90, 102–103, 108, 110–111, 114–115, 117, 124, 126–127, 130–131, 149–150, 155–156, 160, 167, 169, 178, 182, 187, 192, 195–197
Urbanski, Adam, 110

W

Walmartization of schooling, 12
Walton Foundation, 113
war, 4, 8, 34–35, 42, 55, 60, 71, 83, 88–91, 94–99, 101–102, 111, 113, 139, 146, 171
Washington, D.C., 16, 19, 104, 115–116, 124, 126, 131–132, 134, 137, 151, 169, 194
Webster, Noah, 175
welfare, 3, 33–35, 41, 43, 106, 111, 144, 172, 174, 180

For Product Safety Concerns and Information please contact our EU representative GPSR@taylorandfrancis.com
Taylor & Francis Verlag GmbH, Kaufingerstraße 24, 80331 München, Germany

www.ingramcontent.com/pod-product-compliance
Lightning Source LLC
Chambersburg PA
CBHW070259230426
43664CB00014B/2580